Fourth edition. Fifth printing with expanded, revised and updated information

www.marineguides.com

D o c k s
and
Destinations
Coastal Marinas and Moorage

A User-Friendly© West Coast Cruising Dock-to-Dock
Destinations Guide
Puget Sound to Ketchikan
Docks • Facilities • Services
• Launch Ramps

Peter Vassilopoulos

By The Same Author
Anchorages and Marine Parks*
Antiques Afloat
from the Golden Age of Boating in British Columbia

A West Coast Best Seller

Seagraphic Publications • Vancouver Canada

Photographs, text, drawings and diagrams copyright 1994/1998 Peter Vassilopoulos.
Seagraphic Publications Ltd. Vancouver, Canada. Box 1312, Delta, BC. V4M 3Y8.
In the USA: Box 984, Point Roberts, WA. 98281-0984
Prepress graphics and typesetting Seagraphic Publications Ltd.
Photo scanning and production assistance–Stephanie Bold.
Printed in Canada.
Photographs by author unless otherwise indicated.

The information in this book is accurate and correct as far as can be determined. All cautions and docking information is provided without guarantee and it is up to the boat operator to ensure the proper use of navigational charts and other aids to navigation. Depths are approximate where recorded and should be verified by use of charts, depth sounders, BC Sailing Directions, Small Craft Guide and other sources. Maps and diagrams are approximate and not to scale and should not be used for navigation purposes. Hydrographic Charts should be used at all times when navigating waterways, bays, coves, harbours and marinas. The publisher and author is not liable for marine operations leading to accident, damage or injury in any way connected with reference to this guide. It is intended purely as a reference to available facilities at marinas on the coast.

© Peter Vassilopoulos 2000 by Seagraphic Publications Ltd. All rights reserved. No part of this book may be reproduced or transmitted in any form by any means without the permission of the publisher, except by a reviewer, who may quote brief passages or show any one diagram in a review unless otherwise arranged with the publisher.
First Printing–August 1994
Second Printing–March 1995
Third Printing–March 1996. (Revised–2nd edition)
Fourth Printing–October 1998. (Revised–3rd edition)
Fifth Printing–Dec 2000. (Revised–4th edition)

Library of Congress (Registered)
Canadian Cataloguing in Publication Data:

Vassilopoulos, Peter, 1940–
   Docks and Destinations
   ISBN 0-919317-28-6   4th revised and expanded edition

1. Marinas–British Columbia–Pacific Coast–Guidebooks. 2. Marinas–Washington (State)–San Juan Islands–Guidebooks. 3. Pacific Coast (B.C.)–Guidebooks. 4. San Juan Islands (Wash.)–Guidebooks. I. Title.
FC3845. P2A3 2000   797.1'09711'1   C00-911269-3
F1089.P2V37 2000

Copies available from marine stores, marinas and book stores. Distribution and acquisition enquiries to Seagraphic Publications (604) 943-4198.
email: *divermag@axion.net*

Peter Vassilopoulos

Docks and Destinations

A coastal guide to marinas and moorage facilities in the Pacific Northwest

Featuring the San Juan Islands, the Gulf Islands, Desolation Sound and North of Cape Caution to Ketchikan, Alaska. Plus the west coast of Vancouver Island, Puget Sound and Hood Canal.

Includes the San Juan Islands, the Strait of Georgia,
the Lower Mainland, Howe Sound, the Sunshine Coast,
Desolation Sound, Johnstone Strait, Knight Inlet,
Queen Charlotte Strait, Fife Sound,
Alert Bay area, Rivers Inlet to Prince Rupert and
Vancouver Island Quatsino Sound to Sooke, Juan de Fuca Strait,
Admiralty Inlet, Hood Canal,
Puget Sound.

Cover: A tranquil place at Fair Harbor in the protected waters of Puget Sound.

PREFACE

Since the introduction in 1994 of the first edition of *Docks and Destinations* I have had the opportunity to revisit many parts of the coast, rediscovering some secluded anchorages (see *Anchorages and Marine Parks*) and making new friends at marinas and in the boating community along the way. It appears those using this guide have found it useful, as intended, for providing quick reference to facilities and information on places they had not known previously. I am gratified my work has been of value and that I have been able to share some knowledge with those who are out and about in their boats. I encourage new boat owners to enjoy our local waters and to do so in safety.

This guide covers marinas and docks with and without services. Use it whenever approaching any of the ports in order to know what dock layout and services are available. Mariners have found it particularly useful for telephoning ahead for reservations. Please refer to Anchorages and Marine Parks (Seagraphic Publications 1998) for comprehensive coverage of the anchorages and marine parks on the BC coast and in the San Juan Islands.

Boat owners are kindly asked to observe proper etiquette on the water and at the various marinas and other facilities. At some places there are severe water shortages and mariners are requested to use available water with discretion. Garbage cannot be disposed of easily at most island locations and mariners are asked to not leave their garbage at the docks. Expectations by mariners of the marina operators can sometimes be unreasonable. Please consider the difficulties under which people on the coast have to function. Their season is extremely short—about two and a half months to possibly three months of the summer holidays. They have to make a living and cover their annual costs in those short months. They have to bring in supplies from varying and often long distances. This means not only the produce and groceries which they offer for sale but also their materials to build and maintain their properties. And remember they have established themselves in an area of wet wintery conditions where the slightest neglect results in a quick return of their property back to nature. There are many competent people working at marinas but staff who assist for summer are not always experienced and it is difficult for them to know the specific preferences of individual arriving boat operators. The facilities found along the coast are usually the mom and pop type of businesses and mariners arriving on their doorsteps in need of replenishment are more than welcome, giving the operators an opportunity to meet people and communicate on a friendly, personal level.

You are on holiday. Relax. Be patient. Give them a friendly greeting and you will be gratified with their welcoming response. Operators who welcome you with a grunt rather than a warm, friendly smile, are rare on the coast. If you do come across any such operators, try to be understanding (most people have their bad days once in a while), or just respond by trying an alternative facility next time.

Boating friends and acquaintances have offered advice on what to include and change in this

4

A cove, a marina and a marine park–at Jarrell Cove in Puget Sound.

edition. I thank them for their input and have used some of their suggestions. While the final format is mine alone, the input from boating friends has definitely influenced it. I must thank the following for their help:

My wife Carla, Walter and Rita Lee, Henry and Jeanne Karcz, Chris and Sue Fraser and those fellow boat owners who have told me or reminded me about places I may otherwise have missed. Thanks also to Pacific Yachting Magazine, Boat Journal, Nor'Westing and others which have had kind reviews on the previous editions. Thanks to the friendly neighbours at marinas we have used as home base and destinations. Thanks to the many readers of the previous editions who reported back to me with information on changes and variations at coastal facilities. And a special thanks to the marina operators who have responded to my faxes and calls to confirm the information.

In producing this new edition of Docks and Destinations it is my sincerest hope that you will use it to expand your boating horizons in finding new and interesting destinations and convenient and safe overnight moorage.

New material for this edition includes marinas in Juan de Fuca Strait, Puget Sound and Hood Canal. Some new aerial photographs have been included for which I must express appreciation to Heinz Bold. I believe that these, presented as large as the format of this book will allow, combined with the diagrams and text, will provide the mariner with an easy reference to the various facilities and destinations that I have included. The guide continues to provide functional, user-friendly, easy access to information needed, and guidance on available facilities.

Like its companion guide, Anchorages and Marine Parks, it is designed to provide guidance but not to remove the joy of exploring for yourself. It is intended to encourage you to moor at a marina and go exploring ashore where walking the local roads and trails provides good exercise. Thanks to Stephanie Bold for scanning photographs and to my wife Carla for assisting me contact marinas by phone and fax for verification of the new information gathered for this edition. Thanks also to the marinas themselves for checking the information.

I stated previously that I didn't believe Shakespeare with his copious collection of adjectives and flamboyant superlatives could have found adequate description for some of our landscapes, waterfalls, mountain peaks and deep waterways. In retrospect, he probably could have, but not I. For me it is the use of photographs and other illustrations that help reveal the charm of the islands and inside passages of the area known as the Pacific Northwest. The best descriptions have been coined in the names of some coastal places such as God's Pocket, Village Island, Minstrel Island, Bones Bay, Telegraph Cove, Kingcome, Ocean Falls and many others.

Top: Preedy Harbour on Thetis Island with a view towards Chemainus on the east coast of Vancouver Island. Mariners stopping at Thetis Island can take the ferry from this bay to Chemainus for a day excursion to the shops or to view the famous murals for which the town is known internationally. Centre: Lighthouse on Green Island en route from Prince Rupert to Ketchikan. Right, top: Small docks like this public one on North Pender Island offer limited, temporary moorage. Right: Sidney Spit–popular and busy in summer.

MARINAS–GUEST MOORAGE

Guest Docks and Marinas

From Sailpast to Summer

Many home marinas are exclusively for privately owned pleasure boats. Here they are stored and maintained throughout the year. As the dawn breaks each year on a new spring and the chill of winter is diminished owners and yacht club members in particular take to scrubbing and polishing their boats in preparation for a colourful sailpast followed by as many boating weekends and prolonged periods away as possible. Cruising to general destinations such as the the San Juans, the Gulf Islands or Desolation Sound is the trend. Frequently there are no specific plans for overnight moorage other than a vague intention to stop if there is suitable anchorage or moorage at one of several possible overnight shelters. Increasingly, and with more boats converging on popular destinations, it is becoming essential that reservations for moorage be made in advance.

This guide is intended to help mariners decide where to stop in safe, sheltered moorage overnight and where services, needed by the boat owners or their crews, can be readily acquired. To this end it provides phone numbers, details of marina facilities and other pertinent information.

Heading Out

Mariners heading north from Puget Sound marinas each summer face some long, exposed passages, current and tide rips off Whidbey Island or the open waters of Juan de Fuca Strait. Lake Washington boat owners are faced with the challenge of locking through the Hiram M. Chittenden locks, while La Conner mariners contend with strong currents through the Swinomish Canal. Victoria and vicinity mariners require a passage around an often rough and tide-ripped Trial Islands and up through a sometimes testy Haro Strait before they reach the placid waters off Sidney. Fortunately most Victoria residents can take one look out to sea and determine the ease of passage. Checking with the tide and current tables is always sound logic to ensure a comfortable beginning of a cruise.

Sidney and Saanich Inlet mariners are in much the same position, but they have the advantage of being where they are going without even leaving the dock (that is—practically in the heart of the Gulf Islands). And the same applies to Maple Bay, Ladysmith and Nanaimo. Mariners in these areas have enviably easy access for extended seasonal periods to the anchorages and marinas of the Gulf Islands but often look farther afield for their major trips. Their favoured distant destinations include Desolation Sound and beyond. For them access out of their marinas is subject to little more than a decision to go. Swift currents and windy conditions through some passages could delay the more cautious and slower travelling mariner leaving from any of these latter destinations, but usually little compromises their departure and returning plans. At Nanaimo mariners, locals and visitors alike, may await the slack at Dodd Narrows before venturing south into the islands, or may stay at the docks while seas off Entrance Island settle after a storm before crossing the Strait or en route north.

Vessels at marinas on the Sunshine Coast or at places north of Nanaimo are already part way to cruising in Desolation Sound or beyond. Be sure to check your marine charts for area WG and ensure it is safe and that no military exercises are in progress before crossing this part of the Strait of Georgia.

Mariners on the Vancouver side of the Strait of Georgia may spend days monitoring weather forecasts prior to a major trip, and certainly will listen to the reports on VHF prior to any other departure. Wind and wave height is of utmost interest, tidal changes and currents can be critical and even openings of fishing to the commercial industry can affect one's plans to set off on a voyage. Vessels leaving Vancouver and Port Moody are subject to the currents under Lions Gate bridge and Second Narrows.

Leaving False Creek is quite straight forward and bumpy conditions off Stanley Park are the quick indicator that worse stuff lies ahead, usually at Point Atkinson. Boats departing Richmond and running down the North Arm of the Fraser may reach open water before determining that it was not such a good idea to leave the dock. One can sometimes tell from the wind force at the marina whether there is likely to be rough conditions out of the river, but how rough? Listen to the reports on VHF before leaving. And one can always wait in Coward's Cove for conditions to ease.

Most vessels from these Vancouver and Richmond areas have Howe Sound as their playground. The facilities in Howe Sound are among the best on the coast and increasing numbers of yachtsmen are finding enough satisfaction in spending time at places on Bowen Island or at Gibsons that they decline to cross the Strait to the Gulf Islands other than for extended trips. Out of Surrey or Delta, on the other hand, the Gulf Islands are closer than Howe Sound. And mariners mooring their boats at Ladner, Crescent Beach or Point Roberts can be in the midst of the Gulf Islands in less than an hour (a little longer in a sail boat or displacement trawler). But leaving the Fraser River is one of the biggest challenges on the west coast. (Returning may be another.) The currents at the Sand Heads lightship are vicious at times. A receding tide near low water, especially against a west or northwesterly moderate breeze (don't even think about a strong wind or worse) can be dangerous in the extreme. Refer to the government publication on Weather and Thompson's **Oceanology** for interesting information about current, wind and wave patterns at the river mouth. Bear in mind that while the weather report covers Sand Heads windspeeds it does not provide wave height at the river mouth, a sadly lacking service, especially considering the dangerous nature of the seas at that point. You can always turn back and wait at Steveston for improved conditions or return to your marina, but coming back from across the Strait you reach a point where you are committed.

Leaving Crescent Beach is straight forward enough except that it is a long run across an open bay before entering the Strait. This may be easy and safe when departing, but it is sometimes difficult to assess conditions for returning. Point Roberts is well located for quick, visual assessment of conditions in the Strait and close enough to the San Juan and Gulf Islands that a crossing of the Strait is quick enough even for slower travelling vessels. But it is very exposed to bad weather conditions for a return trip and mariners should carefully determine what they can expect off Point Roberts before leaving the safety of a comfortable mooring on the other side. The use of *Canpass* makes border crossing easier. Enquire at Canada Customs for details on *Canpass*.

Boats cruising to Canada out of other Washington ports have some extra distance to travel through US waters to reach their Canadian destinations. Many simply stay in the San Juan Islands, which have numerous well run marinas and boating facilities. Vessels passing through en route to Canada have to be mindful of wind and tidal conditions at several passages, but with careful VHF weather monitoring and the ability to wait out unfavourable seas, at safe and interesting places, the passage can be most pleasant.

Canadians travelling to the San Juans and Puget Sound are equally subject to monitoring sea conditions. Know where you are headed and check the route before you leave. Watch for obvious current-swept waterways and check the tide and current tables. When cruising any unknown waters check what other boats are doing. If there are no other boats about be particularly cautious and double check the current predictions and weather reports.

Vessels travelling across the border, unless they have a US cruising pass and/or subscribe to *Canpass* must stop at a customs dock for clearance and should carry their clearance reporting number for checking back into their home country.

Once you have managed to clear your marina and the possible obstacles of weather, currents and tide you are on your way to the fabulous San Juans, Gulf Islands, Desolation Sound or beyond. Or try some of the interesting places in Puget Sound or on the west coast of Vancouver Island.

South to North

The format of this book takes the reader in a south to north progression from one dock to the next, beginning in the San Juan Islands. Vancouver Island west coast information is arranged from north to south. It concludes by continuing south from Juan de Fuca Strait to Olympia. The intention is to provide a logical sequence of references to fuel stops or overnight moorage en route to a final destination.

Information accompanying the graphics and photographs is up to date but constant changes are being made at various marinas. This book will be revised and updated periodically depending on the frequency and extent to which coastal facilities are altered or improved.

The author welcomes your cruising tips and observations for future editions.

Doing it right.

Marinas are a home away from home. When you tie up to a dock at a private marina you are in effect stopping in to visit other boat owners and the owners and operators of the marina. What you do and how you operate your vessel says a lot about you and a lot about your experience as a mariner. Your reception from marina managers and fellow boat owners will be determined by the impression you create from the moment you nudge your boat up to the dock.

Some boat owners, and often this applies to novices, don't really care how they are perceived by others. Those same people also tend to not learn from their errors. For mariners who wish to fit in, be they newcomers or old hands, here are some basic tips, but first, take an accredited boating course and obtain your operator's proficiency certificate:

During the peak months of summer telephone ahead for reservations. Remember changes are being made constantly and you can expect to find new additions at some docks, name and phone number changes, different regulations, revised services and other variances from the information contained in this guide. Please note the changes for your own convenience.

Before you arrive at a marina ensure you are not passing other installations at speed. Slow down well before you reach the dock. Sitting at a dock in West Sound in the San Juans once I saw a large boat came by at full speed leaving a wash in excess of two feet that caused some damage at the dock. He was heading for a club dock at the head of the bay and had totally ignored the existence of the marina tucked in behind the island to his starboard. That same week I saw a similar sized vessel do the same thing entering Bedwell Bay.

Before you enter the marina establish exactly where your assigned slip is. In many marinas you can call on VHF for slip assignment. The dock photographs and diagrams in this book should help you easily locate the slip or general area of the slip to which you have been assigned. As you approach your slip note effects of current and wind and plan your docking manouvres accordingly. It's always easiest to angle in towards the dock against the flow of water or direction of the wind. If you are backing your boat into a tight slip it is even more essential that you are aware of these conditions. Have your crew at the ready and prepared for landing.

Play it the way the pros do. They attach a line to a centre cleat and hold the end coiled in one hand as they step ashore. Snubbing the line to a cleat on the dock when the boat is close to that cleat will keep it there and prevent the bow or stern from breaking away and swinging out, as often occurs when only a line at the bow or the stern is used. Have fenders down at a height compatible with the height of the docks and positioned one ahead of the centre cleat and one near the stern. Once the boat is stopped the skipper can casually step ashore, secure the bow and stern lines and adjust fenders at leisure.

Crew: Other people may offer assistance. Usually they expect to be handed a line and all too often when they take it they totally destroy your docking plan. This is usually done by yarding on the bow line, bringing the bow in too close to the dock disabling you from handling the stern. You don't have to pass them a line. Do so if absolutely necessary or when the skipper has the boat docked. No harm saying to a person "here is the line, please just hold it" or have two docksiders haul in bow and stern simultaneously. Don't try to look as though you are proficient if you cannot pull it off. You are better off to say to anyone watching as you are approaching your slip that you are new at this and would appreciate some experienced help in docking. You'll be surprised how readily people will come to your aid and how pleasant they will be when you are up front about your docking abilities.

Docking is just the beginning. You will not enamour yourself or your crew to anyone at

Downtown Vancouver. Looking east across False Creek from Granville Island's Pelican Bay.

the dock if you yell, either at them or at your crew. At many marinas there are full-time personnel employed to assist boaters docking. They are not always the most experienced but as long as you follow some of the above advice their assistance will enable you to perform a good landing.

If you are docking parallel to a long open dock, tie up your boat in such a way that you allow maximum room for the next boat coming in. If you have a dinghy in the water tuck it in under the bow of your boat while you are not using it in order that you leave room for the next boat.

Anchoring off and going ashore to visit a marina and its facilities, perhaps to have a meal, a snack or browse for some souvenir is a common practice during summer. Also common is the individual who goes ashore only to drop off a huge bag of garbage. On small, remote islands, this is a major problem. If you are a mooring guest you may do well to assess how convenient it is to leave garbage behind, even though some places have disposal bins. If you know you are continuing to a mainland facility soon, save the garbage for that stop. The same applies to water. If you are travelling to an island with limited water resources fill up before going there and use water sparingly. Do not use scarce, island water to wash your boat.

Some boat owners have been known to tie up at a marina for long periods during the day, fill up with water, perhaps use the facilities such as shower and laundry and then take off and anchor across the bay for the night. There are times when such use of moorage has denied a prospective overnight moorage customer space to tie up. Marinas have a very limited season in which to prosper and mariners who cause lost overnight moorage will not be appreciated.

Most marina operators will be happy to have you stop for a short period if you don't plan to spend the night. Some have a charge per hour. Others, like government docks, allow two hours free and then an overnight charge is levied. If you make use of marinas and their services as a paying guest you will help ensure their survival for the future.

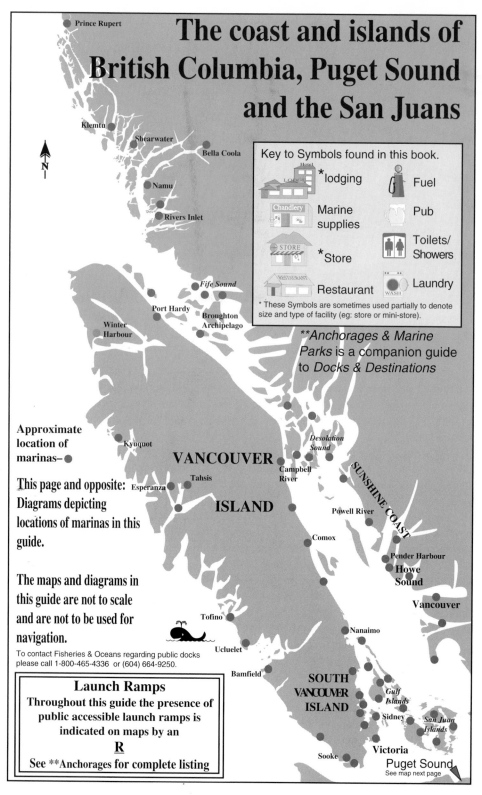

The coast and islands of British Columbia, Puget Sound and the San Juans

Prince Rupert

Klemtu

Shearwater

Bella Coola

Namu

Rivers Inlet

Fife Sound

Port Hardy

Broughton Archipelago

Winter Harbour

Key to Symbols found in this book.

*lodging

Fuel

Marine supplies

Pub

*Store

Toilets/ Showers

Restaurant

Laundry

* These Symbols are sometimes used partially to denote size and type of facility (eg: store or mini-store).

**Anchorages & Marine Parks* is a companion guide to *Docks & Destinations*

Approximate location of marinas–

Kyuquot

VANCOUVER

Desolation Sound

Campbell River

SUNSHINE COAST

This page and opposite: Diagrams depicting locations of marinas in this guide.

Tahsis

Esperanza

ISLAND

Powell River

Comox

Pender Harbour

Howe Sound

The maps and diagrams in this guide are not to scale and are not to be used for navigation.

Tofino

Vancouver

Nanaimo

To contact Fisheries & Oceans regarding public docks please call 1-800-465-4336 or (604) 664-9250.

Ucluelet

Bamfield

SOUTH VANCOUVER ISLAND

Gulf Islands

Sidney

San Juan Islands

Victoria

Sooke

Puget Sound

See map next page

Launch Ramps

Throughout this guide the presence of public accessible launch ramps is indicated on maps by an

R

See **Anchorages for complete listing

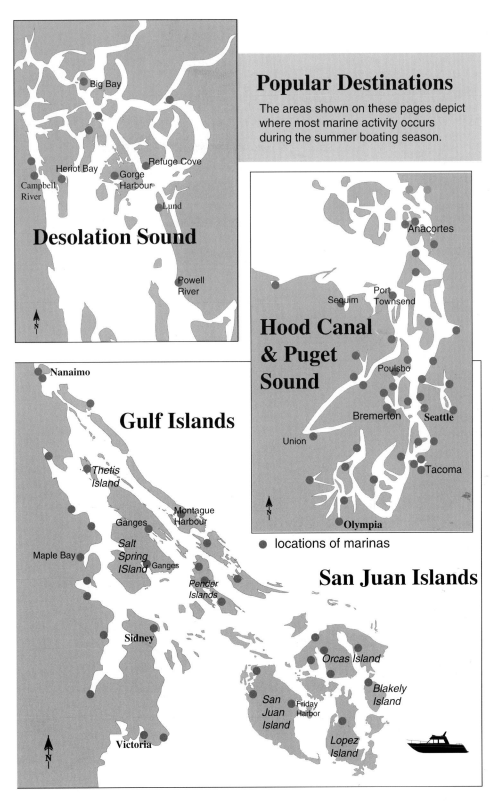

Desolation Sound

Big Bay

Refuge Cove

Heriot Bay

Gorge
Harbour

Campbell
River

Lund

Powell
River

Popular Destinations

The areas shown on these pages depict where most marine activity occurs during the summer boating season.

Anacortes

**Hood Canal
& Puget
Sound**

Sequim

Port
Townsend

Poulsbo

Bremerton

Seattle

Union

Tacoma

● locations of marinas

Olympia

Gulf Islands

Nanaimo

Thetis
Island

Ganges

Montague
Harbour

Salt
Spring
ISland

Ganges

Maple Bay

Pender
Islands

San Juan Islands

Sidney

Orcas Island

Blakely
Island

San
Juan
Island

Friday
Harbor

Victoria

Lopez
Island

13

Historic buildings and places of interest can be found adjacent to many waterfront landings such as the Orcas Hotel, top, and the West Sound Store, above.

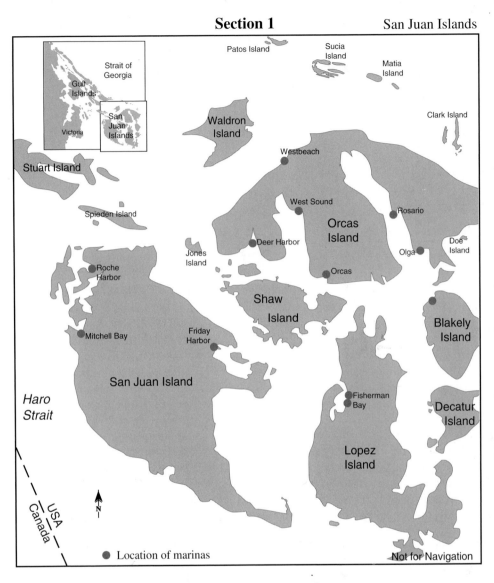

Location of marinas   Not for Navigation

San Juan Islands

Journeying into the San Juans mariners have the pick of some outstanding marinas, fine restaurants, well-stocked marine, grocery and hardware stores as well as arts and crafts centres. There are fast food places, ice cream vendors, pubs, hotels, good accommodations and rustic bed and breakfast places. There are walking and hiking trails and roads as well as car, bicycle and motor scooter rentals. Some stops include dining at places such as the restaurant at Deer Harbor or the quaint West Sound Store and Deli for a good bowl of soup, a sandwich, salad or dessert. At Friday Harbour there is such a wide choice of

restaurants as well as other stores it would take an entire vacation to enjoy the place to its fullest. The annual Jazz Festival on the last weekend in July is a busy time so get in early or keep away if you want to avoid crowds. A more tranquil place may be Fisherman Bay with its good anchorage and marinas, nearby Lopez Village and pleasant dining facilities. Roche Harbor is a busy customs port and attracts some of the larger cruising yachts to its busy marina. It's a place to visit if you like to look longingly at some of those mega vessels that frequent and even monopolize it. The Hotel De Haro usually has fine dining and it's entertaining to watch the evening color ceremony at sundown. Fascinating history of the islands include the early explorations of the Spanish, the presence of the English and the famous Pig War which nearly led to an international confrontation between the British and Americans. One of the more charming remnants of recent history of the islands is Rosario Resort on Orcas Island. A stop at this facility will provide sheltered moorage as well as a chance to acquaint yourself with its splendid history.

A short or long stay in the San Juans can provide a complete vacation, and many Canadians make the trip once in a while just as their American counterparts are steaming through the San Juans en route to the Canadian Gulf Islands and points beyond.

Above left and right: Friday Harbor.
Opposite centre: At Lopez Village.
Right: The marina at Roche Harbor with anchorage in Garrison Bay beyond.
Note inset showing extended docks. See following page.
Left: Rosario Resort on Orcas Island.

16

A smart crew will not pass dock lines to someone on shore until the skipper is good and ready. Spectators who are eager to assist often are inexperienced and will pull on the bow line, throwing the skipper's manouvres totally out of control. It is best only to pass someone ashore a line connected amidships, and only when it is really necessary, such as when wind or current are pushing the boat away from the dock.

Roche Harbor

Roche Harbor
Resort & Marina

Kevin Carlton
Box 4001, Roche Harbor,
Washington. 98250
Phone: (360) 378-2155 Fax (360) 378-9800
1 800 451-8910   Cel: 317-8573
Chart 18421/33   VHF call 78A
email: roche@rocheharbor.com
Web: www.rocheharbor.com
Marina services:
Moorage. 377 permanent and transient
slips to about 180 feet. **Pumpout** facilities.
Power at docks: 20 30 50, 100 amps.
Water. Fuel : Gas, diesel. Propane. Oil.
Customer services:
Showers, laundry, washrooms
Public phones ashore. Phone hook up.
Walking: Road access walking, cycling.
Adjacent and nearby facilities: Store–
groceries, a wide range of provisions.
Hotel, fine dining, accommodations. Arts
and crafts. Clothing, apparel, gifts,
groceries. Ice, fishing tackle, licences,

marine supplies. Moped rentals. Horse
riding. Hiking trails. Boat rentals, kayaks.
Good fishing nearby. Pool and tennis
courts. Jazz festival late July–call for
information. Fourth of July celebrations
and fireworks. Color ceremony each
sunset.   Coffee wagon.
   All facilities open March through October. Moorage and basic facilities open
year round–partial during winter. Launch
ramp nearby. Taxi or bus service to island
centres and ferry to Anacortes. Airfield.
Major Customs Port of Entry.

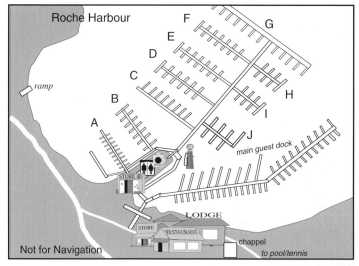

Roche Harbour

F
G
E
D
C
B
A
H
I
J

ramp

main guest dock

STORE

LODGE
STORE
RESTAURANT

chappel
to pool/tennis

Not for Navigation

Below: Facilities at Roche Harbour include the well stocked store whose name commemorates the historic Lime Stone company for which Roche Harbour was founded. Opposite, below: Approaching the fuel dock.

Hotel de Haro is the historic landmark at this famous harbor. It is a magnificent building exemplifying the type of construction and opulence of its day. There is a lot to see and do at Roche Harbor. The resort is a museum in its own right, its buildings dating back to 1886. It was founded in conjunction with the adjacent lime kiln and barrel manufacturing company.

Roche Harbor Marina

Snug Harbor Marina

Friday Harbor

San Juan

Island

Not for Navigation

Friday Harbor

Port of Friday Harbor

**Box 889, Friday Harbour,
Washington. 98250
Phone: (360) 378-2688
Chart 18434. 18421. Waterproof #43**

**VHF 66A (US mode)
Marina services:
Moorage.** Guest and permanent.
Power at docks: 30 amp.
**Water.
Fuel dock adjacent:** Gas, diesel, propane.

Customer services:
Pump-out station.
Laundry, showers, ice, bait.
Public phones ashore.
Nearby church/es: multi-denominational.
Pharmacies and other necessities.
Scuba diving arrangements and charters–
ask at nearby dive store or marina for
details.

Walking: Road access walking, cycling,
car and scooter rentals.
Entertainment:
Regular annual music festival late July,
Pig War Barbecue in June. Many other
events.
Nearby facilities: Ferry to Anacortes.
Marine stores–charts, marine hardware,
supplies, books, fishing licences, tackle,
etc. Post office, liquor, restaurants, banks,
accommodations, pubs and specialty
stores. Golf, cinema, airport.

Note:
*When arriving at Friday Harbor from
Canadian waters first check in at the
customs dock on the breakwater.
The flag up means the office on the dock is
open. Down means you can check in at the
office ashore or by telephone if that office
is closed. Then proceed to dock A for slip
assignment or call on VHF 66A.*

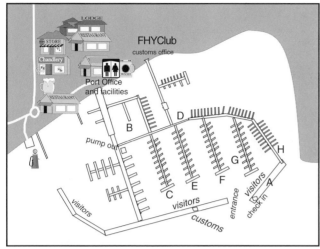

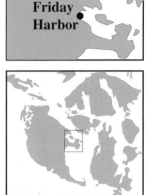

Not for Navigation

Major Customs Port of Entry:
Phone (360) 378-2080.
Or 1 800-562-5943

Friday Harbor

This large marina is one of the busiest in the Pacific Northwest. It is a major customs stop entering United States waters for Canadian boat operators and one of the major centres for returning American mariners. Located on the east side of San Juan Island it competes with Roche Harbor as a customs stop but the two are vastly different. Friday Harbour has a large town comprising everything from city hall to cinema, super-markets to specialty shops, hardware store, marine chandleries and a wide variety of restaurants, pubs and bistros. As a major ferry landing, Friday Harbor sees the coming and going of a vast number of people: islanders, cyclists coming to visit, campers, boaters and fly-in sightseers. During summer crowds of boaters flock to the town for the major event of the year, the Summer Jazz Festival. A Pig War barbecue is held in June.

For the boat owner there is fuel, moorage, water, showers, laundry, 30 amp electrical service and all the amenities one could imagine necessary for a major stopover. There are two anchorages in the immediate proximity of the huge marina, one adjacent to the north west marina entrance and the other out in the middle of the harbor.

21

Snug Harbor

Snug Harbor Marina Resort

Dick Barnes (owner Glenn Kalmus)
**2371 Mitchell Bay Rd., San Juan Island,
Washington. 98250**
Phone: **(360) 378-4762 Fax 360 378-8859.**
Chart: **Waterproof #43. 18421**

Marina services:
Moorage. 71 slips. Guests welcome.
Power. 15, 20, 30 amp.
Water.
Fuel : Gas. Repairs. Marine supplies.
Customer services:
Garbage bins.
Shower, laundry. By arrangement.
General store, groceries, provisions, charts,
books, clothing, gifts, hardware, marine,
fishing equipment. Public phones ashore.
Walking: Road access walking.

Adjacent Facilities: Accommodations.
Ten self-contained, fully equipped bunga-
lows. RV park. Launch ramp. Scuba charters,
whale watching.
Note: Rocks in entrance. Channel to left.
Depth 3' at zero tides.
Use large scale chart or Waterproof #43 for
navigating inside Henry Island.
Nearest customs at Roche Harbor.

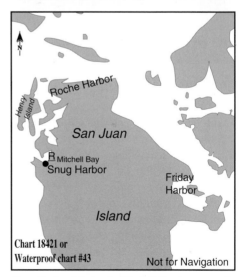

Chart 18421 or
Waterproof chart #43
Not for Navigation

*Snug Harbor Marina in Mitchell Bay is protected
from the open waters of Haro Strait by a shallow
entrance and drying reef. The channel at zero
tides drops to three feet. The bay lies south of
Roche Harbor.*

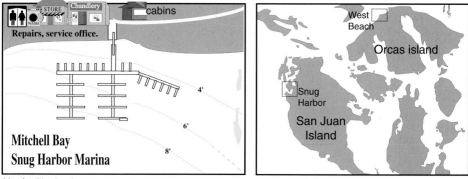

Mitchell Bay
Snug Harbor Marina

Not for Navigation

Below: West Beach Resort

Orcas Island

Charts 18432, 18421

West Beach Resort

Tim and Liz Hance
190 Waterfront Way,
Eastsound, Washington. 98245
Phone: (360) 376-2240 fax (360) 376-4746
Toll free (877) 937-8224
email: *vacation@westbeachresort.com*
Web: *www.westbeachresort.com*
Marina services:
Moorage. Transient boats to 26'.
Water. Fuel: Gas. Propane, ice.

Customer services:
Fish cleaning facility. **Showers, laundry.**
Resort. Store, coffee shop. Charts, books,
fishing tackle, bait. Stove oil, kerosene.
Entertainment: Walking–road access. Good
scuba diving in vicinity.
Adjacent Facilities: Accommodations.
18 self-contained, fully equipped bungalows.
RV park. Scuba airfills. Public phone.
Launch ramp guests only (fee includes park-
ing for trailers). Seasonal Beach Grill.

Deer Harbor

Deer Harbor Marina

Mike Douglas, manager
Box 200, Deer Harbor, Orcas Island
Washington. 98243
Phone: (360) 376-3037 Fax: 376-6091
Charts 18421/34 VHF call 66 (US mode)

Marina services:
Moorage. Transient and permanent.
Power at docks: 15 amp.
Water.
Fuel: Gas, diesel.
Customer services:
Barbecue area. Accommodations.
Showers, washrooms. Ice.
Public phones ashore.
Walking: Road access walking, cycling.

Entertainment:
Heated swiming pool and spas. Small boat rentals, whale watching tours, kayaking, sunset cruises and fishing charters.

Adjacent facilities: Store–groceries, deli and provisions. Store–gifts, postcards, clothing and arts and crafts. Sean Paul's restaurant–elegant dining.
Taxi service to island centres and ferry to Anacortes. Seaplane service to Seatac.

Note:
Clear customs for USA destinations at Roche Harbor or Friday Harbor.

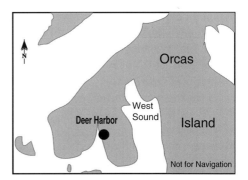

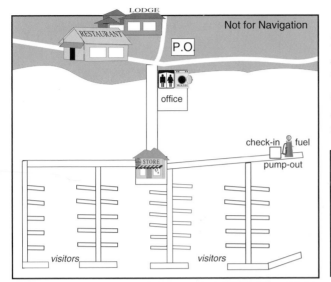

This is a busy marina in summer. It is designed and operated for visitors and has amenities for boaters on the move.
Nearby restaurants cater to the marine crowd.

Opposite: check-in and fuel dock at Deer Harbor. This photo shows marina busy in season. North fingers superimposed on photo taken before docks added. Inset above: off-season photo shows current marina layout. Private marina to the left.

Deer Harbor

This cosy corner of Orcas Island is a pleasant stopover at docks that face a semi-protected open bay. Most wind conditions do not bother boats at the marina but a southerly or south westerly wind may cause a bit of movement, especially off season. In season many boats visit the docks to stay overnight and enjoy excellent cuisine at nearby restaurants. The marina offers fuel, water, showers, ice, snacks and groceries. A resort located just across the road offers accommodations and spa amentities.

West Sound

West Sound Marina

Mike & Peggy, Ian, Betsy Wareham.
Box 119, Orcas Island
Washington. 98280
Phone: (360) 376-2314
Chart 18421/34 VHF call 16
Hazard: Island reef near guest dock.
Marina services:
Moorage. Some transient moorage.
Power at docks: 15, 30 amp.
Water. Pumpout
Fuel: Gas, diesel, oils.
Customer services:
Marine ways and repairs. Major shipyard.
Complete marine chandlery.
Showers, washrooms. Ice. Public phone.
Walking: Road access walking, cycling.
Nearby facilities: Store–deli and provisions. Light meals. Bed and Breakfast.
Taxi service to island centers and ferry
to Anacortes. West Sound Yacht Club.
Small public dock at head of bay.

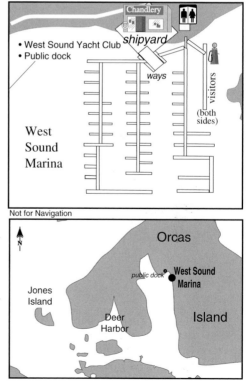

West Sound

This protected moorage is largely for long term resident boats. However, it has an excellent marine service facility with 30 ton travel lift and comprehensive repair services. It has a well stocked marine store and the buildings ashore include a large, modern, heated bay where refinishing and mechanical work can be done in any weather conditions. The facility caters to all of the San Juan Islands with a 24 hour emergency service. Transient moorage accommodates a number of boats on a 250 foot finger that is an extension of the fuel dock. Gas and diesel are available and are generally priced competitively with fuel at places such as Friday Harbor. It has a pump out station.

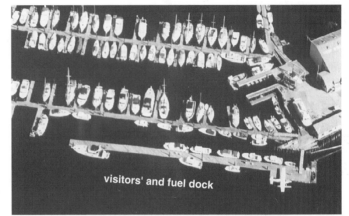

visitors' and fuel dock

A short walk up the road there is a deli which serves light meals at lunchtime. An island taxi service out of East Sound is available for transportation to other parts of Orcas Island such as Orcas ferry landing or the town of East Sound. The facility is owned and operated by Mike and Peggy Wareham, son Ian and daughter Betsy. The chandlery offers Johnson outboard products, fishing gear, marine supplies of a wide variety, propane and ice.

Note:
Clear customs for USA destinations at Roche Harbor or Friday Harbor.

Note the docks at the head of the bay. One is the yacht club and the other a public dock.

public

West Sound Marina

fuel

private

Orcas Landing

Russel's Store (Independent operator)
Box 200, Deer Harbor, Orcas Island
Washington. 98280
Phone: (360) 376-4389 (Russel's Inc.)
Chart 18430, 18434, 18421

Fuel dock–Island Petroleum Services
Phone (360) 376-3883.
Moorage. Stopping briefly only.
Water. Fuel: Gas, diesel. Oils.

Customer services:
Stores and facilities ashore. Ice.
Public phones ashore.
Walking: Road access walking, cycling.
Entertainment:
Sightseeing by bicycle popular.
Adjacent Facilities: Stores–groceries, gifts, clothing, arts and crafts. Orcas Hotel nearby. Taxi service to island centres and ferry to Anacortes.

VHF call 66 (US mode)

Orcas Landing

A quaint village at the ferry landing serves the community on Orcas Island. It has an historic hotel as a focal point. The Orcas Island Hotel has rooms and pub and restaurant, the latter of which is reputed to serve excellent meals. Through the week food is served at the pub or at the pub's outdoor terrace area. Changes and improvements should provide greater comfort. The dock at Orcas is for transient mariners

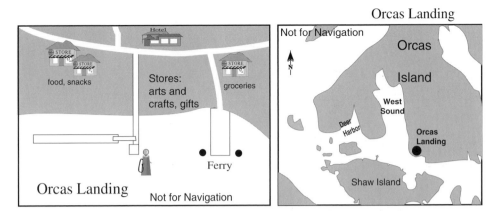

only. It is long and accessible both sides although the shoreward side has a narrow entrance and if a boat is tied up at the end entry for anything but a small boat would be tight. Fuel is available at the dock as well as other marine products and services. On shore there is a gift and craft store, Russels, which has a wide selection of wares. The settlement is popular among transient mariners and land based visitors alike. Summer sees thousands of cyclists, campers and motorists arriving on the island in a constant stream off the ferries. At Orcas it is a common sight for crowds of vacationers to be lining up for their trip home mingling with those just arriving as they flood into hotel, craft stores, grocery store, fast food restaurant, ice cream store or other facilities.

Left: The small craft dock at Orcas Landing.
Below: Orcas Landing with Russel's and other buildings adjacent.
Opposite: The ferry at Orcas Island. The dock for small craft can be seen clearly to port of the vessel.

Rosario Resort Marina

Harbor Master
Orcas Island
East Sound, Washington. 98245
Phone: (360) 376-2222 Fax 376-3038
Chart 18421, 18430, 18434.
email: *info@rosarioresort.com*
Web: www.rosarioresort.com
Marina services:
Moorage. Guest and permanent. **Fuel.**
Power at docks: 30, 20 amp. **Water.**
Customer services:
Laundry, showers, ice, bait.

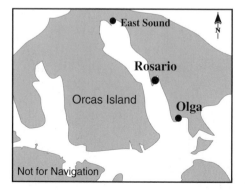

VHF 78A

Public phones ashore. Garbage bins.
Hotel, pub, spa, pool (indoor and outdoor),
retaurants–fine dining or casual. Gift shop.
Accommodations and all hotel services.
Nearby church.
Scuba diving arrangements and charters–
ask at dive store or marina for details.
Walking: Road and trail access walking.
Car rentals.

Entertainment:
Regular live music, organ recitals in the
historic mansion. Slides and Rosario
history narration. Golf nearby. Tennis
courts. Kayak tours. Air tours. Whale
watching tours. Fishing charters.
Adjacent facilities: Cascade Bay Cafe
and grocery store, supplies. Rental cars.
Kayak rentals.
Note: Reservations recommended for
marina or resort, in peak summer months
particularly. **Mooring buoys** and anchoring landing fee includes passes to spa and
pools. **Launch ramp.**

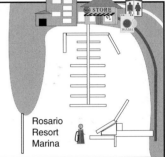

The Rosario docks (inset left) are protected behind a breakwater with a fuel dock at the entrance. The mansion, lower, looks over the sweep of East Sound. Above, right: The store at Olga. Lower: The landing at Olga.

Rosario Resort

There is sheltered moorage at the docks behind the breakwater. Mooring buoys are not necessarily sheltered from the wind and waves that blow up East Sound some afternoons. The hotel is a feature of the San Juan Islands with a colourful history and excellent restaurant. Facilities include water, showers, store and a swimming pool with hot tubs.

Robert Moran, who built Rosario Resort after retiring in 1904, was a former shipbuilder in Seattle. He used shipbuilding methods and materials in the construction of the mansion. The building's walls are made of 12 inch concrete and the roof is sheathed in copper. Windows are 7/8 inch plate glass and many sections of the interior are panelled in mahogany. One of the resort's major features is the Kimball pipe organ, said to be the largest installed in a private residence in the United States. The mansion was listed in the National Register of Historic Places in 1979. The estate was sold in 1938 and the current ownership created the resort in 1960.

Rosario is the closest sheltered marina for accessing East Sound, a bustling village that attracts many visitors annually, mostly by ferry. There are restaurants, stores, banks, post office, medical clinic, movie theater, pharmacy, churches, galleries and many other facilities. East Sound airport provides tours for visitors wanting a lofty look at the islands.

The town of Olga (photo right) has a quaint village store and community docks. Stop and dine at the village arts co-op restaurant.

A sign on the dock reads: "Dock maintained with community labor and moorage fees collected after 6 pm." It is exposed and not recommended for overnight unless you are certain of favourable weather.

31

Blakely Island

Blakely Island General Store and Marina

Richard and Norma Reed
Blakely Island
Washington. 98222
Phone: (360) 375-6121 Fax 375-6141
Chart 18421 18430
email: blakely@rockisland.com
Web: *www.rockisland.com/~blakely/*
Marina services:
Moorage. Guest moorage.
Fuel: Gas, diesel.
Power at docks: 30 amp.**Water.**
Customer services:
Showers, laundry, washrooms.
Store. Provisions. Groceries.
Clothing, gifts. Tackle, bait. Fishing reports taken. Licences. Ice. Hot dogs, snacks. Patio. Banquet and meeting space. Public phones ashore.
Garbage disposal for customers.

Adjacent facilities: Covered barbecue pits in cabana on the waterfront. Pet area–All dogs to be kept on leash please.
Cleaning facilities–sink and power. Club bookings, facility day use. Lawn Games.
Note:
Entrance depth to 8' at zero tides. Fuel dock accessible either side.
Covered docks at entrance are private.
Clear customs for USA destinations at Roche Harbor or Friday Harbor.

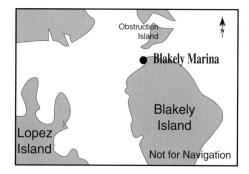

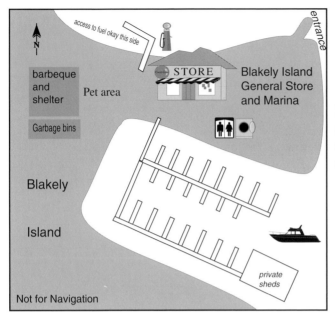

The entrance is narrow and shallow at low tide. The level of the water drops to 8 feet but it is an easy passage.

Left: The store at Blakely Marina with the patio out front. It faces the open passage and overlooks the fuel dock.
Below: The fuel dock is accessible from either side.

Blakely Marina

There is no access to the rest of the island, which is privately owned. The marina has facilities for guest boats and a sheltered bay where a number of boats can moor. Access is limited to higher tides for deep draft vessels. The depth through the channel is 8' at zero tides. A current runs past the entrance. This is a beautifully landscaped island and although most of it is private the scenery is enjoyable from the marina or the patio ashore.

Fisherman Bay

Charts 18421/30/34

Islands Marine Centre

Ron & Jennifer Meng
**Box 88, Lopez Island,
Washington. 98261
Phone: (360) 468-3377 Fax 468-2283**
email: *imc@rockisland.com*
**Marina services:
Moorage.** Guest moorage on the south side
of marina.
Power: 30 amp.
Water.
Fuel: Next door at Lopez Islander Resort.
Boatyard. Repairs and service. Haulouts.
15 ton travel lift. Launch ramp.

**Customer services:
Showers, washrooms**
Yacht sales and service. Various makes of
outboard motors and boating equipment.
Marine chandlery, hardware, charts,
clothing, gifts, electronics, fishing tackle
and information. Licences. NAPA store.
Ice. Public phones ashore.
Walking: Road access walking, cycling.

VHF channel 69.

Entertainment: Golf nearby. Picnic and
barbecue area. Bicycle rentals. Wine
tasting at nearby vineyards.
Adjacent facilities: Lopez Village less
than one mile. Stores–groceries, provisions, inn, meals, accommodations. Lopez
Islander Resort and restaurant next door.
Courtesy van service to ferry, airport, golf,
by arrangement.

Note:
Customs Port of Entry at Friday Harbor
or Roche Harbor.

Islands Marine
Center

Chandlery

Ramp   Travelift

T1
to
T 10

Not for Navigation   *Guest moorage on T dock (south)*   **T 10**

The entrance, above, to Fisherman Bay
is narrow and shallow, but deep enough
for a safe passage for most craft at low
tides. A sign on marker number five
reminds mariners to round marker
number eight inside the bay leaving it to
starboard. It is located not far from the
outer floats of Islands Marine Center
docks shown in the distance and to the
right in the aerial photograph, opposite
lower. The chandlery and service
facility at Islands Marine Center
appear in the photo below.

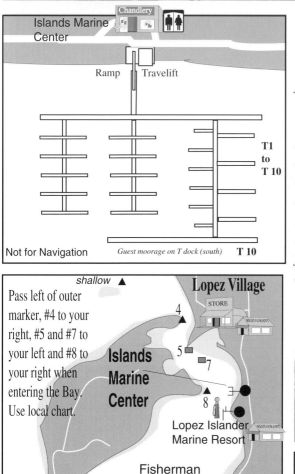

shallow ▲   **Lopez Village**

STORE

Pass left of outer
marker, #4 to your
right, #5 and #7 to
your left and #8 to
your right when
entering the Bay.
Use local chart.

**Islands
Marine
Center**

4
5
7
8

Lopez Islander
Marine Resort

Fisherman
Bay

Not for Navigation

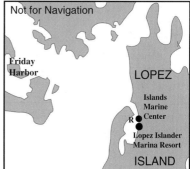

Not for Navigation

Friday
Harbor

LOPEZ

Islands
Marine
Center
R
Lopez Islander
Marina Resort

ISLAND

Lopez Islander Resort & Marina

Bill & Earle Diller. Kathy Casey, Mgr.
Box 459, Lopez Island,
Washington. 98261
Phone: (360) 468-2233 Fax 468-3382
Charts 18421/30/34
Dock 468-3383 VHF 78
www.lopezislander.com
Marina services:
Moorage. Guest mooring.
Power: 30, 50 amp.
Water.
Fuel: Gas, diesel
Sea plane float

Customer services:
Showers, laundry, washrooms.
Store on dock, groceries, provisions,
charts, clothing, gifts, books, bread, fishing
tackle. Ice. Public phones ashore.
Courtesy phone on dock.
Hotel accommodation–28 rooms. Swimming
pool. Hot tub. Conference and banquet
facilities. Salmon fishing and scuba diving
charters. Wildlife & whale watching.
Restaurant lounge (360) 468-2234. Patio
service. Espresso bar. Dockside welcome
package June to September.
Walking: Road access walking, cycling.
Entertainment: Golf nearby. Hot tub.
Bicycle and kayak rentals and guides.
Adjacent facilities: Lopez Village less than
one mile. Stores, arts and crafts, churches,
accommodations. 5 miles to ferry service.
Float plane calls at marina.

Lopez Islander
Marina Resort

Lopez Island Vineyards are open to the public and wine tasting is available June to September 7, Wednesdays to Sundays from 12 noon to 5pm. Other months on Fridays and Saturdays. The vineyards are a short distance beyond the Lopez Island village and a reasonable walk or a quick drive away. Lopez wines are made from local Madeleine Angevine, Siegerrebe and from Yakima Valley Chardonnay and Cabernet Sauvignon/Merlot.

Lopez Island is one of the easiest islands in the San Juans for cycling. Bicycle rentals are available adjacent to Lopez Islander Marina and Islands Marine Center. An extensive road system allows wide exploration of the many interesting things to see and do on the island.

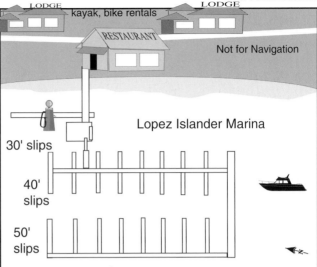

LODGE kayak, bike rentals LODGE

Not for Navigation

RESTAURANT

Lopez Islander Marina

30' slips

40' slips

50' slips

View towards the entrance of Fisherman Bay

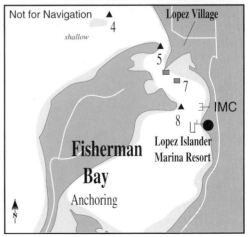

Not for Navigation ▲ Lopez Village
4
shallow
5
7
IMC
8

Fisherman Bay

Anchoring

Lopez Islander Marina Resort

Clockwise from top: A view out of Fisherman Bay from the marinas. The fuel dock at Lopez Islander Marina, two scenes at Lopez Village–a craft store and the village inn. Lopez Islander Marina is the facility on the left of the two marinas in the lower photo on the opposite page.

Point Roberts

Traveling South?
See section 14 for marinas
from Blaine to Olympia.

Point Roberts Marina

Bruce Gustafson
713 Simundson,
Point Roberts, WA. 98281
Phone: (360) 945-2255 Fax (360) 945-0927
Charts: Cdn: 3492, 3463. US: 18421
email: *prmarina@whidbey.com*
Web: *www.prmarina.com\prmarina*
Customer Services:
Moorage 24' to 125'.
Fuel: gas, diesel, propane.
Water, Power 30, 50 amp, **Showers, laundry, washrooms.** Public phones. Restaurant. Chandlery, bait, tackle, fishing licences, repairs, service. **Pumpout** facility at guest dock. Workyard. Haulouts–35 ton travelift, monorail sling hoist–boats to 22 feet. US Port of Entry. Customs.

Mostly for permanent moorage. There is space for visiting vessels at the long finger in the entrance channel as well as other slips, mostly on H dock. Phone for reservations.

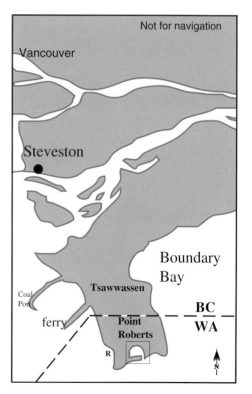

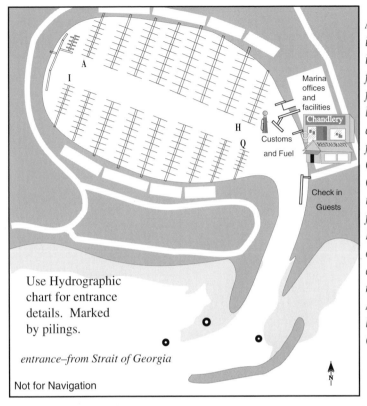

A

I

H

Q

Marina
offices
and
facilities

Customs

Chandlery

RESTAURANT

Customs
and Fuel

Check in
Guests

Use Hydrographic
chart for entrance
details. Marked
by pilings.

entrance–from Strait of Georgia

Not for Navigation

N

Although this marina is not in the San Juan Islands, it is very near. Access to it from the islands is closest from Sucia Island. It is a large centre for repairs and provides a good stop for access to the British Columbia mainland. Customs requires reporting when landing from Canadian ports. Point Roberts is on the tip of a peninsula which is attached to the BC mainland.

A nearby border crossing by land takes you into Greater Vancouver.

Coastal Marine Parks
(see *Anchorages and Marine Parks* published 1998)

Marine Parks in the San Juan Islands and British Columbia offer tranquil and delightful moorage. They have been established for use by the general public and attract hikers, backpackers, cyclists, RV campers and mariners. Many parks have picnic and overnight camp sites with trails and beaches. Some have docks adequate to moor dinghies only, some to moor a number of small to medium sized craft and others none at all. Most have mooring buoys for safe overnight mooring. Flat fees are levied for use of docks or mooring buoys. These change periodically but at present they are about $5 per mooring buoy per night and the charges usually apply from 3 pm to 8 am in the San Juans and after 6 pm in Canada.

The authorities ask that parks be respected and kept clean. Garbage should not be disposed of unless there is a specific disposal station. Sewage should not be discharged in marine park anchorages and noise should be limited to daylight hours. There are marine park hosts at some Marine Parks and in BC their presence will be indicated by the flying of a BC Parks Marine Park Host burgee. The host is usually a member of a power squadron, a yacht club, a sailing association or is an individual who has volunteered to assist visitors to the parks.

In Washington State it is possible to purchase an annual moorage permit which allows use of mooring buoys and docks at the various locations throughout the year without further fee. Fees are in effect year round at some facilities while at others only between May and September. In the San Juan Islands these include Sucia Island, Stuart Island, Jones Island, James Island and Matia Island.

For more information on marine parks in US waters contact Washington State Parks Headquarters, PO Box 42664, Olympia, WA. 98504–2664 (360) 753-5771.
In Canada, RR #6, 2930 Trans Canada Hwy, Victoria BC. V9B 5T9. (250) 387-4363.

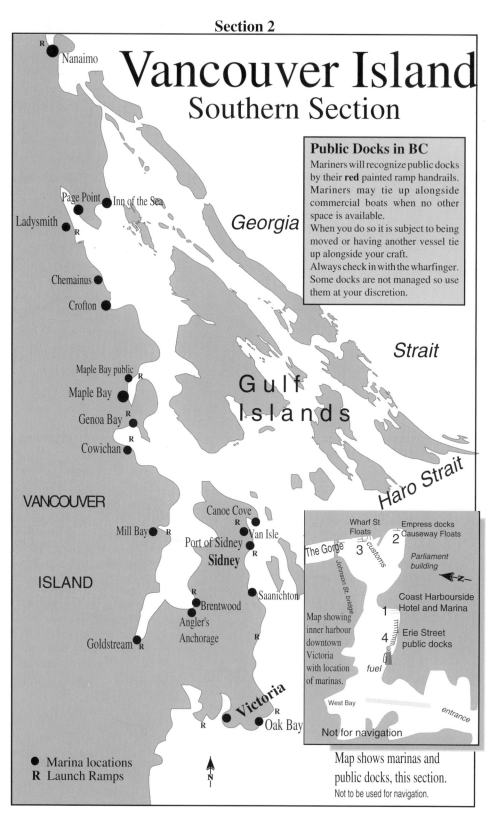

Vancouver Island
Southern Section

Georgia

Public Docks in BC

Mariners will recognize public docks by their **red** painted ramp handrails. Mariners may tie up alongside commercial boats when no other space is available.

When you do so it is subject to being moved or having another vessel tie up alongside your craft.

Always check in with the wharfinger. Some docks are not managed so use them at your discretion.

Strait

R Nanaimo

Page Point   Inn of the Sea

Ladysmith   R

Chemainus

Crofton

Maple Bay public   R

Maple Bay

Genoa Bay   R

Cowichan   R

G u l f
I s l a n d s

Haro Strait

VANCOUVER

Canoe Cove   R

Mill Bay   R   Van Isle

Port of Sidney   R

Sidney

ISLAND

Brentwood   R   Saanichton

Angler's
Anchorage   R

Goldstream   R

Victoria

R   Oak Bay
R

Wharf St
Floats

The Gorge

Johnson St. bridge

3   customs

2   Empress docks
    Causeway Floats

Parliament building

Coast Harbourside
Hotel and Marina

1

4   Erie Street
    public docks

fuel

Map showing
inner harbour
downtown
Victoria
with location
of marinas.

West Bay

entrance

Not for navigation

● Marina locations
R Launch Ramps

N

Map shows marinas and
public docks, this section.

Not to be used for navigation.

Above: Victoria's Causeway floats in front of the Empress Hotel.

Victoria

The Coast Harbourside Hotel and Marina. 1

Gale Windle
**146 Kingston St., Victoria,
BC, V8V 1V4
(250) 360-1211 Fax (250)360-1418
Chart 3415, 3440, 3462, 3313**
email: g.windle@coasthotels.com
Fuel: (at adjacent fuel dock) gas, diesel.
Marina Services: Moorage. Visitors welcome. Reserve in summer. **Water** at dock.
Power: 30, 50 amp. Pumpout. **Garbage disposal. Laundry, showers, washrooms.**
Accommodations, restaurant, spa, sauna, at adjacent hotel.
Service, stores available nearby–several blocks to downtown Victoria.

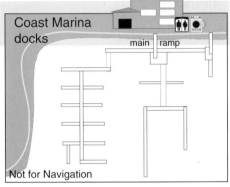
Not for Navigation

Photo shows docks at Coast Harbourside Marina. They have been expanded and opened to visitors.

There are many reasons to put into Victoria. It is a major customs port with a customs dock alongside the large public marina on Wharf Street. After clearing customs it is usually easy to find a slip at the public dock. Another public dock with limited space on either side of a single slip is located just before the Johnson Street bridge. Additional moorage under the same control as the Wharf Street dock is located right in front of the Empress Hotel. Good moorage is also available at Coast Harbourside Hotel and Marina. Beyond the Johnson Street bridge is The Gorge, and if you are ever in Victoria a slow cruise up there in your runabout or dinghy can make for a pleasant excursion.

Wharf Street floats

Causeway Floats. 2

Cathrine Featherby
1002A Wharf Street,
Victoria, BC, V8V 1Y4
(250) 363-3273 Fax 363-3224
Chart 3313, 3440, 3415, 3462   VHF 73
Marina services:
Moorage: Transient moorage.
Caution: Adjacent Seaplane landing area.
Water at dock.

The Empress Hotel is located opposite the Causeway floats.

Power: 30 amp.
Laundry, showers, washrooms.
Garbage disposal,
Customer services:
Customs/phone. Nearby city downtown within walking distance. Hotel Empress across the street. Walking–promenade.
Entertainment.
Downtown Victoria.
Adjacent or nearby services:
Ferries, seaplane services, customs. Hospital, banks, bank machines, car rentals, post office, swimming pool, telephone, taxi service.

Throughout summer there are various forms of entertainment ongoing on the promenade and in the city. This is a busy, small marina and additional moorage is available at the Wharf Street dock. *Photo previous page.*

Hotel

Government Street

A B C D E F G

Causeway floats.

As far as Victoria is concerned there is not only a wide variety of stores but also the charm of an array of British styled shops, pubs and restaurants. British imports are the speciality and if the atmosphere of old England does not strike you immediately go and reserve afternoon tea at the Empress Hotel. Tourists flock to Victoria each summer and the attractions, apart from the above, include the Royal BC Museum, parliament buildings, wax museum, undersea gardens, scenic London-bus tours and much more. There are festivities, shows and numerous public events in the city throughout summer.

Opposite: The docks at Wharf Street are probably the first place most mariners look for moorage. The alternatives are in front of the Empress Hotel, at Coast Harbourside Marina or at Erie Street– which is mostly occupied by commercial boats.

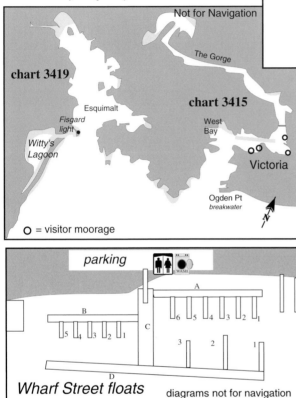

Not for Navigation

chart 3419

The Gorge

Esquimalt

chart 3415

Fisgard light

West Bay

Witty's Lagoon

Victoria

Ogden Pt breakwater

N

O = visitor moorage

The diagram left shows Victoria Harbour in relation to the adjacent Esquimalt harbour where dock facilities are occupied by the Canadian military.

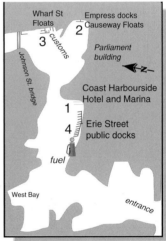

Wharf St Floats

Empress docks
Causeway Floats

3

2

customs

Parliament building

W–Z

Johnson St. bridge

Coast Harbourside Hotel and Marina

1

4

Erie Street public docks

fuel

West Bay

entrance

parking

WASH

A

B

6 5 4 3 2 1

C

5 4 3 2 1

3 2 1

D

Wharf Street floats

diagrams not for navigation

Caution: Seaplane landing area on approaches to Victoria Harbour

Wharf Street Floats. 3

Cathrine Featherby
**1002A Wharf Street,
Victoria, BC, V8V 1Y4
(250) 363-3273 Fax 363-3224
Chart 3313, 3415, 3440, 3462   VHF 73
Marina services:
Moorage**: Transient moorage.
Reserve in summer.
Water at dock.
Power: 30 amp.
**Laundry, showers, washrooms.
Garbage disposal.
Customer services:**

Customs/phone.
Nearby city downtown
within walking distance.
Hotels nearby. Walking–promenade.
Entertainment.
Downtown Victoria, Old City blocks and Chinatown. Scuba diving at Breakwater.
Adjacent or nearby services:
Ferries, seaplane services, customs.
Hospital, banks, bank machines, car rentals, post office, swimming pool, telephone, taxi service.

Erie Street Public docks 4.

Wharfinger
**12 Erie Street, Victoria,
BC, V8V 1Y4.
Ph: (250) 363-3760 Fax (250) 363-6947
Chart 3313, 3415, 3440, 3462 VHF 73
Marina services:
Fuel:** (at adjacent fuel dock) gas, diesel.
Mechanic and services available from local
and nearby marine operators and facilities.
Moorage: Permanent moorage and
overnight slips. Reserve in summer.
Water at dock. **Power:** 20 amp **Garbage.
Laundry, showers, washrooms.**
Waste oil disposal. Tidal Grid.
Nearby:
Accommodations, stores, banks, post office,
dive shops, car rentals, boat rentals, groceries, hardware, restaurants, swimming pool.

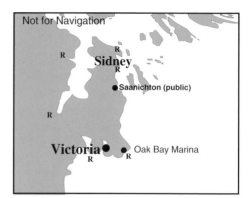

Not for Navigation

Below: Erie St Public dock in Victoria.

Mary Tod Island

*Oak Bay Marina opens off Baynes Channel in the lee of Discovery Island.
Watch for Lewis Reef on the northbound approaches to the entrance.*

Oak Bay Marina

Steve Huxter
**1327 Beach Drive, Victoria, BC,
V8S 2N4 (250) 598-3369**
Phone: (250) 598-3366 Fax (250)598-1361
Chart 3313, 3440, 3424, 3462 VHF 68

Hazard: Rocky entrance. Shoals and shallows–marked with buoys. Consult charts.
**Marina services:
Fuel:** Available at adjacent fuel dock.
Mechanic and services available from local and nearby marine operators and facilities.
Moorage: Permanent moorage and
overnight slips. Reserve in summer.
Water at dock. **Power:** 15 amp, 30 amp.
**Laundry, showers, washrooms.
Customer services:** Customs/phone.
Nearby village. Oak Bay Avenue. 6–8 blocks.
Chandlery. Tackle shop. Gift shops
and others within walking distance.
Deli at marina. Restaurant–dining.
Walking road and beachfront.

44

Going north–from Victoria

The fabled Gulf Islands are steeped in history and folklore and there are books on many subjects dealing with these fascinating islands as well as the San Juans. But this guide is not intended to keep you reading reams of historic notes, rather it encourages you to pick up the more complete works of other authors who have spent far more time researching those subjects for publication. As you make passage along the east shore of Vancouver Island, stopping possibly in Victoria or Sidney to clear customs, you unfold places of interest and people of charm and character that will please you. You may prefer to tie up at a dock and take in the local facilities. Victoria has the charm of British styled stores, pubs and restaurants. British imports are the speciality and if the atmosphere of old England does not strike you immediately go and reserve afternoon tea at the Empress Hotel. Tourists flock to Victoria each summer and the attractions include the Royal BC Museum, parliament buildings, wax museum, undersea gardens, scenic London-bus tours and much more. Try also the Port of Sidney, Canoe Cove or Van Isle Marina. All three have good restaurants including places where you can sit and

In the Victoria Harbour moorage options include the Causeway floats in front of the Empress Hotel. This location gives the visiting mariner the opportunity to see the best of the city. Victoria boasts one of the top tourism billings in Canada, with its very British atmosphere highlighted by pedigree pubs, London open-top buses and High Tea at the Empress.

take in the magnificent crimson summer sunsets. Consider the Blue Peter at Tsehum Harbour, the Stonehouse Pub at Canoe Cove or any of a variety in Sidney including the hotel on the waterfront.

In Saanich Inlet stop at Anchorage Marina and take your dinghy around to Butchart Gardens for a day of strolling in one of the most magnificent masterpieces of landscaping anywhere. Pull into Mill Bay and walk up to the local shopping centre for some tasty cappuccino or shopping at the well-stocked Thrifty Store. Continue up the coast through Genoa Bay for a safe overnight stop and fine dining, or visit Maple Bay for good moorage and a sumptuous meal at the marina restaurant.

Port Sidney

Port Sidney Marina
9835 Seaport Place,
Sidney, BC. V8L 4X3
or P.O. Box 2130,
Sidney, BC. V8L 2P6
Phone: (250) 655-3711
Fax: (250) 655-3771
Charts 3313, 3476, 3441, 3462
VHF 68

Marina services:
Fuel not available. Fuel docks at Tsehum Harbour and Canoe Cove (nearby, north) Mechanic and services available from local and nearby marine operators and facilities. Marine stores on dock and uptown Sidney.
Moorage: 300–400 slips. Permanent moorage and plenty of overnight slips. Reserve in summer. Excellent moorage. Also dockominium ownership available.
Water at dock. **Pumpout.**
Power at docks: 50, 30, 20, 15 amp.
Laundry, showers, washrooms.
Activities dock–reserve for group private functions.

Customer services:
Nearby churches, post office, general stores, books, charts, fishing licences, tackle, bait, fresh produce, groceries, bakery, butchery, hardware, dry cleaning, liquor, pharmacy, clothing, gift stores all within walking distance.
Numerous restaurants, coffee shops, bistros and cafes.
Walking trails or road access.
Some beachfront walks.
Town streets and waterfront roads allow views while walking.
Kayak and other small craft rentals available. Scuba diving arrangements and charters, whale watching–ask marina for details.
Water taxi service to other marinas.
International airport nearby.

Entertainment.
Nearby historic Butchart Gardens.
Sidney Museum summer hours–7 days per week. Features whales with murals and other historic exhibits.
Golf, tennis and other recreation nearby.

Saanichton, Sidney Public.
Transport Canada dock
Chart 3313, 3441, 3462
Manager • Float length 10 m
Lights •
South of Sidney–Restaurants, shops, medical centre, churches. (not walking distance).
Ferries nearby to BC mainland and US ports.

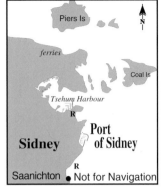

The Port Sidney Marina attracts many boaters from BC and Washington. It is a busy customs port and allows access to the many shops and services in the town.

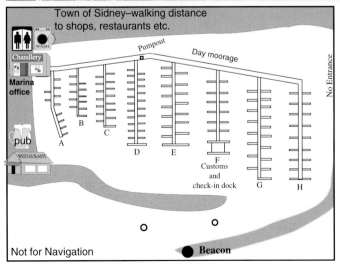

The aerial photograph above and the diagram left show the magnitude of the marina and the layout of the docks. Note: Even slip numbers on northwest side of slips. Odd numbers on southeast side.

47

Tsehum Harbour

Van Isle Marina

Mark Dickinson
**2320 Harbour Rd., Sidney,
BC. V8L 2P6.
Phone: (250) 656-1138
Fax: (250) 656-0182**
email: *info@vanislemarina.com*
www.vanislemarina.com
Hazard–Rocks inside marked by beacons.
Customs services.
Designated marina for courtesy customs clearance. Customs dock. Phone on dock.
Marina entrance.
From around breakwater at entrance to Tsehum Harbour. Most visitor moorage is at east end of fuel and adjacent floats.
Marina services:
Guest Moorage
Fuel: Gas. Diesel. Stove oil: PetroCanada fuel dock. Outboard mix. **Pumpout**
Water at dock. Multiple outlets.
Power: 50, 30, 15 amp. 120, 208 amp available. Public phone–ashore and on docks. Marine store on fuel dock. (250) 656-1138. Waste oil disposal, holding tanks pumpout, Ice. Charts, fishing tackle, licences, bait, life jackets etc.

Charts 3313, 3476, 3441, 3462 VHF 68

Mechanic and services available from local and nearby marine operators and facilities. Haulouts. Philbrooks Shipyard within marina complex. Casual dining in Dock 503 Waterfront cafe ashore. Yacht sales and service in marina complex. Boatlift within marina to 20 tons. Philbrooks boatlift 150 tons or 120 feet.
Docks can accommodate craft to 185 feet. Large permanent marina with many overnight mooring slips. Many facilities ashore. Reserve in summer.

Customer services:
Laundry, showers, washrooms.
Nearby church/es, licenced restaurant/s. Nearby fine restaurants open 7 days a week. Walking trails or road access. Some beachfront walks. Town streets and waterfront roads allow views while walking. Scuba diving arrangements and charters– ask marina for details.

Looking northwards over Tsehum Harbour. The fuel dock at **Van Isle Marina** *can be seen in the lower centre of the photograph.* **Westport Marina**, *upper right of bay, also offers some transient moorage.*

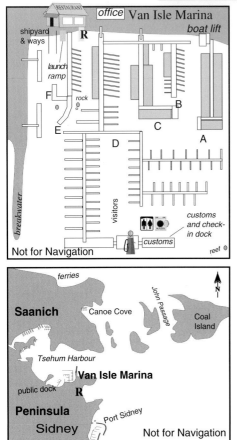

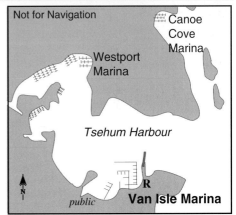

Tsehum Harbour

(Shoal Harbour Public)
Sidney, Vancouver Island.
Fish & Oceans
Chart 3310, 3476, 3441.
Managed • Float length: 318 m
Ramp • Breakwater • Garbage •
Waste oil disposal • Parking • Water •
Lights • Power • Telephone • Wash-
rooms • Adjacent marinas, restau-
rants, chandlery, haul outs, marine
repairs and full shipyard services.

Entertainment.
Cablevision available. TV and telephone
hook-ups.
Nearby historic Butchart Gardens. Bus, taxi
and rentals plus water shuttle to downtown
Sidney, easy access to Victoria, airport, ferries. Golf, tennis and other recreation nearby.

Walk Roberts Bay Bird Sanctuary nearby.

Nearby facilities:
Philbrooks Shipyard, All Bay Marine, The
Boat Yard, Jensen Marine, Sidney Marine
Supply. Tanners Books. Restaurants.
Tsehum Harbour Government dock nearby.

Canoe Cove

Canoe Cove Marina

Dock Manager
**2300 Canoe Cove Rd. Sidney,
BC. V8L 3S6
Phone: (250) 656-5566
Fax: (250) 655-7197**

Customs services.
Designated marina for courtesy customs clearance. Phone on dock.
Marina:
Some visitor moorage. Phone ahead to reserve overnight space.
Hazard: Rocks in north entrance marked by poles. Narrow waterway to fuel dock. Go Slow. Use right-of-way.
Marina services:
Fuel: Gas. Diesel. Stove oil. Propane. Ice. Marine chandlery: Charts, fishing tackle, licences, bait, life jackets etc.
Mechanic and services available from local and nearby marine operators and facilities. Haulouts. 35 ton travel lift. 65 ton ways.
Moorage: Large permanent marina with limited overnight moorage slips. Reserve.

Chart 3313, 3441, 3476, VHF 68

Water at dock. Multiple outlets.
Power at docks: 50, 30, 20, 15 amp.
Laundry, showers, washrooms.
Customer services:
Customs dock/phone. Coffee shop. Pub and restaurant. Artist studio. Walking neighbourhood roadways. Scuba diving arrangements and charters–ask marina for details.
Public pay phones ashore.

Entertainment.
Nearby historic Butchart Gardens. Bus, taxi and rentals plus water shuttle to downtown Sidney, road access to Victoria, airport. Golf, tennis and other recreation nearby.
Adjacent facilities: (The Stonehouse Pub–phone 656-3498) open 7 days a week.
Nearby: BC Ferries Swartz Bay to Vancouver and Gulf Islands.
Churches in Sidney and nearby.

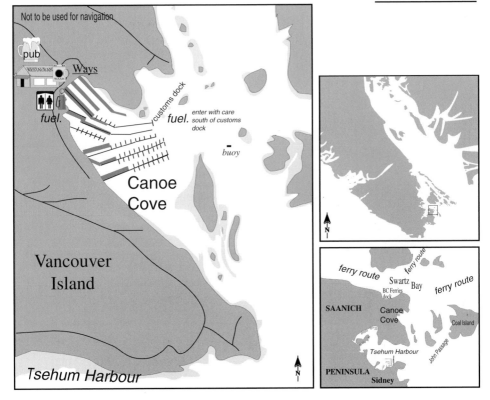

Canoe Cove

This cosy marina is a classic, with many permanent resident boats and little room for guests. Mariners stop in for fuel at the dock tucked away between docks C and D or to clear customs. There is a homey cafe for breakfast or lunch and early light dinner in the summer. For finer fare the Stonehouse Pub a short way behind the marina has an atmosphere that matches its good dining. Special events are celebrated at the restaurant with appropriate meals for the occasion.

The large boat yard adjacent to the marina has haulout and dry storage space and is operated by the service centre at the head of dock C. The ways will allow haulouts of larger vessels and the travel lift caters to more average sized boats. A chandlery situated near the cafe carries a wide range of items for repairs, service and annual maintenance.

The property is quite extensive with a resident artist and a well-known yacht brokerage company. It is the home of the Canoe Cove shipyard.

Many boat owners at the marina commute by ferry from the mainland and other parts taking advantage of the marina's close proximity to some of the most favoured cruising destinations on the coast and in the nearby islands.

Piers Island, Sidney (public)

Transport Canada dock
Chart   3313, 3476, 3462, 3441
Manager • Float length 63 m
Used primarily for local residents' access.
Opposite BC Ferries Swartz Bay terminal (Sidney).

Brentwood Bay
Chharts 3313, 3441, 3462

Brentwood Inn Resort

Mike Keepence
7172 Brentwood Drive, Brentwood Bay, BC. V0S 1A0
Phone: (250) 652-2413
Fax: (250) 652-2402

Customs services.
At adjacent Anglers Anchorage Marina. Phone on dock.

Marina Entrance.
Hazard–Reef off outer dock. Best route keep marker to starboard. Approach dock from ferry terminal. Check your chart.

Marina services:
Convenience store: Ice, fishing tackle, licences, bait, some provisions.
Mechanic and services available from local and nearby marine operators and facilities can be arranged.

Moorage: 65 slip permanent marina with limited overnight moorage. Reserve.

Water at dock. Multiple outlets.

Power at docks: 30, 15 amp.

Laundry, showers, washrooms.

Customer services:
Nearby church/es, Dockside restaurant and pub with view. Deck open in good weather and restaurant open 7 days a week.
Restaurant, speciality–seafood.
Walking trails or road access. Some beachfront and parkland trails.
Professional fishing guides available.
Rental runabouts - 16 footers.
Scuba diving arrangements and charters– ask marina for details.
Public pay phones ashore.

Entertainment.
Nearby historic Butchart Gardens.
(Dinghy in to Butchart Gardens)
Bus, taxi and rentals to downtown Sidney, easy access to Victoria, airport, ferries.
Golf, tennis and other recreation nearby.

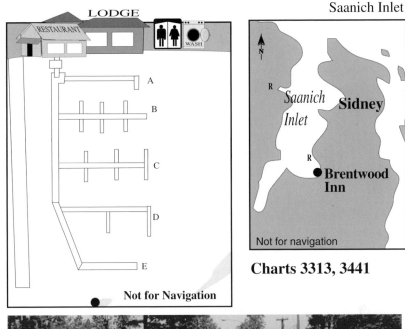

LODGE

RESTAURANT

WASH

A

B

C

D

E

Not for Navigation

R

Saanich Inlet **Sidney**

R

● **Brentwood Inn**

Not for navigation

Charts 3313, 3441

Opposite: Brentwood Inn marina docks.
Above: A waterfront restaurant dock is tucked
in north of the ferry landing adjacent to
Brentwood Inn. Small to medium boats only and
it is shallow at low tide.

Adjacent facilities:
Restaurant–with dock for boat in customers.
Fuel at Mill Bay, Goldstream or Sidney.
Launch Ramp nearby on native land.

Public dock

Brentwood Bay
Saanich Inlet
Transport Canada dock
Chart 3313, 3441
Manager • Float length 22 m
Adjacent: Private marina and
Angler's Anchorage Marina
Walk in adjacent park.
Used mostly by commercial traffic
for loading.

Angler's Anchorage

Angler's Anchorage Marina

Mark Tigchelaar
933 Marchant Rd. RR #1,
Brentwood Bay, BC. V8M 1B5
Phone: (250) 652-3531
Fax (250) 652-9923

Canada Customs
Designated marina for courtesy customs clearance.
Phone on dock.
Marina Entrance:
Near Brentwood Inn Marina–refer to chart 3313 for navigation.

Marina services:
Mechanic and services available from local and nearby marine operators.
Repairs can be arranged.
Moorage: Large permanent marina with limited overnight moorage slips.
Water. Power at docks: 30, 15 amp.

Chart 3313, 3441, 3462
VHF 68

Customer services:
Laundry, showers, washrooms.
Nearby church/es.
Dockside marine restaurant.
Public pay phones ashore.

Entertainment.
Nearby historic Butchart Gardens.
Bus, taxi and rentals to downtown Sidney, easy access to Victoria, airport, ferries.
Walking trails or road access. Some beachfront walks.
Golf, tennis and other recreation nearby.

Adjacent facilities:
Brentwood Inn Resort/Marina.
Government dock. Restaurants.
Shopping in nearby Brentwood Bay.
Launch ramp nearby on native land.

This marina is the closest facility to Butchart Gardens. Stop at the marina, where overnight moorage is available, and take your dinghy to the dock at the Gardens. Or enquire about the ferry service.

Pictured above: The dock and fuel pump at Goldstream. View looks north towards entrance of Saanich Inlet.
Opposite: Angler's Anchorage Marina.

Goldstream

Goldstream Boathouse
Mark Aitken and Doug Spence
2892 Trans Canada Highway, RR 6,
Victoria, BC. V9B 5T9
Phone: (250) 478-4407
Chart 3313, 3441, 3462 VHF 68

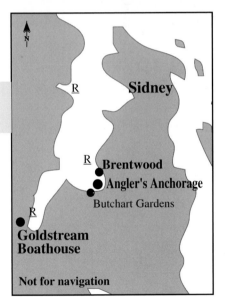

Marina services:
Fuel: Gas. Oil filters, etc.
Marine supplies. Marine repairs. Haulouts.
Moorage. Transient available.
Water at dock.
Power at docks: 30, 15 amp. (For transient moorage customers–15 amp.) **Washrooms.**
Customer services:
Nearby church/es
Road access walking. Parkland trails at Goldstream Park nearby.
Rental boats. Bait, ice, tackle, fishing licences. Groceries, snacks.

Scuba diving arrangements and fishing charters–ask marina for details.
Public pay phones ashore.
Entertainment.
Historic landmark boathouse.
Butchart Gardens.
Bus, taxi and car rentals to downtown Victoria. Golf nearby.
Adjacent facilities:
Campsites. **Launch ramp.**

Mill Bay

Mill Bay Marina

Fred and Marilyn Laba
Box 231 740 Handy Road,
Mill Bay, BC. V0R 2P0
Phone: (250) 743-4112

Marina services:
Fuel: Gas. Diesel.
Water at dock. Multiple outlets.
Power at docks: 15 amp. Multiple outlets.
Laundry, showers, washrooms.
Boats for rent. Charters. Bed & breakfast.
Marine supplies. Ice, fishing tackle,
licences, bait.
Mechanic and services can be arranged.
Moorage: 158 plus slips–permanent marina
with 540' overnight moorage. Reserve.

Customer services:
Nearby church/es. Road access walking.
Some nearby river and beach trails.
Rental boats. **Launch ramp (2 ramps).**

Mill Bay public dock

Fisheries & Oceans
Phone (250) 743-9764
Chart 3313, 3441, 3462
Manager • Float length 15 m

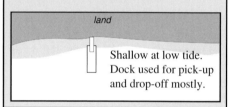

land

Shallow at low tide.
Dock used for pick-up
and drop-off mostly.

Photograph shows Mill Bay Marina. Note the two
launch ramps. The one to the right is a public ramp.

Chart 3313, 3441, 3462   CB 10

Shopping centre and grocery store nearby
(Thrifty) will deliver purchases to your boat.
Public pay phones ashore.
Entertainment.
Across inlet to Butchart Gardens.
Bus, taxi and rentals to downtown Victoria.
Golf nearby.

56

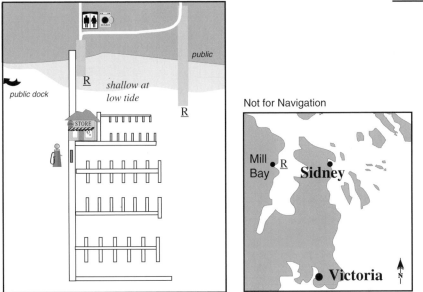

public

shallow at low tide

public dock

STORE

Not for Navigation

Mill Bay
Sidney
Victoria

Mill Bay Marina

The shopping centre at Mill Bay has good grocery shopping as well as a variety of interesting stores, arts and crafts, restaurants, espresso and coffee shops among others.

The centre is an easy walk from the marina. The main float to the south includes a fuel dock and overnight moorage for larger vessels. Small craft will be assigned slips inside.

Right: Public docks. Left: Masthead Marina.

Cowichan

Numbers identified in photo on page 64

1. Cowichan Bay Public

Harbour Authority/Wharfinger
General Delivery,
Cowichan Bay, B.C. V0R 1N0
Phone: (250) 746-5911
Fax 748-7122
Marina services:
Water at dock. Multiple outlets.
Power at docks: 15 amp. Multiple
outlets.
Washrooms.
Telephone.
Moorage: Overnight available. Check in
on arrival or reserve.
Nearby services:
Showers, laundry, boats for rent. Char-
ters. Bed & breakfast. Marine supplies.
Ice, fishing tackle, licences, bait. Boat lift,
liquor store, post office, bank machine,
pub, restaurant, shops, swimming pool,
taxi, hardware, grocery.
Mechanic and services can be arranged.

Chart 3313, 3441, 3462   CB 10

Nearby church/es. Road access walking.
Some nearby river and beach trails.

2. Masthead Marina

1705 Cowichan Bay Road,
Cowichan Bay, B.C. V0R 1N0
Phone: (250) 748-5368 Fax 748-5855
Marina services:
Garbage disposal.

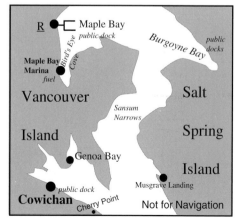

Cowichan

Masthead Marina left of jetty.

Looking west from the public docks

Water at dock. Multiple outlets.
Power at docks. Multiple outlets.
Restaurant.
Moorage: Overnight available. Check in on arrival or reserve.
Nearby services:
Showers, laundry, washrooms, boats for rent, charters, accommodations. Marine supplies. Ice, fishing tackle, licences, bait. Boat lift, liquor store, post office, bank machine, pub, restaurant, shops, swimming pool, taxi, hardware, grocery. Art gallery, potter, jeweller.
Mechanic and services can be arranged.
Nearby road access–walking. Some nearby river and beach trails. Kayak and mountain bike rentals.

Update Information courtesy Sue Wells.

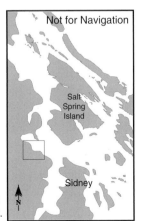

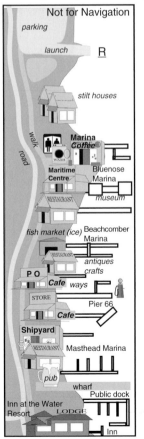

Cowichan Harbour is a working wharf. Visitors are welcome to stop and experience its ambience. The atmosphere of the village is captivating. No need for typical gift stores and tourist boutiques. Moor at the public docks when the fishing fleet is away. And at other marinas in the Bay subject to space being available.

Photo opposite page shows Masthead Marina (left) and the public dock (right).

59

3. Pier 66 Marina

1745 Cowichan Bay Road,
Cowichan Bay, B.C. V0R 1N0
Phone: (250) 748-8444 Fax 748-8444
email: *rufus@islandnet.com*
Marina services:
Fuel: gas, diesel, premix, ice, oil, bait,
licences. **Garbage disposal.**
Water at dock. Multiple outlets.
Power at docks: 15 amp. Multiple outlets.
Telephone. Marine supplies, boat rentals,
charts, fishing licences, bait and tackle.
Moorage: Overnight available. Check in on
arrival or reserve.
Nearby services:
Showers, laundry, charters. accommoda-
tion, boat lift, post office, bank machine,
pub, restaurant, shops, swimming pool, taxi.
Tidal grid. Mechanic and services can be
arranged. z Nearby church/es. Road access
walking. Some nearby river and beach trails.

4. Beachcomber Marina

1759 Cowichan Bay Road,
Cowichan Bay, B.C. V0R 1N0
Phone: (250) 748-6789
Marina services:

Water at dock. Multiple outlets.
Power at docks: 30 amp. Multiple outlets.
Garbage disposal.
Washrooms.
Boat lift, telephone.
Moorage: Overnight available. Check in on
arrival or reserve.
Nearby services:
Showers, laundry, charters. Bed & break-

fast. Ice. Marine supplies, hardware, groceries, charts, tackle, boat rentals, fishing
licences, bait. liquor store, post office, bank
machine, pub, restaurant, shops, swimming
pool, taxi.

Mechanic and services can be arranged. Nearby church/es. Road access walking. Some nearby river and beach trails.

5. Bluenose Marina

1765 Cowichan Bay Road,
Cowichan Bay, B.C. V0R 1N0
Phone: (250) 748-2222 Fax 748-8982
Marina services:
Water at dock. Multiple outlets.
Power at docks: 15 amp. Multiple outlets.
Washrooms. Laundry. Shower.
Garbage disposal.
Telephone, restaurant, taxi.
Moorage: Overnight available. Check in on arrival (plus 5 mooring buoys).

Nearby services:
Boats for rent. Charters. Accommodation. Marine supplies. Ice, fishing tackle, bait, fishing licences. Boat lift, liquor store, post office, pub, shops, swimming pool, taxi, hardware, grocery.
Mechanic and services can be arranged. Road access walking.
Some nearby river and beach trails.

6. Inn at the Water Resort

Howard Johnson Coast Inn Resort
1681 Botwood Road,
Cowichan Bay, B.C. V0R 1N0
Phone: (250) 748-6222 Fax 748-7122
Small dock located adjacent to entrance of the public marina. Hotel overlooks docks.
Marina services:
Water at dock.
Power at docks: Multiple outlets.
Washrooms, showers.
Telephone. Ice.
Car rental. Accommodation. Swimming Pool. Restaurant. Pub. Taxi service.
Moorage: Overnight available. Check in on arrival or reserve.
Nearby services:
Laundry, boats for rent, launching, charters. Bed & breakfast.
Marine supplies. Fishing tackle, licences, bait. Boat lift, liquor store, post office, bank machine, shops, hardware, grocery. Mechanic and services can be arranged. Nearby church/es. Road access walking. Some nearby river and beach trails.

Cherry Point

1241 Cherry Point Drive,
Cobble Hill, B.C. V0R 1L0
Phone: (250) 748-0453
Marina services:
Garbage disposal.
Water at dock.
Power at docks: 30 amps.
Washrooms.
Telephone. Camping, boat launch, boat charter. RV facilities.
Moorage: Overnight available. Check in on arrival or reserve.
Nearby services:
Mechanic and services can be arranged. Road access walking.
Cherry Point Marina is located on the approaches to Cowichan–not shown in diagrams.

Genoa Bay

Genoa Bay Marina

Will, Ben Kiedaisch
RR #1 5100, Genoa Bay Rd, #1
Duncan, BC., V9L 5Y8
Phone: (250) 746-7621
1 800-572-6481 Fax: (250) 746-7621
www.genoabaymarina.com
Hazard: Entering bay keep to port of day
beacon. Avoid shore-side reef–marked.

Marina services:
Moorage. Large marina with permanent and transient moorage.
Water at dock. (Please conserve)
Power at docks: 15 amp.
Laundry, showers, washrooms.
Ice. Repair service available.

Customer services:
Restaurant. Licenced. Breakfast, lunch, dinner. Also patio service. Barbecue area. Tenting.
General store: groceries, fishing gear, licences, fresh baked goods.

Charts 3313, 3441, 3478, 3442, 3462

VHF 68

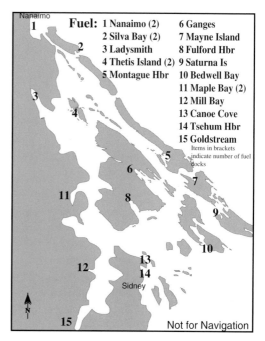

Nanaimo
Fuel:
1 Nanaimo (2)
2 Silva Bay (2)
3 Ladysmith
4 Thetis Island (2)
5 Montague Hbr
6 Ganges
7 Mayne Island
8 Fulford Hbr
9 Saturna Is
10 Bedwell Bay
11 Maple Bay (2)
12 Mill Bay
13 Canoe Cove
14 Tsehum Hbr
15 Goldstream
Items in brackets indicate number of fuel docks
Sidney
Not for Navigation

Above: Genoa Bay Marina in the spring.
Left: The restaurant sits on the bank overlooking the marina.
Opposite is an aerial view of the bay.

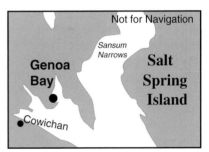

Gifts. Kayak rentals. Video rentals.
Art and crafts gallery.
Public pay phones ashore.
Entertainment:
Road access walking or cycling. Nearby hiking trails.
Adjacent facilities:
Anchorage. Yacht Sales.
Launch ramp.

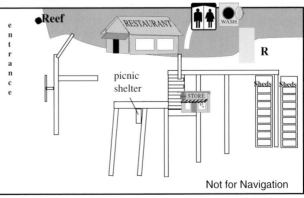

63

Maple Bay

Maple Bay Marina
Ted McLeod & Bill Neapole
6145 Genoa Bay Road,
Duncan, BC., V9L 1M3
Phone: (250) 746-8482
Fax: (250) 746-8490

Marina services:
Fuel: Gas, diesel. Marine repairs, service.
CNG. Propane. Maple Bay Marine Centre
(Jim Young & Ron Goss).
Marine supplies. Diving, towing.
Fishing gear, licences, charts, bait. Ice.
Guest and permanent moorage.
Water at dock.
Power at docks: 15, 20 amp.
Laundry, showers, washrooms.

Customer services:
Shipyard Pub & Restaurant. Licenced.
Patio service.
Gift Shop. General Store. Beauty salon.
Road access walking or cycling trails.
Scuba diving arrangements and charters–ask
marina for details. Kayaking.
Public pay phones.

Charts 3313, 3478, 3442 VHF 68
3441, 3462

Daily float plane service.

Entertainment.
Restaurant. Outdoor breakfast adjacent to
marina buildings available on weekends.

Adjacent facilities:
Excellent bed & breakfast accommodations
nearby. Custom yacht work available.

Maple Bay
Fisheries & Oceans public dock
Phone (250) 746-7101
Chart   3310, 3478, 3441, 3462
Manager • Float length 46m
Water • Lights • Public phone •
Launch ramp.
See photograph on opposite page.
.

store
(closed)

R
Maple Bay
public dock

**Bird's Eye
Cove Marina**

Cove Yachts

fuel

fuel Maple Bay
Marina

Vancouver
Island

Chandlery
WASH | STORE

RESTAURANT
pub

Maple Bay Marina

A   B   C   D   E   F
fuel

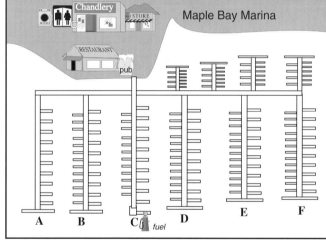

*The public float, (above)
at Maple Bay is in the
outer bay before ap-
proaching Bird's Eye
Cove. The general store at
the government float was
not operating in 2000.
Lower left: Models
displayed at the annual
Classic and Wooden
Boat festival at
Maple Bay.*

R
Maple Bay
public dock

fuel
(2)
Maple Bay
Marina

Salt
Spring
Island

Genoa Bay

Cowichan

Not for Navigation

65

Birds Eye Cove Marina (left) is a popular fuel stop. Service and repairs at adjacent Cove Yachts. Maple Bay Marina, (previous page) at the head of the bay, is a major moorage and fuel stop with available marine supplies.

Bird's Eye Cove Marina

Bob and Nancy Walker
6271 Genoa Bay Rd, RR1 Duncan, BC. V9L 1M3.
Phone (250) 748-4255 Fax (250) 748-2319
Marina Services:
Some transient moorage.
Fuel dock–all fuels and oils. Tackle, some supplies.
Service and repairs adjacent.
Open year round.
Nearby:
Maple Bay marina–store, restaurant, pub.

Cove Yachts (1979) Ltd.

Phil and Alexandra Pidcock
Cove Marina, 6261 Genoa Bay Road
Duncan BC V9L 5Y4
(250) 748-8136 Fax 748-7916
Travel lift. Ways. Commercial and pleasure craft work. Marine supply store.

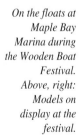

On the floats at Maple Bay Marina during the Wooden Boat Festival. Above, right: Models on display at the festival.

Crofton, Chemainus, Ladysmith

An overnight stop at the sheltered harbours of Crofton and Chemainus can be a memorable experience. The government docks have room for transient boats in the summer. Off season if there is no room to tie up it is possible, preferably for not too long a stay, to come alongside a docked fishing boat. Fishermen generally do not object to having a boat moored temporarily alongside them. However you may prefer to be tied directly to the dock for easier access to and from your moored boat.

At Ladysmith, within easy walking access from the government docks, one can find many store facilities and boating requirements, supplies and services and a touch of coastal history. It is an old coal mining town named for the town in South Africa which was under siege during the Boer War and relieved by the British coincidental to the founding of Ladysmith in BC. Its naming also honoured the charitable wife of Sir Harry Smith, governor of the Cape Province of South Africa.

Across the harbour the docks at Page Point are most hospitable to recreational boats. During summer a steady stream of craft call at the lodge for overnight moorage, fuel and very limited supplies. Also a regular clientele check in for the sumptuous meals served

Top: Crofton docks are emptier of fish boats in summer than winter, providing lots of guest moorage. Above: Chemainus looks busy but there is sometimes space to tie up. Prepare to raft to other boats.

at the lodge. Moorage is sheltered and the docks are available specially for visiting boats.

From Ladysmith it is easy and quick to access several outstanding destinations. Among them are Telegraph Harbour, Wallace Island, Chemainus and Pirate's Cove. Some interest-

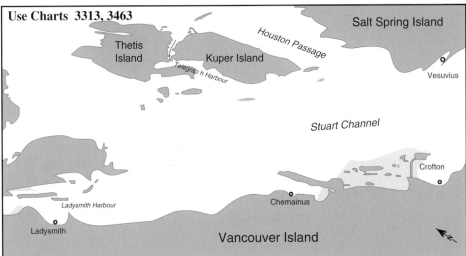

Public docks Crofton to Ladysmith

ing stops in this general area include North Galiano, Vesuvius, Crofton and Retreat Cove.

Visit Wallace Island Marine Park nearby for its excellent paths and scenery, for its history and protected overnight moorage. It's a cross-roads for people on the move, enjoying the outdoors by boating, canoeing and tenting. The park attracts many boats every season and many campers take advantage of the recreational facilities provided by the Parks Branch and maintained by Power and Sail Squadron members.

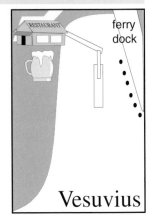

Vesuvius

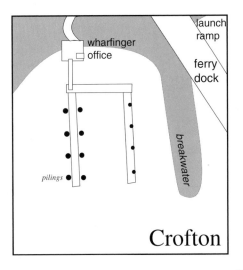

Crofton

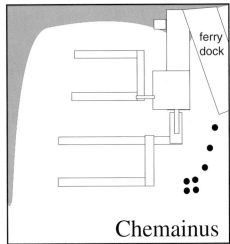

Chemainus

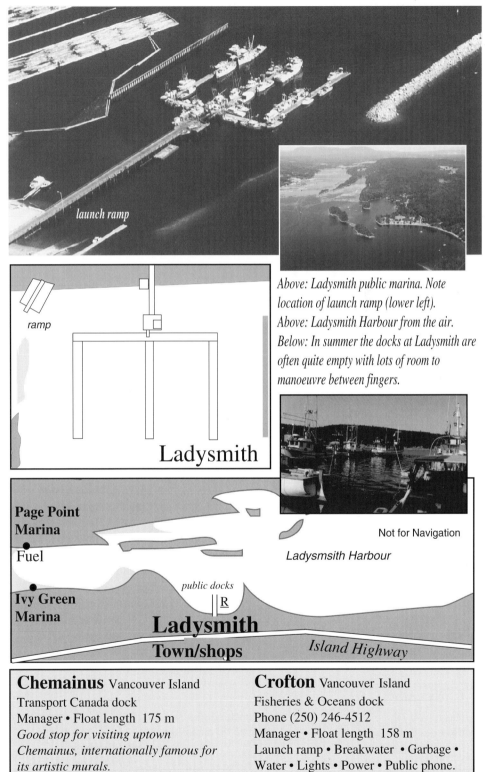

launch ramp

Above: Ladysmith public marina. Note location of launch ramp (lower left).
Above: Ladysmith Harbour from the air.
Below: In summer the docks at Ladysmith are often quite empty with lots of room to manoeuvre between fingers.

ramp

Ladysmith

Page Point Marina

Fuel

Ivy Green Marina

public docks

R

Not for Navigation

Ladysmsith Harbour

Ladysmith

Town/shops

Island Highway

Chemainus Vancouver Island

Transport Canada dock
Manager • Float length 175 m
Good stop for visiting uptown Chemainus, internationally famous for its artistic murals.

Crofton Vancouver Island

Fisheries & Oceans dock
Phone (250) 246-4512
Manager • Float length 158 m
Launch ramp • Breakwater • Garbage •
Water • Lights • Power • Public phone.

Ladysmith Harbour

Page Point Inn and Marina

Lawrence and Lexi Lambert
4760 Brenton-Page Road, RR #1
Ladysmith, B.C, V0R 2E0
Phone: (250) 245-2312 Fax: 245-7546

Marina services:
Fuel: Gas. Diesel. Propane.
Service available. Marine supplies.
Fishing gear, licences.
Guest moorage, 1400 feet dock space.
Water at dock.
Power: 15amps. 30 amps to be added.
Laundry, showers, washrooms.

Customer services:
Restaurant. Fine dining. Licenced.
Also patio service.
Gift shop.
Public pay phones ashore.
Daily float plane service accessible and stops
at marina for pick-up.

Chart 3313, 3475, 3443, 3463 VHF 68

Entertainment.
Cycles free with room rental. Canoes,
rowboats. Car rentals. Road access walking
or cycling. Golf nearby, arrangements–ask
at marina for details.

Adjacent facilities:
Excellent bed and breakfast accommodations at lodge. Make reservations ahead in
summer months.
Short boat trip to Ladysmith–stores–stop at
government dock opposite/south just inside
entrance to Ladysmith harbour.

*This facility for many years was known as
Manana Lodge. The property is on Page
Point, from which it now takes its name.
Not to be confused with Page's Marina in
Silva Bay.*

Ladysmith,	
Vancouver Island	Launch ramp • Breakwater • Grid • Garbage •
Fisheries & Oceans dock	Waste oil disposal •
Phone (250) 245-7511	Water • Lights • Power • Public phone •
Manager • Float length 213 m	Near uptown restaurants, shops.

Ivy Green

Page Point

Page Point Inn and marina offers outstanding overnight sheltered moorage, fuel, restaurant and many amenities.

On the west side of Ladysmith Harbour, Ivy Green Marina offers some overnight moorage. The marina also has a launch ramp and adjacent marine service facilities.

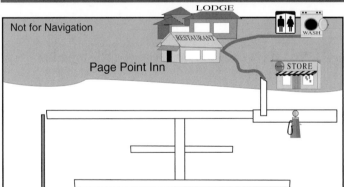

LODGE

Not for Navigation

RESTAURANT

Page Point Inn

WASH

STORE

Not for Navigation

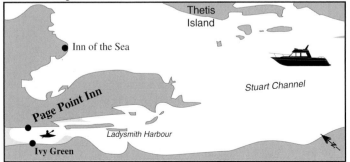

Thetis Island

Inn of the Sea

Stuart Channel

Page Point Inn

Ladysmith Harbour

Ivy Green

Inn of the Sea Resort

Carol Radloff
3600 Yellow Point Road,
Ladysmith, BC. VOR 2E0
Phone (250) 245-0239
Fax (250) 245-1349
Chart 3313, 3443

Hazard: Reef extends out
from the point. Give
wide berth and approach
from the south-east.
Consult chart.

Marina services:
Guest, limited moorage.
Reservations advised.
No water at dock.
Power at docks: 15
amp.
Mooring buoys.
Laundry, showers, wash-
rooms at lodge.

Customer services:
Restaurant. Lounge. Breakfast, lunch,
dinner. Licenced.
Luxurious shore accommodations. Heated
outdoor pool.
Road access walking or cycling. Nearby

walking trails.
Public pay phones ashore.
Entertainment.
Tennis, canoeing, swimming, jaccuzi.
Adjacent facilities:
Bed & breakfast accommodations at
lodge.

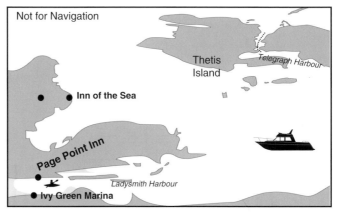

Not for Navigation

Thetis
Island

Telegraph Harbour

Inn of the Sea

Page Point Inn

Ladysmith Harbour

Ivy Green Marina

Ivy Green Marina

Box 88, 1335 Rocky Creek Rd.
Ladysmith,
B.C, V0R 2E0
Phone: (250) 245-4521
Marina services:
Showers, washrooms. Haulout and repairs.
Launch ramp.

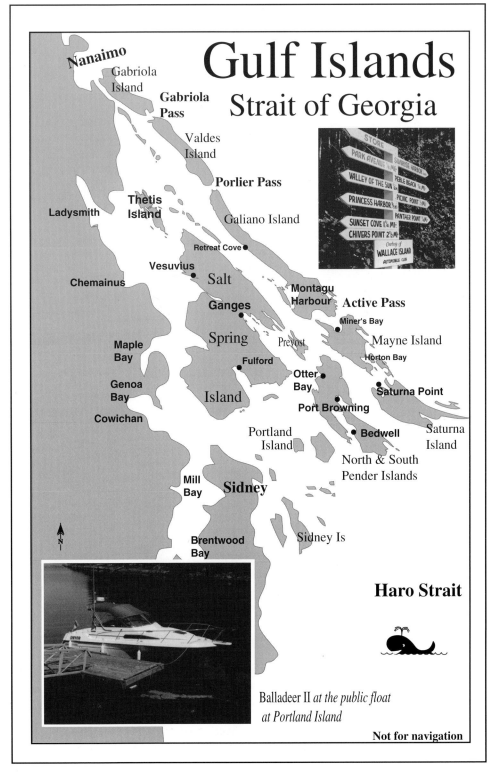

Gulf Islands
Strait of Georgia

Nanaimo

Gabriola Island

Gabriola Pass

Valdes Island

Porlier Pass

Thetis Island

Ladysmith

Galiano Island

Retreat Cove

Vesuvius

Chemainus

Salt

Ganges

Montagu Harbour

Active Pass

Miner's Bay

Mayne Island

Maple Bay

Spring

Prevost

Genoa Bay

Fulford

Horton Bay

Island

Otter Bay

Saturna Point

Cowichan

Port Browning

Portland Island

Bedwell

Saturna Island

North & South Pender Islands

Mill Bay

Sidney

Brentwood Bay

Sidney Is

N

Haro Strait

Balladeer II *at the public float*
at Portland Island

Not for navigation

STORE
PARK AVENUE
SUNRISE HARBOR
VALLEY OF THE SUN
PEBLE BEACH
PRINCESS HARBOR
PICNIC POINT
PANTHER POINT
SUNSET COVE 1¼ MI
CHIVERS POINT 2½ MI
Courtesy of
WALLACE ISLAND
AUTOMOBILE CLUB

Salt Spring Island

Top: The church at Fulford Harbour was built using materials carried to the island in canoes. Above: Looking up Fulford Harbour from across Portland Island.

The islands in the lower Strait of Georgia known as The Gulf Islands offer many anchoring and mooring alternatives. The diagram on the previous page shows the main archipelago which makes up the group of islands that are most popular for overnight use. Note the cautions in the following text but always be mindful of weather conditions and forecasts.

Salt Spring Island is the largest of the Gulf Islands and has most facilities and amenities similar to mainland and Vancouver Island centres.

74

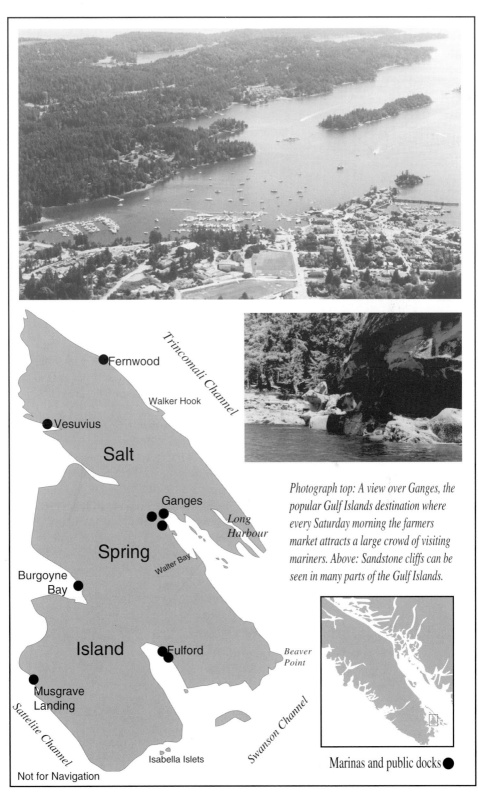

Fernwood

Trincomali Channel

Walker Hook

Vesuvius

Salt

Ganges

Long Harbour

Spring

Walter Bay

Burgoyne Bay

Island

Fulford

Beaver Point

Musgrave Landing

Satellite Channel

Swanson Channel

Isabella Islets

Not for Navigation

Photograph top: A view over Ganges, the popular Gulf Islands destination where every Saturday morning the farmers market attracts a large crowd of visiting mariners. Above: Sandstone cliffs can be seen in many parts of the Gulf Islands.

Marinas and public docks ●

Fulford Harbour

Chart 3313, 3478, 3441/2, 3462

Fulford Harbour Marina

Woodcor Enterprises
**#5–2810 Fulford-Ganges Rd.,
Salt Spring Island,
BC. V8K 1Z2   VHF 68
Phone: (250) 653-4467 Fax: 653-4457**
email: *fulfordmarina@saltspring.com*
Web: *www.saltspring.com/fulfordmarina*

Marina services:
Moorage: Guest and permanent.
Large breakwater float.
Fuel: Gas, diesel, oil.
Water at dock. All slips.
Power at docks: Multiple 30, 20 amp.
Customer services:

Public phone ashore.
Showers, washrooms. Laundry.
Entertainment.
Island tranquility. Eagles, herons, otters and seals. Tennis courts, waterfront gazebos and barbecue area. Walking, beaches.

Nearby facilities:
BC Ferries to Sidney. Government docks. Places of interest: Historic churches. Fulford settlement–arts and crafts, groceries, restaurants, hotel. Walk to Drummond Park. Nearby private museum of Indian Art–Bob Akerman collection and his wife's classic doll collection. Five minutes walk to pub/dining room, grocery store, coffee shop, crafts, parks, ferry. 10 minutes to lake.

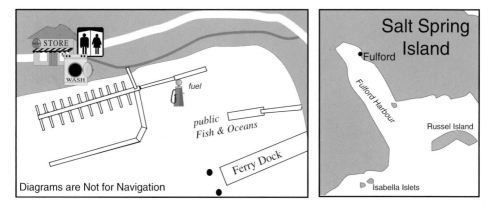

The restaurant at the ferry landing at Fulford, known for many years as Rodrigo's.

An old fuel pump at what was once a busy garden shop in Fulford Harbour

Public docks:
Fulford Harbour, inner dock
Fisheries & Oceans dock
Phone (250) 537-5711
Chart 3313, 3478, 3441, 3442, 3462
Manager – Reid Collins.
Phone (250) 653-4728
• Float length 36 m
• Garbage • Lights • Power • Public phone ashore
Adjacent ferry to Sidney, restaurants, shops.

Fulford Harbour, Outside breakwater.
Transport Canada dock
Chart 3313, 3478, 3441, 3442, 3462
Manager • Float length 16 m
Public phone ashore •
Not recommended for overnight moorage.

At Ganges the Saturday morning market is a great attraction.
Opposite: Fuel dock at Fulford Marina seen from the government dock just across the way.

Ganges

New breakwater now provides docking and access to Ganges. Located adjacent Coast Guard station (see diagrams).

Ganges Marina

Management Seycove Marina
**161 Lower Ganges Road,
Ganges, BC V8K 2T2**
Phone: (250) 537-5242 Fax (250) 538-1719
email: *guinness@saltspring.com*
Marina services:
Moorage: Guest moorage only.
Reservations taken.
Fuel: Gas, diesel, oils–Shell. Other services available.
Water at dock. All slips.
Power at docks: 50, 30, 15 amps.

Customer services:
Public phone ashore. Marina store has some supplies. Ice.
Laundry, showers, washrooms.
Complimentary bikes and baby strollers. Also coffee, muffins and juice mornings and *hors d'oeuvres* on long weekends.

Entertainment:
Ganges Saturday public market.
Crafts and art galleries.
Scooter and car rentals at marina. Walking and cycling on island roads, some nearby waterfront and beachfront access.
Nearby:
Government docks. Shopping centre. Propane. Close to all Ganges facilities. Fresh produce. Bakery. Thrifty Foods (537-1522)– groceries. Restaurants. Anchorages and places of interest. Churches. Arts and crafts. Hotels, bed and breakfast. Bistros. Pubs.

Outdoor restaurant patio at Mouat's in Ganges.

78

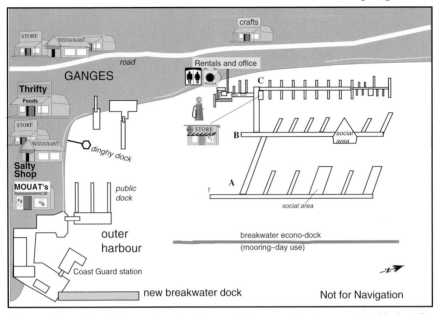

Photograph opposite and diagram above show Ganges Marina occupying a large portion of the bay. The public dock, abutting Mouat's large store building, is located to the right of the marina and adjacent the Coast Guard dock. Moorage is available at the breakwater dock southeast of the CCG station.

Ganges is the business centre and hub of the Gulf Islands. It is not only located on the largest of the Gulf Islands but also it has the largest population of all communities in the archipelago. Salt Spring Island residents and visitors by boat or by road via the BC Ferries system use Ganges as a shopping and cultural centre.

Activities on Salt Spring Island as well as arts and crafts attract many visitors each summer. The morning farmers market held on the waterfront every Saturday has become a colourful attraction. The work of local artists can be seen and bought in the several art shops and galleries in Ganges. Shopping at Mouat's historic store provides opportunity to stock up on the items you need for your boating comfort, safety and convenience. The many other speciality stores in the town will provide hours of pleasurable shopping or window shopping. And the restaurants are of a variety that will enable you to select from a wide range of menus. Hastings House, one of the top restaurants in Canada, is located in Ganges.

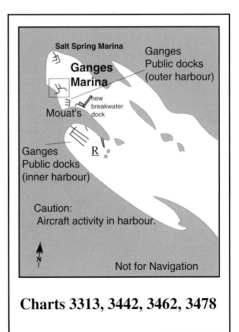

Charts 3313, 3442, 3462, 3478

Salt Spring Marina

Lesley Cheeseman (mgr), Dick Durante.
124 Upper Ganges Rd.,
Salt Spring Island, BC. V8K 2S2
Phone: 1 800-334-6629 (250) 537-5810
Pub: 537-5559 Fax (250) 537-9100
Chart 3313, 3462/3, 3478 VHF 68
Marina services:
Moorage: Guest and permanent.
Haulouts, towing and other services.
Water at docks.
Power at docks: Multiple 30, 15 amp.
Customer services:
Marine pub. Public phone ashore.
Marina store has chandlery, fishing licences
and tackle. Marine service.*
Showers, washrooms. laundry,
souvenirs, coffee, ice, bait, fishing gear.
Budget car rentals.
Entertainment.
Ganges Saturday public market.
Arts. Galleries.
Scooter, kayak and boat rentals.
Walking on island roads, some nearby
waterfront and beachfront access.

Adjacent and nearby facilities:
Moby's Pub. Shopping centre.
Anchorages and places of interest:
Churches, arts and crafts, groceries,
restaurants, hotels, bed and breakfast.

---

* Harbours End Marine & Equipment Ltd

Barry Green
122 Upper Ganges Rd.,
Salt Spring Island, BC. V8K 2S2.
Phone(250) 537-4202 Fax 537-4029
Marine Sales and Service, chandlery.

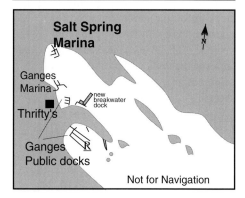

Salt Spring Marina
Ganges Marina
new breakwater dock
Thrifty's
Ganges Public docks
N
Not for Navigation

Hastings House restaurant will take reservations and collect you at your boat for a meal that will cost you a lot but provide you a memorable gourmet experience that will be hard to match.

Boat services include temporary stopping if space permits, at the government dock on the north side of the town or in the harbour. Private marinas Ganges Marina and Salt Spring Marina provide overnight and extended mooring with power and electricity at the docks and laundry, showers and toilets on shore.

Salt Spring Marina offers also a large restaurant and pub at the head of the dock and activities such as boat, bicycle and scooter rentals, as well as boat repairs and service. Harbour's End Marine and Equipment is an authorized dealership for several brands of engines and other equipment and is located right at the marina just opposite Moby's pub and restaurant. Ganges Marina nearby sells fuel.

Market at Ganges attracts crowds on Saturday mornings throughout the cruising season. Merchants from local stores and local artisans conduct business from these outdoor stalls, offering a wide range of crafts and merchandise along with some tasty snacks and refreshments.

Not for Navigation

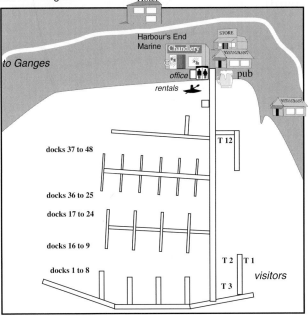

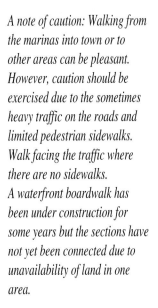

A note of caution: Walking from the marinas into town or to other areas can be pleasant. However, caution should be exercised due to the sometimes heavy traffic on the roads and limited pedestrian sidewalks. Walk facing the traffic where there are no sidewalks.
A waterfront boardwalk has been under construction for some years but the sections have not yet been connected due to unavailability of land in one area.

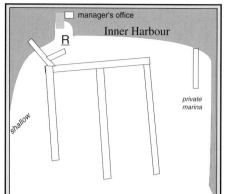

The outer harbour public docks and the Ganges waterfront. Mouat's, Thrifty's, The Salty Shop and other stores are located here.

Ganges, Salt Spring Island Public docks.

Ganges Boat Harbour (Inner Harbour)
Fisheries & Oceans dock
Phone/fax (250) 537-5711
Manager • Float length 326 m
Launch ramp • Breakwater • Garbage •
Waste oil disposal • Water • Lights •
Power • Public phone • Washroom •
Showers.
Adjacent to restaurants, shops.

(Outer dock and Coast Guard)
Transport Canada dock
Float length 24 m
Aircraft Float • Water • Lights • Power •
Public phone ashore •
Adjacent restaurants, shops.
Fuel dock adjacent.
Marinas, fuel, services nearby.

Ganges, (Outer Harbour)
Fisheries & Oceans dock
Manager–*check in at office in Inner Harbour for stays over two hours* • Float length 41 m • Garbage • Water • Lights •
Public phone ashore •
Adjacent to restaurants, shops.
Phone (250) 537-5711–for all public docks at Ganges.

Charts 3313, 3478, 3442, 3462

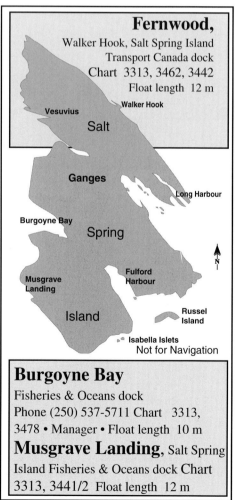

Fernwood,
Walker Hook, Salt Spring Island
Transport Canada dock
Chart 3313, 3462, 3442
Float length 12 m

Vesuvius

Walker Hook

Salt

Ganges

Long Harbour

Burgoyne Bay

Spring

Musgrave Landing

Fulford Harbour

Island

Russel Island

Isabella Islets
Not for Navigation

Burgoyne Bay
Fisheries & Oceans dock
Phone (250) 537-5711 Chart 3313, 3478 • Manager • Float length 10 m

Musgrave Landing, Salt Spring
Island Fisheries & Oceans dock Chart 3313, 3441/2 Float length 12 m

new breakwater

Top: Inner Harbour behind the breakwater on the south side of Ganges. Note the small private marina to the right.
Above: View of Ganges Outer Harbour small dock right of Ganges Marina (centre). Inner Harbour far right. Salt Spring Marina far left.
Left: Boats at the outer harbour public dock.
Inset: The harbour shuttle at Ganges.

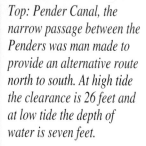

Top: Pender Canal, the narrow passage between the Penders was man made to provide an alternative route north to south. At high tide the clearance is 26 feet and at low tide the depth of water is seven feet.

Centre: Port Washington general store which closed down in the past decade after serving passing vessels since the early 1990s is now an art gallery. The floats will accommodate several small to medium sized boats but are exposed to washes from passing ferries and some wind conditions. Information on page 92.

Bottom: One of the fuel stops in the Gulf Islands is at Bedwell Bay.

The Pender Islands

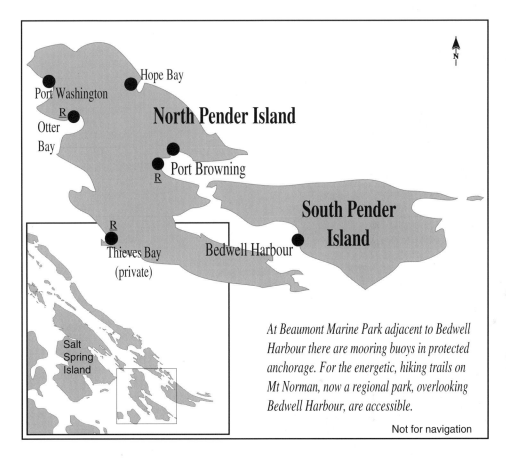

Hope Bay

Port Washington

R

Otter
Bay

North Pender Island

R Port Browning

R

Thieves Bay
(private)

Bedwell Harbour

South Pender Island

Salt
Spring
Island

At Beaumont Marine Park adjacent to Bedwell Harbour there are mooring buoys in protected anchorage. For the energetic, hiking trails on Mt Norman, now a regional park, overlooking Bedwell Harbour, are accessible.

Not for navigation

The Pender Islands are blessed with beautiful, unspoilt and charming features and are centrally located in the Gulf Islands, providing moorage, anchorage and safe stops for all boat operators. One of the main harbours of the Penders is Bedwell: resort, marina and customs stop.

Pender Canal, separating South from North Pender, is a narrow passage which curves its way under a low bridge that connects the two islands. At high tide boats will clear the bridge if they are no taller than 26 feet.

Otter Bay is another of the Gulf Islands' major ports for recreational boating. It has a fully operational marina with good docks and a store that has local crafts, paintings, clothing, books, some fresh produce, canned goods and frozen foods among other items. The marina office sells fishing licences and can provide information on local island services such as mechanical, towing, bed & breakfast and ferries schedules. A large lawn is a playing field for the children and several picnic tables have been placed along the waterfront. If you want a catered meal go to the golf club nearby for breakfast or take in one of the local restaurants whose dinners are legendary.

Bedwell Harbour

Bedwell Harbour Resort

Bill James
**RR #1 South Pender Island,
BC., V0N 2M0**
Phone: (250) 629-3212
Fax: (250) 629-6777
email: *bedwell @islandnet.com*
Web: *www.islandnet.com/~bedwell/*
Customs service.
Customs. Phone (250) 629-3363.
Officials on duty office and other hours.
Marina services:
Fuel: Gas, diesel, ice. Service.
Moorage. Large marina with mostly
transient moorage.
Water at dock–limited supply.
Power at docks: 15, 30 amp.
Laundry, showers, washrooms.
Tackle shop on dock.
Customer services:
Restaurant. Pub. Breakfast, lunch, dinner.
Licenced. Also patio service. Swimming
pool. Lodging. General store: Fishing gear,
licences, charts, bait. Fresh baked goods.
Gifts. Groceries.
Tennis raquets available. Bicycle rentals.
Road access walking or cycling. Nearby
hiking trails.
Public pay phone ashore.
Entertainment.
Live music weekends, summer. meals at
poolside. Tennis courts.
Fireworks July 1.
Adjacent facilities:
Play area. Pet area.Beaumont Marine Park.
Camping, hiking. Mooring buoys. Nearby
Mt. Norman is accessible by trail.

This is one of the main American
entrances to Canadian waters in British
Columbia. It is a busy customs port
throughout the summer months June
through September. It is essential that
visiting vessels clear customs at an
official entry port before stopping elsewhere in Canada. And Bedwell is one of

Opposite and right: Bedwell Harbour Island Resort and marina.
Below l & r: The marine pub and patio with general store to the left. The pool overlooks the marina.

the most used entry ports for vessels arriving, including returning Canadians, out of the San Juan Islands or Puget Sound. The facilities at Bedwell are as comprehensive as you will find anywhere in British Columbian waters. The docks are extensive and power and water are available, the latter not for washing boats due to the relative short supply from its on-island source. A fuel dock serves gas and diesel and other marine products and the marina, as part of the shoreside resort, offers access to the swimming pool and other amenities included with one's moorage. Showers, laundry, a general store, restaurant, snack kiosks, and a marine bar and bistro make up most of other facilities. There is a hotel which is popular for visitors arriving by boat or by road via ferries from Sidney or the mainland, as well as town-houses which are home to their owners who mostly use them at weekends.

Chart 3313, 3477, 3441 VHF 68

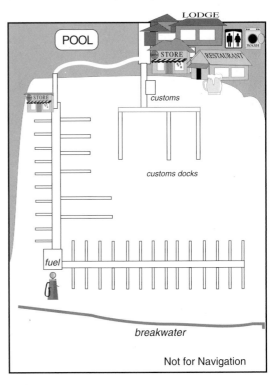

POOL

LODGE

STORE

RESTAURANT

WASH

STORE

customs

customs docks

fuel

breakwater

Not for Navigation

Port Browning

Port Browning Marina

Lou Henshaw
General Delivery,
North Pender Island.
BC, V0N 2M0
Phone: (250) 629-3493

Caution: Narrow, shallow Pender Canal
divides the two Pender Islands.
Check chart and tides.

Customs: check in at Bedwell Harbour.

Marina services:
Moorage. Large marina with permanent
and transient moorage.
Water at dock.
Power at docks: 15 amp.
Laundry, showers, washrooms.
Reservations advised summertime.

Customer services:
Pub. Restaurant. Breakfast, lunch,
dinner. Licenced. Also patio service.

Chart 3313, 3477, 3441/2   VHF 68

Swimming pool. Cold beer and wine store at
marina.
Minimarket marine store. Ice, groceries,
charts. Fishing gear, licences, charts, bait.
Fresh baked goods. Gifts. Groceries.
Road access walking or cycling. Take care
walking the narrow island road.
Good beach access.
Public pay phones ashore.

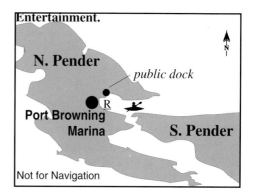

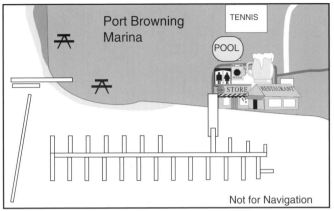

Docks and facilities at Port Browning include pub, store, restaurant, pool and tennis courts. A large expanse of lawn is used frequently in summer for yacht club or group gatherings and regular weekend lamb or pork barbecues.

Saturday market at nearby shopping complex. (Below)

This is the nearest marina to the North Pender Island shopping centre and supermarket.

Swimming pool, large lawn, camping.
Tennis, golf, nearby.
Saturday morning early farmers' market at nearby shopping plaza and at the island community centre.

Nearby facilities:
Tru Value Foods supermarket (250) 629-8322 (delivery to marina possible, and shopping centre nearby. Wide range of services, liquor, bank, art, gifts, dairy products, bakery. Restaurants, B&Bs, accommodations on the island. Check at shopping centre. Small craft launch ramp located on the beach near the marina. Air strip adjacent shopping centre.

Browning Harbour (public)
North Pender Island
Fisheries & Oceans dock
Phone (250) 629-3423
Chart 3313
Manager • Float length 27 m
Store, shopping complex nearby.
Port Browning Marina is located almost directly opposite.

Otter Bay

Otter Bay Marina

Kay and Chuck Spence
General Delivery,
North Pender Island.
BC., V0N 2M0
Phone: (250) 629-3579 Fax 629-3589
Hazard: Keep clear and to starboard of green spar U 57.

Marina services:
Launch ramp (small craft).
Moorage. Large marina with permanent and transient moorage.
Water at dock. Use sparingly please.
Power at docks: 30, 15 amp.
Laundry, showers, washrooms.
Reservations advised summertime.

Customer services:
Store. Gifts, bait, ice, limited groceries.
Charts. Fishing tackle, licences.
Garbage disposal.
Road access walking or cycling.

Chart 3313, 3441/2 VHF 68

Take care walking the narrow island road.
Public pay phones ashore.
Cabin sleeps 4–5 people.

Entertainment.
Eagles, herons, otters and seals.
Bicycle, boat and kayak rentals.

Adjacent facilities:
BC Ferries dock.
Picnic tables, barbecue area.
Gazebo.
Deck on breakwater at marina.
Golf course–10 minutes walk. The club coffee shop/restaurant serves good meals.
Islander Restaurant nearby. Also arts and crafts, cappuccino, espresso bar at Galloping Moon Gallery. (250) 629-6020.

Crew off anchored boats welcome ashore for a small fee.

Otter Bay Marina is a very popular resort. Week ends in mid summer and on holidays are booked well in advance. For many years Otter Bay operated with minimal dock space and limited service. When Chuck and Kay Spence took over running the facility they set about enlarging the docks, replacing the buildings on shore and adding amenities to make a visit to the bay a more enjoyable experience. They have achieved this and more with the provision of a swimming pool, coffee bar and store. The pool has hours set aside for adult use only which is popular among those needing to relax undisturbed while they bathe during a hot day.

Otter Bay was not always the laid back cruising destination it is today. At one time it flourished as a fishing centre featuring such establishments as cannery, saltery and reduction plant. But in 1963 it took on a new life as a marina and by 1972 it had moved to the ownership of Bob Melville who many of today's cruising yachtsmen got to know quite well. After nearly twenty years Bob and Karen Melville moved to the BC Interior when David Bromley bought the marina and the Spences took over managing it. The Melvilles left a legacy at Otter Bay in the way of Karen's flower and vegetable garden as well as the fruit trees that can be found on the property.

Chuck and Kay Spence have created their own legacy with the additions they have made to the property. Their arts and crafts selection, the covered barbecue area and their friendly welcome to moored guests has become their trademark.

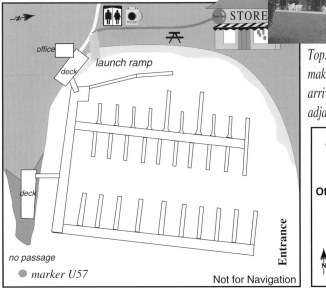

Top: Summer months are busy so make reservations ahead of your arrival. Inset, Above: The store and adjacent pool.

Store now offers art, crafts, gifts, coffees and snacks.

Aerial photo page 84

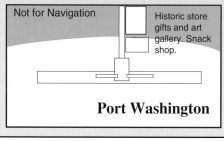

Not for Navigation

Historic store gifts and art gallery. Snack shop.

Port Washington

Port Washington,

North Pender Island
Transport Canada dock
Chart   3313, 3442
Manager • Float length 45 m • Aircraft float • Public phone ashore • Nearby arts and crafts. Walking–island roads. Coffee bar. Snacks, gifts. Fair weather moorage.

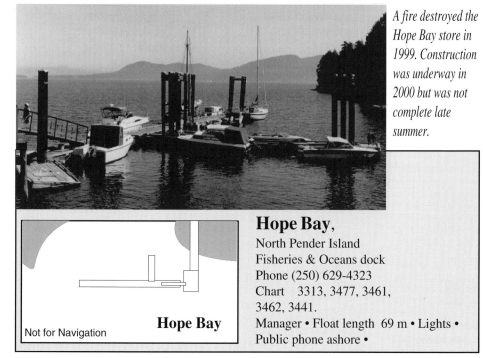

A fire destroyed the Hope Bay store in 1999. Construction was underway in 2000 but was not complete late summer.

Not for Navigation

Hope Bay

Hope Bay,

North Pender Island
Fisheries & Oceans dock
Phone (250) 629-4323
Chart   3313, 3477, 3461, 3462, 3441.
Manager • Float length 69 m • Lights •
Public phone ashore •

Inset: Restaurant and pub overlooking Lyall Harbour at Saturna Landing.

Saturna Point

Saturna Point Landing

& Fuel Dock. Lyall Harbour,
Saturna Island, BC. V0N 2Y0
Phone/fax: (250) 539-5725
Harbour Master:
Gloria Manzano (250) 539-2229
Marina services:
Government dock. Limited space–mostly drop off/pick up. Not intended for overnight.
Fuel: Gas, diesel, outboard mix, oil.
Public phone ashore.
Store and restaurant ashore.
Lighthouse Pub.

Charts 3313, 3473, 3462

Customer services:
General store: fish tackle, hardware, licences, ice, bait. Propane available nearby.
Post office nearby–1 mile
Entertainment.
Annual lamb barbecue July 1st. at Winter Cove. Island tranquility. Eagles, herons, otters and seals.
Adjacent facilities:
BC Ferries. Use caution manouvering when ferry operating. Winter Cove anchorage, Boot Cove: Saturna Lodge and Restaurant. Vineyards on island–enquire at store.

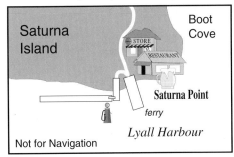

Saturna Island

Boot Cove

STORE

RESTAURANT

Saturna Point

ferry

Lyall Harbour

Not for Navigation

Lyall Harbour (Saturna Point)

Fisheries & Oceans dock
Chart 3310, 3477, 3462
Manager • Float length 62 m
• Lights •
Adjacent facilities include Fuel, restaurant/pub, store.

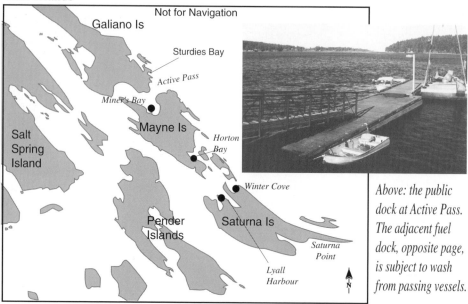

Not for Navigation

Above: the public dock at Active Pass. The adjacent fuel dock, opposite page, is subject to wash from passing vessels.

Active Pass

Scuba diving is popular in Active Pass. However one has to be mindful of the strong current and tide rips as well as the constantly passing ferries. It is best, therefore, if scuba divers use the services of professional dive charter operators rather than attempt diving the pass off their own private vessels.

Fishing in the pass, and particularly at each entrance to the pass is extremely popular and rewarding. However, here again, one should exercise caution due to the passage of

Left: BC ferry going through Active Pass. Opposite: The docks, now operated by the local community, at Miner's Bay and the fuel float. It is open seven days a week for fuel. Other marine services are available through the general store on shore.

ferries. Fishing vessels are obliged to move aside for approaching ferries. Common sense calls for such action to avoid collision and also to aid the ferries in their tight manouvering in the restrictive passage.

When approaching Miner's Bay for fuel, simply steer directly towards the fuel dock. The water shallows off towards the shore but mooring buoys indicate adequate water in their vicinity. Watch for the swells created by passing ferries and other vessels and wait for them to pass before attempting to dock at the fuel dock or the government floats behind the modest wood piling breakwater.

Charts 3313, 3473, 3462

Miner's Bay

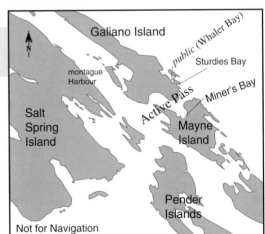

Not for Navigation

Mayne Island, Miner's Bay
Transport Canada dock
Manager • Float length 37 m
Aircraft float • Lights •
Marine Services:
Fuel • gas, diesel, outboard mix. pop,
confectionery. Tackle, bait, propane.
Adjacent restaurants, shops.
Moorage at wharf, slips.
No water or power on docks.
No laundry–No washrooms. Taxi service.
Access to settlement.
Near Ferry service–Gulf Islands to
Mainland/Sidney. Churches nearby.
Groceries, stores, accommodation nearby.
Easy walking on island roadways.
Ferry wash causes some rolling at dock.

Also in Active Pass brief stops are
possible at the small dock in Sturdies
Bay adjacent to the ferry landing.

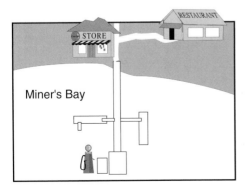

Miner's Bay

Whaler Bay
Fisheries and Oceans dock
Manager • Lights • Power. No facilities.
Limited dock space. Nearby convenience
store, Near ferry dock. Trincomali Bakery
and Deli, Art and Soul Craft Gallery.

Montague Harbour

Charts 3473, 3313, 3342, 3462

Montague Harbour Marina

Graham, Marilyn, Andrew Breeze
RR #1 Galiano Island, BC.
V0N 1P0   VHF 68
Phone: (250) 539-5733 Fax 530-3593
email: montaguemarina@gulfislands.com
Web: www.nwboat.com/montague
Marina services:
Fuel: Gas. Diesel. Marine supplies. Bait, ice.
Transient and permanent **moorage.**
Water. Power: 30, 15 amp at some slips.
Customer services:
Store–groceries, gift shop, island arts and crafts, books, charts, fishing licences, ice, bait and tackle. meals–light fare.
Cafe. Draft beer. Liquor licence.
No off-sales. Espresso bar–sundeck.
Public pay phone.
Adjacent facilities and entertainment:
Marine park at Montague Harbour. Mooring buoys and dock. Extensive walks and camp ground, beaches and picnic facilities. Sea kayak float. Scuba diving good in Active Pass and nearby reefs. Use charter services.

Public docks on Galiano:

North Galiano,
Galiano Island
(Spanish Hills)—Summer only
Fisheries & Oceans dock
Phone (250) 539-2352
Chart 3313, 3443, 3463
Manager • Float length 12 m
Public phone ashore •
Adjacent the old Spanish Hills Store.

Retreat Cove, (photo opposite)
Galiano Island.
Fisheries & Oceans dock
Phone (250) 539-2611
Chart 3313, 3442, 3463
Manager • Float length 24 m

Montague Harbour,
Galiano Island
Transport Canada dock
Chart 3313, 3473, 3462
Manager • Float length 50 m
Adjacent Montague Marina.

Whaler Bay (see page 95)
Galiano Island. Fisheries & Oceans.

*Above: The docks at Montague Harbour Marina.
Right: Store and espresso bar overlooking the docks.
Opposite: Note the more recent expanded buildings seen in the aerial photograph of Montague Harbour Marina.*

Inset right: Retreat Cove.

Retreat Cove

Nanaimo

N

Sidney

Victoria

Spanish Hills

Retreat Cove

Whaler Bay

R

Montague Harbour
Marina

Active
Pass

Launch ramp – R

Galiano Island

97

Pub and restaurant at Vesuvius on Salt Spring Island west side.

Bottom: At the dock in Horton Bay, Mayne Island.

En route up the coast towards Thetis Island and its popular marinas many stop at Wallace Island. The dock (below) is in Conover Cove where you can go ashore and hike the easy trails that run the length of the island.

Horton Bay,
Photo, left. Mayne Island.
Fisheries & Oceans dock
(250) 539-2402
Chart 3313, 3477, 3462
Manager • Float length 60 m
Garbage • Lights •

Telegraph Harbour occupies a central location in the Gulf Islands. The famous "Cut" is located between the two islands.

Thetis Island

There's a waterway in the Gulf Islands that draws boats to the challenge of its shallows. One which lures sailors like the legendary sirens to an ignominious fate of running aground if not onto the rocks, to reach the prize beyond of sheltered anchorage and a fair haven from unexpected squalls and wind. The shallow, narrow passage that separates Thetis Island from Kuper is the eastern entrance to one of the most centrally located and popular anchorages in the Gulf Islands. The canal (known as 'The Cut') lets boats through only at medium to high tides and denies passage to all but the tiniest of craft at low tides. It dries at a one foot tide. But despite the quirks and whims of the famous passage, it is the waterway that experi-enced cruising yachtsmen associate with Telegraph Harbour. Explore the area: take a dinghy ride through the cut and see the shallows for yourself before taking your boat through. The alter-native route into Telegraph is around the bottom of Kuper

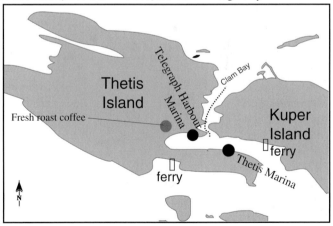

or the top of Thetis. If you are coming from a Vancouver Island base and returning to Vancouver Island after a stay at Telegraph Harbour, the passage is not an issue. But if you are crossing the Strait of Georgia and entering the Gulf Islands through Porlier Pass then the canal is the preferred access to the sheltered harbour. Choose a high tide to approach the canal or plan a longer, but pleasant detour around Thetis or Kuper.

When you arrive in Telegraph Harbour, if you are among the average type of boat owner, the first thing you will do is find moorage, at Thetis Island Marina or at Telegraph Harbour Marina. At the former you may look for the pub, at the latter you will want to moor

Telegraph Harbour

Telegraph Harbour Marina

Ron and Barbara Williamson
Thetis Island, BC,
V0R 2Y0   VHF 68
Phone: (250) 246-9511
Fax: (250) 246-2668

Marina services:
Fuel: Gas. Diesel. Oils.
Marine supplies.
Fishing gear, licences, charts, bait, ice.
3000 feet of moorage.
Water. Limited supply–use sparingly.
Power at docks: 30, 15 amp.
Multiple outlets.

Customer services:
Laundry, showers, washrooms for over-night moored guests.
Store/coffee shop, light meals, groceries, milkshakes, ice cream, baked goods.
Frozen foods, produce, gifts, arts and crafts,

Charts 3477, 3313, 3442, 3463

books, snacks. Continental breakfasts and light meals available in store or on patio.
Boating groups book events/rendezvous.
Playground.
Picnic/barbecue facilities ashore.
Book ahead in summer.

Nearby
Road access walking or cycling.
Some nearby parkland and beach trails.
Public pay phones ashore.
Daily float plane service. Short ferry trip to Chemainus shops and famous murals. Fresh roasted coffee available on island. Home/boat delivery Asian cuisine, pizza. Enquire.
Entertainment.
Recreation building. Volleyball, shuffleboard, horseshoes.
Adjacent facilities:
Bed & breakfast accommodations nearby.

quickly and head up the dock for one of the delicious old fashioned milkshakes for which the marina store has become famous. New owners in 2000 at Telegraph Harbour Marina are Ron and Barbara Williamson, who promise a warm welcome to all mariners. Across the harbour, Paul and Dawn Deacon at Thetis Island Marina, go to great lengths to welcome you and make you feel at home. In fact, so warm is the welcome at Thetis Island that we have found ourselves cancelling our continuation plans in favour of just staying around longer than planned.

Below: A friendly gathering place at Telegraph Harbour Marina.

And extending a visit is a logical choice considering the advantages of being there. The harbour is very protected from winds and weather and available moorage is usually plentiful even in the busy summer period.

When rounding Thetis Island the western entrance to Telegraph Harbour is via Preedy Harbour where seals can be seen sometimes sunning themselves on the rocks just off Foster Point. Thetis Island Marina juts out into the main passage and posted signs effectively call on boats entering Telegraph Harbour to slow down. Thetis Island Marina has a pub and serves meals from a more varied menu than that at Telegraph Harbour Marina. The regular clientele at the two marinas can be quite different, naturally, the pub being more of a social centre and congregating place for those who enjoy the pub atmosphere.

Telegraph Harbour Marina is suitable for

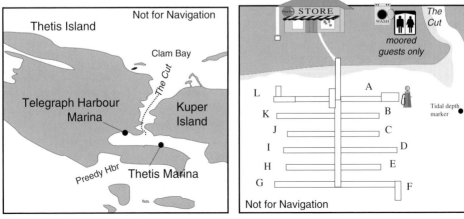

Thetis Island

Thetis Island Marina and Pub

Paul and Dawn Deacon
Thetis Island Marina
General Delivery, Thetis Island
BC, V0R 2Y0
Phone: (250) 246-3464 fax 246-1433
email: *marina@thetisisland.com*
Web: www.thetisisland.com
Marina services:
Fuel: Gas, diesel, propane, kerosene,
stove oil.
Marine supplies: Fishing licences, tackle,
bait, charts, tide tables, ice.
Transient moorage.
Water. Limited supply–use sparingly.
Power at docks: 30, 15 amp. Multiple
outlets.
Laundry, showers, washrooms.
Customer services:
Post Office. Store–groceries, dairy treats,
ice cream. bakery products. Frozen foods,
produce, gifts, arts and crafts, books, snacks.
Restaurant/pub–meals available inside or
on large sunny patio.

Chart 3477, 3313, 3442, 3463
VHF 68

Boating groups book weekend events/rendezvous. Playground. Picnic/barbecue
facilities ashore. Arrange/book ahead in
summer. Good scuba diving nearby.
Nearby church. Road access walking or
cycling.
Saturday morning crafts market–ask marina
for details.
Public pay phones ashore and at fuel dock.
Daily float plane service. Fresh roasted coffee available on the island.

Entertainment.
Short ferry trip to Chemainus shops and
famous murals. Live entertainment in the
pub on long weekends through summer
months. Horseshoe pit, satellite TV. Darts.
At the marina and nearby: Island arts and
crafts, spinning, knitted goods.
Adjacent facilities:
A variety of comfortable bed & breakfast
accommodations are located nearby.

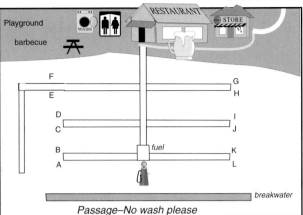

Above: Thetis Island Marina on left protrudes into the passage between Thetis Island and Kuper Island. Below: Thetis Island pub and a view of the docks. Opposite: Aerial view of Thetis Island Marina.

families and family activities. Like most of the Gulf Islands water is in short supply on Thetis and boat owners are asked to use only what they need for refilling their fresh water tanks. Garbage is a problem for marinas but they do allow disposal of garbage by moorage customers. The Thetis Island post office and a propane filling station is located at Thetis Island Marina. The convenience stores at both marinas carry some souvenirs, charts and books as well as a selection of items for replenishment of boating supplies. Other than these stores at the two marinas there are no shops or shopping centres on the island. However, Chemainus on Vancouver Island, which is a short ferry ride away, has a selection of stores and restaurants to please everyone. It is worth the ferry ride to stroll around this artistic Vancouver Island centre. The passenger ferry leaves Thetis Island for the run across Stuart Channel eight times a day.

Not far from Telegraph Harbour Marina is a well-known supplier of fresh roasted coffee—Pot of Gold is open at most times to sell their rich aromatic beans or freshly ground coffee to islanders and visitors alike. Just stroll up to the entrance of their property and make your purchases at the gate stall.

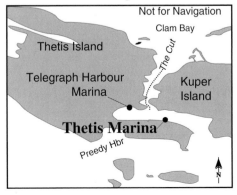

Thetis Island is known for its arts and crafts. Crafts on sale on the island represent the works of various islanders and prices are generally more favourable than those for similar items in the cities. Look for their wares and details at the two marinas.

If you enjoy strolling a walk along any of the Thetis Island roads is relaxing and easy without any significant hills and traffic. Or at low tide you can don your boating boots and go beachcombing along the dry but marshy flats of the canal and watch your fellow boat owners trying their luck in the Cut.

103

Gabriola Island

Nanaimo

Gabriola

Silva Bay

Gabriola Pass

Degnan Bay

Ladysmith

Porlier Pass

Chemainus

Crofton

Vesuvius

Vancouver

Ganges

Active Pass

Island

Sidney

Limited access to the shore is available at the public docks at Degnen Bay.

N

Anchoring in Silva Bay is popular but beware of strong northerlies or north-westerlies that tend to howl into the bay at times causing the need for a watch during the night when anchors drag. Fishing at nearby Thrasher Rock keeps the bay busy throughout summer and quite popular during other months. Page's Marina, which has been around a long time, has some interesting works of art on display as well as casual supplies, books and crafts. The facility is also known as a fuel stop and transient moorage marina.

Not for navigation

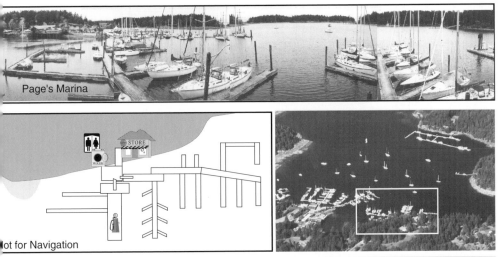

Page's Marina

ot for Navigation

Silva Bay

Charts 3475, 3313, 3443, 3463

1. Page's Marina

Ted and Phyllis Reeve
Site 30 RR #2, Gabriola, BC,
V0R 1X0
Phone: (250) 247-8931
Chart 3475, 3310.
www.island.net/~tpreeve/
email: tpreeve@island.net

Marina services:
Fuel: Gas. Diesel. outboard oil.
Moorage mostly to 30 feet, some larger.
Water at dock. Limited supply.
Power 15 amp.
Customer services:
Rental cottages. Picnic and campground.
Office/store has art, books, etc.
Showers, laundry, washrooms.
Walking road access.
Good scuba diving in nearby locations. Dive
shop ashore, rentals, air fills. (Nick Small).
Mobile repairs, service, available.
Public pay phone.
Entertainment.
Fishing charters can be arranged.
Adjacent facilities: Grocery store at Silva
Bay Boatel.

Page's Marina dock has a large area and easy docking. Located at the end of the passage inside Sear Island. Watch depths at low tide and use a chart when navigating.
Page's has books and art at the office ashore.

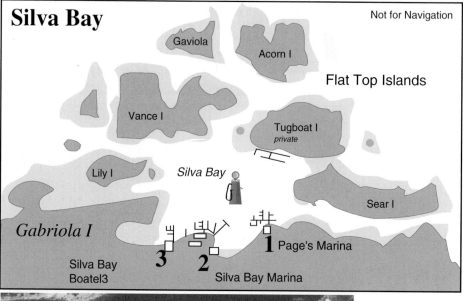

Silva Bay

Not for Navigation

Gaviola

Acorn I

Flat Top Islands

Vance I

Tugboat I
private

Lily I

Silva Bay

Sear I

Gabriola I

3 **2** **1** Page's Marina

Silva Bay
Boatel3

Silva Bay Marina

Aerial photograph shows location of Sterling Resorts Silva Bay Marina with the Silva Bay Boatel docks to its left.

2. Sterling Resorts Silva Bay Marina

Dock Manager
Gabriola, BC,
V0R 1X0
Phone: (250) 247-8662, 247-7649
Chart 3475, 3313, 3463, 3443.

Marina services:
Fuel: Gas. Diesel.Outboard mix.
Moorage, ways, shipyard.
Water at dock.
Power 15 amp. 30 amp.

Customer services:
Store, cafe, restaurant, pub–The Bitter End
phone 247-8606.**Washrooms, laundry, showers**, pool, spa, sauna.

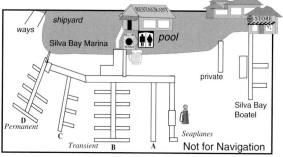

LODGE

ways

shipyard

RESTAURANT

STORE

Silva Bay Marina

WASH

pool

private

Silva Bay
Boatel

D
Permanent

C

Transient B

A

Seaplanes

Not for Navigation

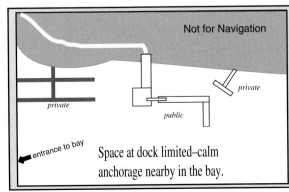

Silva Bay Boatel docks shallow at low tides. Limited space for tie-up.

3. Silva Bay Boatel

Audrey Leloupe
Silva Bay, Gabriola, BC,
V0R 1X0
Phone : (250) 247-9351

Marina services:
Moorage (limited–mostly small boats).
Customer services:
Grocery store. Coffee, light snacks served. Fishing licences, bait, tackle, some hard-

Chart 3475, 3313, 3463, 3443.

ware. Ice, propane. Head depot.
Walking road access.
Good scuba diving in nearby locations.
Public pay phone.
Entertainment.
Fishing charters can be arranged.
Adjacent facilities:
Accommodation in motel. Self-contained kitchenette suites–7 units.

Space at dock limited–calm anchorage nearby in the bay.

Degnen Bay,

Gabriola Island public dock.
Fisheries & Oceans dock

Chart   3313, 3463, 3475
Float length 60 m
Garbage • Lights • Power
• Public phone •
Private docks adjacent.

*Above: View of Newcastle Island from Nanaimo.
Inset opposite page: The channel inside Newcastle Island is lined with marinas.
Inset above: Newcastle Marine Park docks.
Right: A ferry approaching the BC ferries dock in Departure Bay.*

Nanaimo

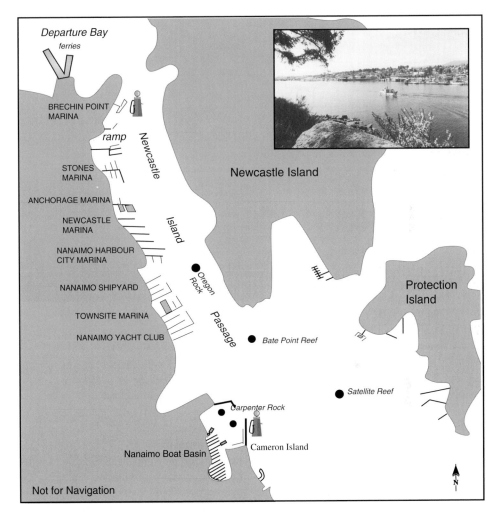

Departure Bay
ferries

BRECHIN POINT
MARINA

ramp

Newcastle

STONES
MARINA

ANCHORAGE MARINA

NEWCASTLE
MARINA

NANAIMO HARBOUR
CITY MARINA

Island

Newcastle Island

NANAIMO SHIPYARD

Oregon
Rock

TOWNSITE MARINA

Passage

NANAIMO YACHT CLUB

Bate Point Reef

Protection
Island

Satellite Reef

Carpenter Rock

Nanaimo Boat Basin

Cameron Island

Not for Navigation

N

Nanaimo and its nearby islands.

Development of the city of Nanaimo has been fast and furious in recent years. Marinas and docks are plentiful with several having been upgraded substantially. The waterfront has undergone a massive face lift and new restaurants and public areas have evolved. There is a regular ferry service between Newcastle Island Marine Park and Nanaimo and another that serves the famous Dinghy Dock Pub on Protection Island. Their docks accommodate boats but space ashore is shared with the non-boating public.

Nanaimo

Fish & chips at the Boat Basin

1. Nanaimo Boat Basin

Andy Pitcher, Harbourmaster

Port of Nanaimo, BC,   **VHF 67**
(250) 754-5053 fax (250) 753-4899
(and Cameron Island Marina)
Port Authority (250) 753-4146

Hazard: When proceeding past Oregon Rock use passage on Newcastle Island side, indicated by sign on mid-channel marker. Consult your chart.

Marina services:

Fuel, Petro Canada: Gas, diesel, mixed gas, ice. Service available.

Moorage: Large civic marina with pleasure boat moorage in summer. In winter docks are heavily used by fishermen.

Reservations taken for 600 foot floating breakwater pier for large vessels and adjacent **Cameron Island Marina** (phone **(250) 755-1216** June to August). Hydraulic crane to 1000 lb .

Water at dock. **Power**: 15, 20, 30 amp. Also 50 and 100 amp.

Laundry, showers, washrooms.
Ice machine. Sani-station **pump out.**

Charts 3457/8, 3313, 3443, 3463,

Customer services:

Customs/phone 24 hour service.

Downtown Nanaimo at doorstep of marina. Road access walking or cycling or vehicle rentals. Public pay phones.

Regular scheduled float plane service to Vancouveer.

Entertainment:

Restaurants, pubs and theatres, arts and crafts exhibits, stores and galleries. Bathtub race every July. Many festive activities.

Fish and chips on dock. Casino nearby.

Adjacent and nearby facilities:

Walkway, plaza and shops. Shipyards, ways, all marine services. Lighthouse Bistro/Pub. Marinas. Newcastle Island Marine Park – docks, walking trails, camping, picnics, BC Ferries to mainland nearby.

Walk on ferries to Newcastle or Protection Islands. Protection Island: Dinghy Dock pub. Anchor off and row to dock. Visit the Dock Shop on waterfront walkway.

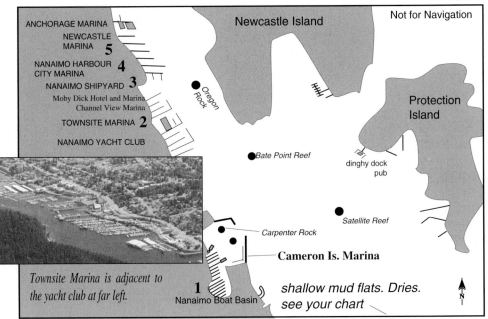

Not for Navigation

ANCHORAGE MARINA
NEWCASTLE MARINA **5**
NANAIMO HARBOUR **4**
CITY MARINA
NANAIMO SHIPYARD **3**
Moby Dick Hotel and Marina
Channel View Marina
TOWNSITE MARINA **2**
NANAIMO YACHT CLUB

Newcastle Island

Oregon Rock

Protection Island

●Bate Point Reef

dinghy dock
pub

Satellite Reef

Carpenter Rock

Cameron Is. Marina

Townsite Marina is adjacent to the yacht club at far left.

1
Nanaimo Boat Basin

shallow mud flats. Dries. see your chart

N

2. Townsite Marina

Dock Manager
20 Townsite Road,
Nanaimo, BC, V9R 4Z9
Phone (250) 716-8801 Fax (250) 716-7288
(see location on diagrams) **Call VHF 73**
Marina services:
Moorage boats 18' to 100 feet. Located adjacent Nanaimo Yacht Club.
Power 30, 50 amps. **Water.** Ice.
Washrooms, Showers, Laundry.
Power 30, 50 amps.

Nearby: Fuel docks, marine chandleries, Downtown Nanaimo. Restaurants, supermarkets, hotels, golf, museum, art gallery. **Note location of Townsite Marina alongside the yacht club.**

Overnight moorage is also available at Channel View Marina (250) 741-0843, and Moby Dick Marina (adjacent).

No wake speeds are enforced in Nanaimo Harbour. Mind the reef and shallows in mid channel marked by a piling with a sign indicating correct passage. Also stay clear of the mud flats in the south end of the harbour.

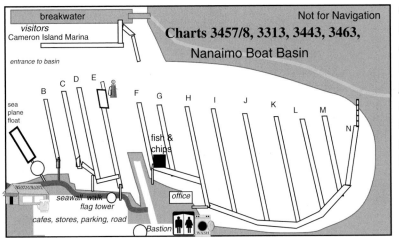

breakwater

visitors
Cameron Island Marina

Not for Navigation

Charts 3457/8, 3313, 3443, 3463,
Nanaimo Boat Basin

entrance to basin

sea plane float

B C D E F G H I J K L M N

fish & chips

RESTAURANT

seawall walk
flag tower

cafes, stores, parking, road

office

Bastion WASH

Dinghy Dock Pub

Dinghy Dock
Floating Marine Pub

Hilda and Bob Banerd
**Box 771, Nanaimo, #8 Pirate's Lane,
Nanaimo, BC. V9R 5M2
Phone: (250) 753-2373 741-8244
Charts 3457/8 3313, 3463.
Boats anchored out call Dinghy Dock
Pub on VHF 18A.
Marina Services**
Tie up space for restaurant/pub.
Season April through October.

Showers. Pub restaurant dining.
Walking on Protection Island. More
moorage and anchoring at Newcastle
Island Marine Park nearby.

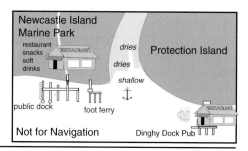

The Dinghy Dock Pub has won awards for excellence. It makes a perfect lunch or dinner stop and occasionally boats will be able to stay overnight. The pub is built on floats and has slips to accommodate eight to ten small to medium sized boats. It is best to anchor out and come to the pub by dinghy. Or, if you are spending the night at Nanaimo take the ferry that leaves regularly from the Boat Basin. Facilities at the Dinghy Dock Pub include showers, laundry and washrooms.

Newcastle Island Marine Park is a short distance away and there are several slips for medium to larger sized boats as well as numerous slips for smaller boats and dinghies. Going ashore at Newcastle Island is a treat, providing lots of treed pathways for hiking, walking or cycling. An interpretive centre functions in summer for the use of students, groups and others interested in the use of the facilities.

The ferry between the Nanaimo Boat Basin and Protection Island leaves the docks hourly, 9:00 am to 11:00 pm.

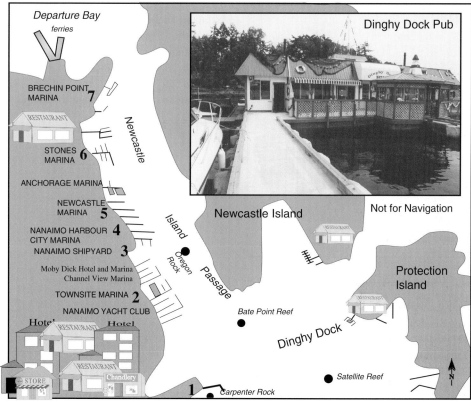

Dinghy Dock Pub (inset). Opposite: Aerial view of location on Protection Island.

3. Nanaimo Shipyard

1040 Stewart Avenue
Nanaimo, BC., V9S 4C9
Phone: (250) 753-1151
Fax: (250) 753-2235
Chart 3313, 3463, 3457/8
email: *rvw@island.net*
Web: *www.island.net/~nsy*

Hazard: Enter Nanaimo via south of Protection Island. From the north/Departure Bay: use correct channel when passing the mid channel rock.
Best passage on Newcastle Island side.
Marina services:
Moorage. Haulouts. Repairs. Vessels to 200 feet.
Chandlery Phone: (250) 753-1244.
All boating supplies.
Water at dock. **Power** at docks.

Charts 3457/8, 3313, 3443, 3463,

Customer services:
Downtown Nanaimo near marina. All facilities and services are available.
Road access walking or cycling.
Vehicle rentals.
Daily float plane service nearby.
Entertainment.
From restaurants, pubs and theatres to arts and crafts exhibits, stores and galleries at Nanaimo. Bathtub race every July.
Adjacent facilities:
Shipyards, all marine services.
Nanaimo Yacht Club reciprocal moorage.
Marinas.
Newcastle Island Marine Park; docks, walking trails, camping, picnics.
BC Ferries to Vancouver.
Ferry to Galiano Island, Newcastle Island and Protection Island.

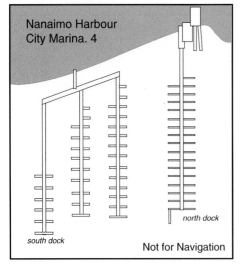

Nanaimo Harbour City Marina. 4

north dock

south dock

Not for Navigation

4. Nanaimo Harbour City Marina

Ron and Susan Mielke
1250 Stewart Avenue,
Nanaimo, BC., V9S 4C9
Phone: (250) 754-2732 Fax: 754-7140
Charts 3457/8, 3313, 3443, 3463,
Hazard: Enter Nanaimo via south of Protection Island.
From the north/Departure Bay watch correct channel when passing the mid channel rock. Passage on Newcastle Island side.
Marina services:
Moorage. Mostly permanent. Haulouts. Repairs, welding. Boatyard. Travel lift.
Water at dock. Ice.
Power at docks: 15, 20 amp
Showers, washrooms.
Customer services:
Downtown Nanaimo near marina. All facilities and services are available.
Road access walking or cycling or vehicle rentals.
Public pay phones.
Daily float plane service.

Entertainment.
From restaurants, pubs and theatres to arts and crafts exhibits, stores and galleries. Bathtub race every July.

Adjacent facilities:
Shipyards, all marine services.
Newcastle Island Marine Park; docks, walking trails, camping, picnics.
BC Ferries to Vancouver. and Galiano.
Ferry to Newcastle and Protection Island.

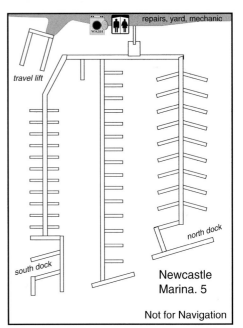

repairs, yard, mechanic

WASH

travel lift

north dock

south dock

Newcastle Marina. 5

Not for Navigation

5. Newcastle Marina

1300 Stewart Avenue
Nanaimo, BC., V9S 4E1
Phone: (250) 753-1431
Fax: (250) 753-2974
Charts 3457/8, 3313, 3443, 3463,
email: *nmarina@nanaimo.ark.com*
Hazard: Enter Nanaimo via south of Protection Island. From the north/Departure Bay: use correct channel when passing the mid channel rock.
Passage on Newcastle Island side.
Marina services:
Moorage. Haulouts. Repairs. Welding. Yard. Storage. Mostly permanent moorage.
Water at dock. **Power** at docks.
Customer services:
Downtown Nanaimo near marina.
All facilities and services are available.
Road access walking or cycling.

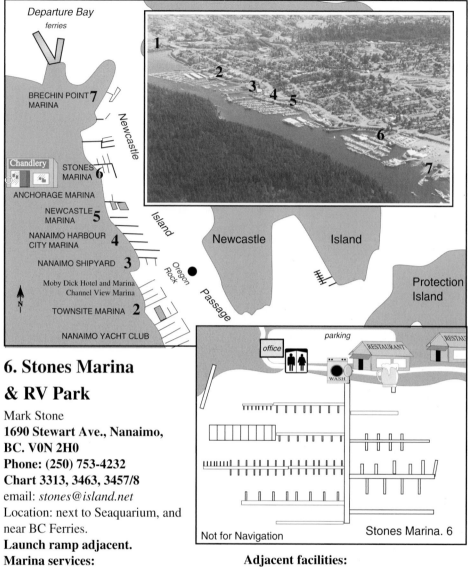

6. Stones Marina & RV Park

Mark Stone
1690 Stewart Ave., Nanaimo, BC. V0N 2H0
Phone: (250) 753-4232
Chart 3313, 3463, 3457/8
email: *stones@island.net*
Location: next to Seaquarium, and near BC Ferries.
Launch ramp adjacent.
Marina services:
Moorage. Transient in summer months.
Power: 15, 30 amp
Water at dock.
Customer services:
Ice. Laundry, showers, washrooms
Pay phone. Garbage disposal. Store. Tackle, fishing licences, bait. Mobile LPG service.
Marine sales. **Pub and restaurant.**
Walking: Road access walking or cycling.
Entertainment.
Nearby access to ferries to Galiano Island, Newcastle and Protection Islands.

Stones Marina. 6
Not for Navigation

Adjacent facilities:
Muddy Waters Pub, restaurant and RV Park.
Brechin Point Marina fuel dock and seaplane float–nearby.

7. Brechin Point Marina

Ph: (250) 753-6122.
Emergency only: After hours Chris at (250) 758-3646 or Doug at (250) 754-2317.
email: *landahl@island.net*
Customs, Seaplanes, marina.
Fuel: Diesel, gas, oils, propane.

Vancouver Area

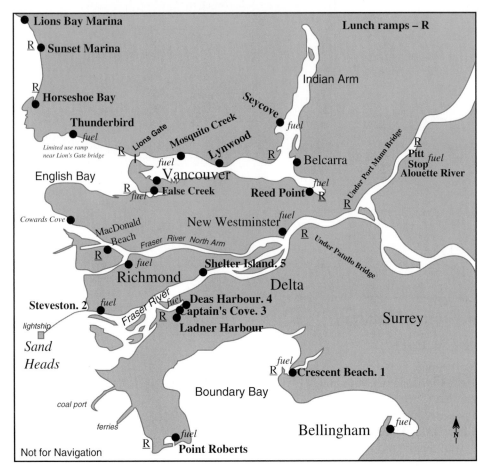

Lions Bay Marina

R Sunset Marina

R Horseshoe Bay

Lunch ramps – R

Indian Arm

Thunderbird
fuel

Limited use ramp
near Lion's Gate bridge

Lions Gate

Mosquito Creek

Seycove
fuel

R

Lynwood

fuel

R

Vancouver

English Bay

R
fuel False Creek

Belcarra

Reed Point
fuel
R

Under Port Mann Bridge

R
Pitt
Stop *fuel*
Alouette River

R

Cowards Cove

MacDonald
Beach

New Westminster *fuel*

Fraser River North Arm

R

R

Under Patullo Bridge

Richmond

R *fuel*

Shelter Island. 5

Delta

Steveston. 2 *fuel*

Fraser River

fuel
R

Deas Harbour. 4
Captain's Cove. 3

lightship

Ladner Harbour

Surrey

Sand
Heads

fuel
R Crescent Beach. 1

Boundary Bay

coal port

ferries

Not for Navigation

R *fuel*
Point Roberts

Bellingham

fuel

N

Marinas in the Greater Vancouver area offer moorage for overnight customers. However, most of them are dedicated to providing permanent moorage and although some have many slips they usually can allocate space as needed during summer when many of their customers' boats are away. Boat operators in transit from southern ports to places such as the Sunshine Coast and Desolation Sound should consider Vancouver's downtown area or False Creek where there are many attractions. In the Fraser River, one can cruise all the way up to Mission or turn off on the Pitt River and enjoy a splendid run into Pitt Lake.

Entering the Fraser River is safe provided you do so when winds are relatively calm and the tide is right. At about maximum low tide with a northwesterly wind you are well advised to wait. Beware of the shallows off the mouth of the river, especially if you do find yourself running into some wind and waves. It is well marked but the shallows actually extend somewhat beyond the markers, especially around the beacon to the south of the lightship.

Stopping at Steveston (public docks) is a treat if you can find moorage and go ashore.

1. Crescent Beach Marina (1967) Ltd.

B.J. Chapman
**12555 Crescent Road, Surrey,
BC. V4A 2V4
Phone (604) 538-9666 Fax 538-7724
Chart 3463.** See map on page 126.
Entrance: Follow markers in long channel
through Boundary Bay, using red right
returning. Moorage (phone for reservations). Water, power 15 amp. **Washrooms,**
public phones. **Fuel:** gas, diesel. Ice.
Chandlery, bait, fishing supplies. Haulout
up to 45' power, 30' sail. **Launch ramp.**

---

2. Steveston *Photo right*

Near the mouth of the Fraser River.
Fisheries & Oceans dock Gulf of
Georgia
Ph/fax (604) 277-4712 Chevron dock.
Charts 3490, 3463
Manager • Float length 778 m
Breakwater • Grid • Garbage • Waste
oil disposal • Parking •
Water • Lights • Power • Public phone
ashore • Washrooms • Showers •
Adjacent city restaurants, shops,
marine stores, chandleries,
repair facilities. Auxiliary Coast
Guard. **Fuel** at three locations.
Additional public docks (Paramount)
for fishing and commercial vessels.
Launch ramp.

Crescent Beach

Fisheries & Oceans dock
Beach float
Chart 3463
Manager • Float length 12 m
Lights • Not a suitable boating stop.

---

3. Captain's Cove Marina

Gina Tweed
**6100 Ferry Road, Ladner,
BC. V4K 3M9
Phone: (604) 946-1244
Chart 3490**
Fresh water moorage at visitor's dock.
Water. Power 15, 30 amps. **Fuel:** gas, diesel, engine and outboard oils. **Showers,
laundry, washrooms.** Public phones. Rusty
Anchor Pub adjacent. Travel lift 30 ton,
repairs, service, storage and workyard, power
wash, painting. **Launch ramp** adjacent.

*Top: Crescent Beach Marina is tucked in the south
curve of Boundary Bay, behind the railway line.
Below: Steveston.*

River House

River House Marina at Ladner. Stop at Captain's Cove (larger boats wait for tide, to pass under bridge)

4. River House Marina

Chris Carroll
5825 60th Ave, Ladner,
BC. V4K 3E2
Phone (604) 940-4496
Limited moorage (mostly permanent).
Some water, power available–15 amps.
Public phones.
River House restaurant and marine pub.
Low bridge beyond Captain's Cove Marina
14' clearance at medium high tide.

5. Shelter Island Marina

Glenn Rae
120–6911 Graybar, Richmond,
BC. V6W 1H3 Ph: 1-877-270-6272
Phone: (604) 270-6272 Fax: 273-6282
Fresh water moorage (permanent). **Water.
Power. Showers, laundry, washrooms.**
Public phones. Marine hardware, repairs,
service. Two travel lifts to 150 tons–vessels
to over 130', 30' beam. Workyard for up to
500 boats. Beer and wine store. Restaurant
and pub adjacent.

6. Bridgepoint Marina

Gary Cross
8831 River Road, Richmond,
BC. V6X 1Y6
Phone (604) 273-8560 Fax: 231-8081
Chart 3491
Fresh water moorage.
Transient visitors welcome.
**Water, power, showers, laundry,
washrooms.** Public phones. Pub, restaurant
on site. Sales adjacent. Fuel dock nearby.

7. Delta Airport Hotel Marina

Bob Dunne
3500 Cessna Drive, Richmond,
BC. V7B 1C7   Chart 3491
Phone: (604) 278-1241 Hotel & Marina
Phone: (604) 273-4211 Delta Charters
Fax Marina: (604) 276-1975
Transient moorage. Water, power.
Public phones. Hotel facilities and services.
Restaurant. Near Vancouver International
Airport, Richmond city facilities, restaurants
and shopping centres.

There the variety of shops, cafes and restaurants will keep you busy for hours. However, there is extremely limited moorage for pleasure craft when the fishing fleet is in.

Going farther up the river there is Captain's Cove Marina for haulouts, repairs and service as well as some overnight moorage, fuel, ice and a pub, The Rusty Anchor, which serves good meals seven days a week. Beyond Captain's Cove is Deas Harbour with its River House restaurant and marina beyond the low bridge of Highway 99. The village of Ladner is tucked away down Ladner Reach which opens off the Fraser at the entrance to Captain's Cove. A large public dock at Ladner welcomes mariners, especially when the fishing fleet is away. Phone (604) 946-8430 for information. Another good facility with marine pub and restaurant is at Shelter Island a little farther up river. If you need a haulout for a large boat or a workyard in which to block it up Shelter Island Marina can provide the necessary facilities.

You could cruise on to New Westminster and return to the Strait of Georgia by going down the north arm of the Fraser. Part way down you will come to Richmond's marinas just after passing under Knight Street bridge and Oak Street bridge. Fuel is available at Vancouver Marina just beyond the swivel bridge on the Middle Arm.

8. Vancouver Marina

John Short
**8331 River Road, Richmond,
BC. V6X 1Y1
Phone: (604) 278-9787 Fax (604) 278-1738
Chart 3491**
No transient moorage. Permanent up to 45' open, 38' covered, Water, power. **Fuel:** gas, diesel, stove oil, engine and outboard oils. Public phones. Repairs, service. Restaurant. Near Richmond city facilities, restaurants.

9. Skyline Marina

Dave Shirley
**8031 River Road, Richmond,
BC. V6X 1X8
Phone: (604) 273-3977
Chart 3491**
Shipwrights. Some transient moorage, water, power–15 amp. Fuel (nearby): gas, diesel, stove oil, engine and outboard oils. Public phones. Repairs, service, chandlery nearby. Nearby Richmond city facilities, restaurants.

Use charts 3490 (South Arm) and 3491 (North Arm)

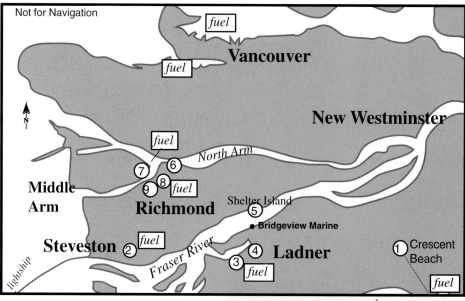

Downtown Vancouver nowadays has plenty of transient moorage. The main visitors' dock at Coal Harbour Marina.

Above: Crescent Beach Marina. There is a fuel dock, a generous launching ramp, maritime service and a convenient store with some boat equipment and supplies available.

1. Harbour Cruises Marina

Jan Andrews
#1 North foot Denman,
Vancouver,
BC., V6G 2W9   Use chart 3493
Phone: (604) 687-9558 Fax: (604) 687-5868
Moorage. **Water. Power** 15, 20, 30 amp.
Fuel (nearby): gas, diesel, stove oil, engine
and outboard oils. **Washrooms.** Public
phones. Chandlery, repairs, service,
nearby. Located next to Stanley Park and
charter vessel basin.

2. Thunderbird Marina(s)

5776 Marine Drive, West Vancouver,
BC, V7W 2S2
Phone: (604) 921-7434 Fax: (604) 921-7486
Charts 3311, 3534, 3481
Limited moorage, **water, power**.
Fuel dock (nearby): gas, diesel, stove oil,
engine and outboard oils. Marine store,
tackle, bait, fishing licences, repairs,
service. 25 ton travel lift for boats to 51
feet. Workyard, storage. *Also downtown*
Vancouver moorage: **Bayshore (West)**
Marina. Guest
moorage, **water,**
power, phones.
Near hotel and
downtown ameni-
ties. Near Stanley
Park.

3. Barbary Coast Yacht Basin

16801 W. Georgia,
Vancouver, BC. V6G 2W6
Phone: (604) 669-0088.
Limited moorage. Large
boats okay. **Power.**
Showers, Laundry,
washrooms.

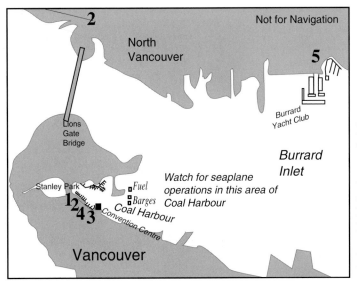

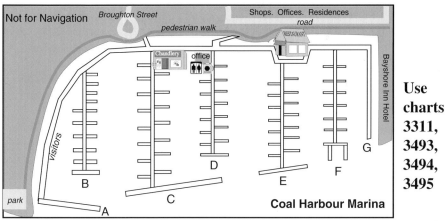

Not for Navigation — Broughton Street — pedestrian walk — Shops. Offices. Residences road — Bayshore Inn Hotel — Chandlery — office — RESTAURANT

Use charts 3311, 3493, 3494, 3495

Visitors — B — A — C — D — E — F — G — park — **Coal Harbour Marina**

Photo, opposite, shows the large basin containing Coal Harbour Marina. To its right are Thunderbird Marina and Harbour Cruises Marina. To its left (not shown) is Barbary Coast Yacht Basin. Foreground shows Royal Vancouver Yacht Club, right of Deadman Island.

4. Coal Harbour Marina

Graham Clarke
1525 Coal Harbour Quay, Vancouver, BC, V6G 3E7
Phone: (604) 681-2628 Fax: 681-4666
email: *coalhbr@seatosky.com*
Web: *www.seatosky.com/coalhbr*
Marina Services   VHF 68
Moorage. Cable vision. **Washrooms. Water. Power** 30, 50, 100, 150 amp.
Fuel (nearby): gas, diesel, stove oil, engine and outboard oils. Vacuum sewage system. Public phones. Wright Mariner Supply–chandlery. Repairs, service–nearby.
Coffee shop, convenience store.
Adjacent to city centre, restaurants, shops.

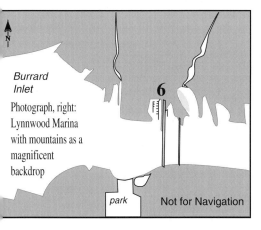

Burrard Inlet

Photograph, right: Lynnwood Marina with mountains as a magnificent backdrop

6

park — Not for Navigation

5. Mosquito Creek

Bill Williams
Ft Forbes Ave., North Vancouver, BC. V7L 4J5
Phone: (604) 987-4113 Fax: (604) 987-6852
Moorage, water, power. **Fuel:** gas, diesel. Washrooms. Public phones. Marine supplies, repairs, service. Crane. 35 ton travel lift. Near North Vancouver restaurants, shops.

Lynnwood Marina

6. Lynnwood Marina

Roger Gibson
1681 Columbia, North Vancouver, BC. V7J 1A5
Phone: (604) 985-1533 Fax: (604) 985-8892
Chart 3311, 3494
Moorage, **water, power**. Ice, bait, fishing tackle, licences. **Washrooms**. Public phones. Chandlery, repairs, service. Painting, storage and work yard, 60 ton travel lift to boats 70' by 18' size.
Restaurant. Services.

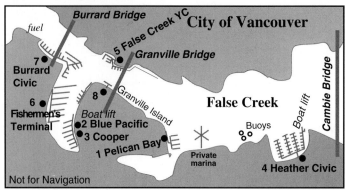

Not for Navigation

1. Pelican Bay Marina
2. Blue Pacific Yacht Charters
3. Cooper Boating Centre.
4. Heather Civic Marina
5. False Creek Yacht Club.
6. Fishermen's Terminal
7. Burrard Bridge Civic
   Marina (Permanent Moorage).
8. Granville Island Public dock.
Note: Manmade Granville Island
is not a true island.

1. Pelican Bay Marina

Michael/Elaine Jensen
**2235 West 32 Ave.,Vancouver, BC. V6L 2B1
Phone: (604) 263-5222 or 729-1442 Fax (604)
683-3444 Chart 3311, 3493. False Creek**
Visitor Moorage. In False Creek on Granville
Island, adjacent to renown Granville Island
Market, theatres, restaurants, shopping.
water, power 30, 50 amps**, washrooms.**
Cable and phone hookups. All marine services available nearby.

2. Blue Pacific YachtCharters

**Phone: (604) 682-2161   (604) 682-5312
Chart 3311, 3493   False Creek**
Moorage, **water, power. Showers.** Garbage
disposal. Nearby market, restaurants.

3. Cooper Boating Centre

**Phone: (604) 687-4110 Fax: (604) 687-3267
Chart 3311, 3493   False Creek**
Moorage, **water, power. Showers.** Garbage
disposal. Nearby market, restaurants.

7. Burrard Civic Marina – mostly permanent moorage.

4. Heather Civic Marina

**600 Stamps Landing,
Vancouver, BC.V5Z 3Z1
Phone (604) 874-2814 Fax: (604) 874-6015
Chart 3311, 3493   False Creek**
Moorage (mostly permanent), **water, power.
Showers, laundry, washrooms.** Public
phones. Pub adjacent, restaurants nearby.
City shops and facilities nearby.
Park, waterfront paths adjacent.
Boat lift at marina.

5. False Creek Yacht Club

**Phone: (604) 682-3292 Fax: (604) 682-3614
Chart 3311, 3493   False Creek**
Moorage mostly permanent. **Water, power,
showers.** Nearby recreational centre.

6. Fishermen's Terminal

**False Creek, Vancouver.
Chart 3311, 3493   False Creek**
Moorage, **water, power. Showers**. Garbage
disposal.

Boat lift on Granville Island
(685-6924) 15 ton capacity.

In Vancouver you have the alternative of an overnight in False Creek or Burrard Inlet. False Creek's
Pelican Bay has facilities including hotel, spa and dining, phones and cable TV at your boat. Near the
entrance of False Creek is the False Creek Yacht Club and opposite is Granville Island with several
overnight options and where you will be able to access the fresh produce market, restaurants and pubs.
Mooring buoys east of Granville Island are designated for use only by visiting offshore cruising yachts.

In Burrard Inlet the marinas are obvious and easy to locate after rounding Brockton Point and
passing the fuel barges. Their location will give you the opportunity to visit downtown Vancouver
within easy walking distance. If you wish to be away from the city, continue down Burrard Inlet and
find your way to Indian Arm or Port Moody. If you prefer to anchor out overnight, go up Indian Arm
to Bedwell Bay and drop anchor. Fuel is available at Seycove Marina in Deep Cove.

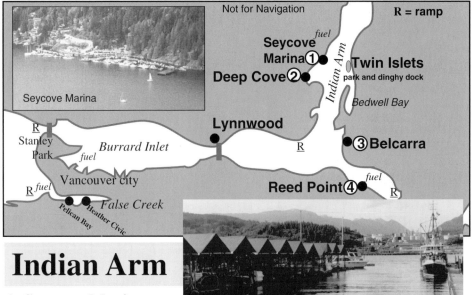

Indian Arm

1. Seycove Marina

2890 Panorama Drive, North Vancouver, BC. V7G 1V6
Phone (604) 929-1251 Fax 929-7862
Chart 3495, 3311
Moorage to 70 feet, **water, power** 15 amp. **Fuel**: gas, diesel. **Washrooms.** Public phones. Chandlery, mobile repairs, service. Nearby Deep Cove village, restaurants.

Charts 3311, 3495 Deep Cove

2. Deep Cove

Diane and Roy Alton-Kaighan
Phone 728-4356 **Overnight moorage.**
Wharfinger 924-2448 • Float length 44 m
Lights • Restaurants, groceries and other services. Adjacent: Deep Cove Yacht Club.

3. Belcarra Park

Parks Board park and floats.
Small dock mostly used for recreational fishing. Kiosk serves snacks, light meals.

4. Reed Point Marina

Dock manager
850, Barnet Highway,
Port Moody, BC, V6H 1V6
Phone (604) 931-2477 Fax 931-2132
Chart 3311, 3494
Marina services:
Fuel: Gas, diesel. Stove oil. Ice, water. Snacks. Bait, fishing licences. Overnight moorage, power 30 amps. 38 ton travel lift, Summer moorage for trailerable boats. Dry storage and work yard. Hamburger stand. Public phone, washrooms. Marine supplies, service repairs, boat rentals.
Yacht sales and service.

Reed Point Marina

Indian Arm

The quaint, old general store at Gambier. It is located not far from the dock at New Brighton.

Howe Sound

This major sound on the coast of BC is one of the most active playgrounds for summer boating. It is the nearest relatively sheltered cruising areas to Vancouver and a popular stop for vessels en route south to north. Large marinas offer safe overnight moorage, and several coves and marine parks provide good-weather anchorage for the thousands of boats that converge on the sound each summer.

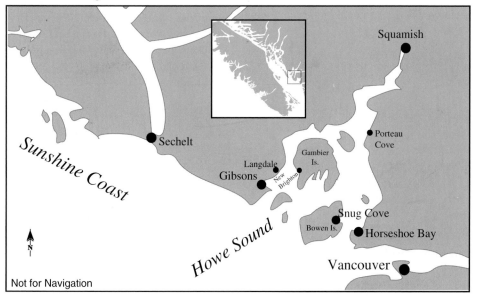

Horseshoe Bay is a busy hub of travelling activity in the summer.

Horseshoe Bay

Charts 3534, 3311, 3526, 3512

Sewell's Marina

**6695 Nelson,
West Vancouver, BC. V7W 2B2
Phone: (604) 921-3474 Fax 921-7027**
*www.sewellsmarina.com
emai: info@sewellsmarina.com*
**Marina Services
Moorage
Fuel:** gas, diesel, stove oil, engine and outboard oils.

**Water at docks
Power** 15, 20, 30 amp.
Washrooms nearby. Public phones, launch ramp. Chandlery, repairs, service, fishing charters, licences, bait, tackle, rentals.
Restaurants, Horseshoe Bay village adjacent– many services available.
Adjacent ferry terminal.

Horseshoe Bay public dock

West Vancouver
Transport Canada dock
Chart   3534, 3526, 3311, 3512
Manager • Float length 64 m
Lights • Power •
Adjacent restaurants, shops, ferries to Vancouver Island and the Sunshine Coast via Langdale/Gibsons.

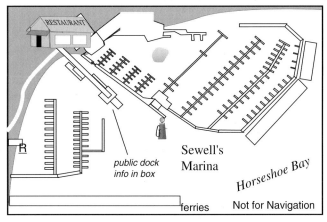

RESTAURANT

B

public dock
info in box

Sewell's
Marina

Horseshoe Bay

ferries   Not for Navigation

Snug Cove

Snug Cove Marina in the centre of the photo. The public dock acts as a breakwater with the ferry landing and Bowen Island Marina to the right.

Union Steamship Co. Marina–Snug Cove

Rondy and Dorothy Dike
P.O. Box 250
Bowen Island, BC, V0N 1G0
Phone: (604) 947-0707 Fax: (604) 947-0708
Chart 3534, 3311, 3526, 3512
VHF call 68
email: *ussc@direct.ca*
Web: *www.steamship-marina.bc.ca*
Hazard: Watch for ferry operations.
Shallows near beach beyond marina docks.
Marina services:
Moorage: 170 slips. Maximum to 220 feet.
Water at dock.
Power at docks: 50, 30 amp.
Showers, public phones, washrooms.
Customer services:
Chandlery. Boating supplies. Gifts, novelties, charts, snacks. Fresh produce, frozen foods, pharmacy, liquor, tackle, bait, hardware, ice and most supplies–at marina or in village. Restaurants, pubs, art and crafts stores, bistro, bakeries, health food and gift and specialty stores.
Entertainment.
Annual summer events include live entertainment, (pub Saturday nights), Bowen Island parade and festival (Saturday prior to Labour Day). Dog Days of Summer (Second Sunday in August). Walking roads and trails on island. Crippen Regional Park has many trails and walks. Including 600 acres surrounding Snug Cove and marina.
Adjacent facilities:
BC Ferries to Horseshoe Bay. Crippen Regional Park. Picnic ashore. Walking trails. Killarney Lake in Crippen Park area. Anchorage in Mannion Bay (temporary).

Balladeer log 1984–The old general store building was being shifted from its street front location to a site a short distance back from the road. It seemed some development is being planned for the settlement of Snug Cove. On a previous visit we had gone inside and inspected the sparse array of goods on the shelves, squeaked across a creaking wooden floor and chatted to the storekeeper.

Soon after, the store was closed to make way for change. Today the building serves as a post office and offices for the Greater Vancouver Regional District. The library was housed in it for some years but was moved to the main street in Snug Cove.

Not for Navigation

Union Steamship Marina

The village

One of the busiest boating centres on the coast, Snug Cove has been developed into a high profile marina and boating haven. Its multi slip dock facility with some 400 slips catering to boats up to well beyond 100 feet in length. The government dock that serves as a breakwater will dock about ten more boats depending on size. The ferry from Horseshoe Bay lands right alongside the government dock. Its wake and wash from the substantial propellers causes a tide-like stream that washes against boats moored to the dock so caution should be exercised when coming or going. When tying up–be sure to secure your boat adequately before leaving it for a walk up to the stores or the park and lake nearby.

The walk through the park is an easy one with well worn pathways as is the stroll up to Killarney Lake. Hiking around the lake is also not too taxing, unless you choose to do so in the middle of summer. Lots of shade helps reduce the discomfort in summertime and the cooler weather out of season does the same. Follow the trail up through the park, along the paved road a short distance to the right and then pick it up again for the stroll to the lake.

The village at the ferry landing is simply known as Snug Cove. Here there are several gift, handicraft and souvenir stores as well as refreshment establishments which include the Whirling Dervish, a light meals and coffee shop, excellent cappuccino and latte. A bakery next door serves coffee to go along with any of the freshly baked bread and pastries available. The long-established restaurant at the lower end of the stores has been serving a variety of simple meals for many years and the restaurant at the main Union Steamship landing boardwalk now offers a wide selection at mealtimes.

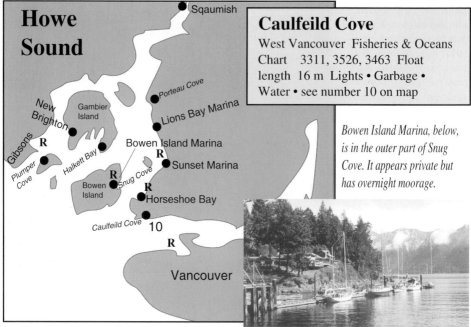

Howe Sound

Sqaumish

New Brighton

Gibsons

Plumper Cove

R

Gambier Island

Halkett Bay

R

Bowen Island

Snug Cove

R

Porteau Cove

Lions Bay Marina

Bowen Island Marina

R

Sunset Marina

R

Horseshoe Bay

Caulfeild Cove   10

R

Vancouver

Caulfeild Cove
West Vancouver Fisheries & Oceans
Chart   3311, 3526, 3463 Float
length 16 m Lights • Garbage •
Water • see number 10 on map

Bowen Island Marina, below, is in the outer part of Snug Cove. It appears private but has overnight moorage.

Lions Bay Marina
Ken Wolder
**Lions Bay, West Vancouver,
BC. V0N 2E0
Phone: (604) 921-7510
Chart 3311, 3526, 3512**
Moorage, water, power at fuel dock.
Fuel: gas, engine and outboard oils. Washrooms. Public phones. Launch ramp, store–marine supplies, ice, snacks, fishing licences, bait.
Closed Tuesdays and Thursdays

Sunset Marina
Sue Rauter
**34 Sunset Beach, West Vancouver, BC.
V7W 2T7
Phone: (604) 921-7476 Fax (604) 921-7477
Chart 3311, 3526, 3512**
Wet and dry moorage, water, power at gas dock. **Launch Ramp, marine store.**
Fuel: gas, engine and outboard oils. Tackle, fishing licences. Washrooms. Public phones. Repairs, service, power wash. Tackle, bait, ice. Restaurant. Parking.

Bowen Island Marina
Norma and Dennis Dallas
email: norma@bowenisland.com
**RR #1, A-1, Bowen Island,
BC V0N 1G0
Phone/fax: (604) 947-9710
Chart 3311, 3526, 3512, 3534 VHF 16**
Marina located to starboard on approaches to Snug Cove, just before ferry landing. Limited transient moorage. Reservations. Moor alongside main dock (marked). Fishing licences, bait, tackle.
Hazard: Ferry dock alongside. Watch operations and propeller turbulence from vessels while at dock.

Plumper
Cove
marine
park

rock

The marine park at Keats Island includes the Plumper Cove docks (below), seen beyond the ridge in the lower right of the photograph. The islands provide shelter from most conditions but occasional westerlies blow in causing some discomfort when anchored or tied to mooring buoys.

Parks in Howe Sound

Halkett Bay

All weather anchorage
(some wind conditions).
Dinghy dock,
camping sites, toilets, hiking.

Porteau Cove

Temporary moorage.
Buoys mark location of artificial reefs.
camping/picnic sites, water, toilets, beach,
scuba diving (wrecks as artificial reefs).

For more information on marine parks see
Anchorages and Marine Parks
(Seagraphic Publications)

Plumper Cove

All weather anchorage
(some wind conditions).
8 mooring buoys. **Boat docks,**
camping/picnic sites, water, toilets, beach.
hiking. Fishing nearby at the Cut.

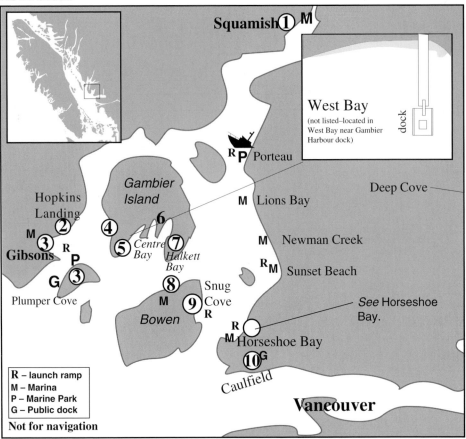

Howe Sound Public Docks

1. Squamish

Fisheries & Oceans dock
Phone: (604) 892-3908
Chart   3311, 3534, 3526
Manager • Float length 118 m
Garbage • Water • Lights • Power • Public
phone ashore • Near city restaurants,
shops, churches, services and facilities.
Yacht club may allow some transient
moorage.

2. Hopkins Landing

Transport Canada dock
Chart   3311, 3526, 3512
Manager • Float length 17 m
Lights •

3. Keats Island

Transport Canada dock
Chart   3311, 3526, 3512
Manager • Float length 15 m
Water • Lights •

4. New Brighton

Gambier Island
Transport Canada dock
Chart   3311, 3526, 3512
Float length 120 m •
Lights • Public phone •
Walking–island roads.
Nearby store.
Ferry service to Langdale/
Gibsons.

The new walkway and the gazebo on the breakwater at Gibsons and a view of the marina from uptown.

Gibsons Landing Harbour Authority

Box 527 Gibson's, V0N 1V0
Phone: (604)886-8017 fax 886-1347
Chart s 3534, 3311, 3526, 3512   VHF 68
email: glha@sunshine.net
Transient moorage available.
Pumpout. Washrooms, Showers, laundry.
Launch ramp near • Breakwater • Aircraft float • Garbage
• Waste oil disposal • Water • Lights • Power 30 amps •
Nearby restaurants, shops. Contact Fred Strom.

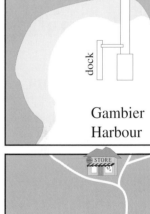

6. Gambier Harbour
Gambier Island
Transport Canada dock
Chart   3311, 3526, 3512
Float length 30 m
Lights • Showers •

6. Port Graves
Gambier Island
Transport Canada dock
Chart   3310, 3512, 3526
Manager • Float length 10 m

7. Halkett Bay
Gambier Island
Transport Canada dock
Chart   3311, 3526, 3512
Float length 17 m
Adjacent marine park

8. Mount Gardner Park
Bowen Island
Fisheries & Oceans dock
Chart   3311, 3526, 3512
Float length 17 m

9. Snug Cove
Bowen Island
Transport Canada dock
Chart   3534, 3311, 3481, 3512, 3526
Manager •
Float length 105 m
Garbage • Lights • Power • Public phone ashore •
Washrooms ashore • Adjacent Union Steamship Marina.
Near village arts and crafts, bakeries, restaurants, shops.
All services. Ferry to Horseshoe Bay.

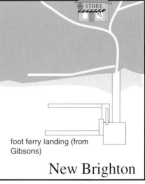

New Brighton

Not for Navigation

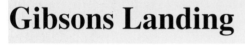

Gibsons Landing

Gibsons Marina

Art McGinnis
**P.O. Box 1520, Gibsons,
BC, V0N 1V0**
Phone: (604) 886-8686
Fax: (604) 886-8686
Charts 3534, 3311, 3526, 3512 VHF 68

Marina services:
400 permanent and transient berths. Dock A
– main visitor dock.
Water at dock. Many outlets.
Sani-station (pumpout).
Power at docks: 15 amp at all slips.
Launch ramp.

Customer services:
Laundry, showers, washrooms.
Marine supplies at chandlery/marina office.
Fishing gear, licences, charts, bait,
ice, repair accessories, books, binoculars.
Nearby church/es multi-denominational.

Post Office: Walk to stores in village, also
pharmacy and other necessities.
Scuba diving at Sechelt up the Sunshine
coast. Ask for information.
Public pay phone ashore.
Walking: Road access walking or cycling.
Waterfront walk, partial around bay. Walk,
cab or bus up to main shopping centre.
*Hourly bus service between Langdale ferry,
Gibsons and Sechelt.*

Entertainment.
Fishing excellent at The Cut a short run from
the marina. Museum, local stores. Art gal-
leries. Book stores (Coast Books).
Adjacent facilities:
Fuel: Gas, diesel, oils. Outboard mix.
Service, haul-outs.
Marine repairs available–mechanic on call.
Marine and boat equipment sales. Bank ma-
chines, gifts, arts and crafts, snacks. Vehicle
rentals. Public dock–see previous page.

From the new gazebo on the Gibsons breakwater. Note the old breakwater in the aerial photo opposite page.

Right: A view of Gibsons Landing public docks new offices and facilities on the wharf.

STORE

RESTAURANT

WASH

Chandlery

pumpout

Smitty's Marina

grid

public

R

A

pub

B

C

D

gazebo

E

F

Gibsons Marina

G

Not for Navigation

Gibsons to Squamish

Gibsons today is a busy community of residents, transient ferry travellers, business people and boat operators docking their craft at Gibsons Marina. This large facility is one of the biggest and best of its kind in local coastal waters. It provides all services required by mariners from the chandlery store at the head of the dock to nearby repair facilities. The marina offers power and water, showers and laundry, fish cleaning, bait, tackle and accessories. In the waterfront village of Gibsons Landing there are stores, restaurants, a

Squamish

Moorage in Squamish

The Squamish Yacht Club has moorage alongside the public marina. There is often adequate room to tie up at the public docks and sometimes a yacht club member will invite you to stop for a while at their facilities, provided there is room. Many mariners tie up to log booms in the area but be careful not to hinder any work in progress if you do. Stop and enquire at the Yacht Club if the government docks are full.

Photos: Views from the public docks alongside the Squamish Yacht Club.

pub, post office, pharmacy, museum and convenience stores. A very handy delicatessen is located near the marina for excellent specialty items and a sit down cup of tea or coffee. Craft and art stores have become a major attraction.

From Gibsons to Squamish takes you either up the eastern shore of Howe Sound, where you can see numerous waterfront homes or small settlements, or up the western side with its islands and passages. One of the major landmarks on the steep-sloped eastern shore is Britannia Beach with its scarred hillside from former mining operations.

The passage up the western shore passes from Gibsons via New Brighton on Gambier, privately owned club facilities of Thunderbird Yacht Club and Burrard Yacht Club at Ekins Point and McNab Creek opposite.

Sunshine Coast
Howe Sound to Desolation Sound

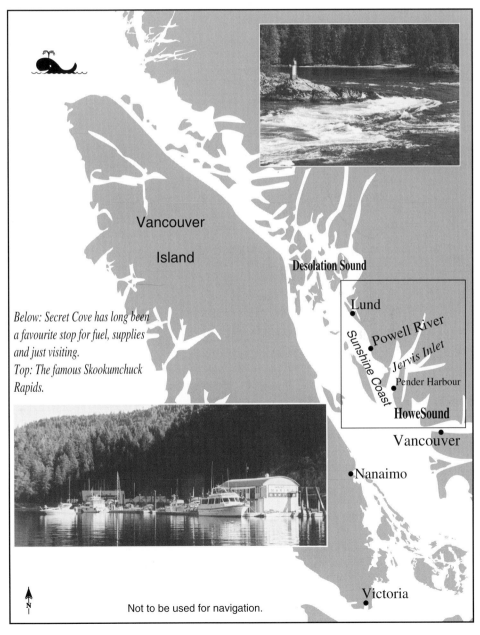

Vancouver

Island

Desolation Sound

Lund

Powell River

Sunshine Coast

Jervis Inlet

Pender Harbour

HoweSound

Vancouver

Nanaimo

Victoria

Below: Secret Cove has long been a favourite stop for fuel, supplies and just visiting.
Top: The famous Skookumchuck Rapids.

Not to be used for navigation.

N

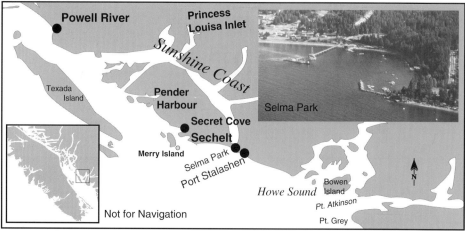

Above: Secret Cove Marina. Inset: Hotels, their docks and the waterway to Buccaneer Marina in Secret Cove.

Opposite page: The fuel dock at Secret Cove and boats at the marina. Inset, top : Selma Park at Sechelt.

Port Stalashen Marina

Art McGinnis *(see also Gibsons Marina)*
1585 Field Road, Sechelt
BC, V0N 3A1
Phone: (604) 885-4884 Fax: (604) 885-3103
Toll free 1-888-850-0111
Charts 3311, 3512.   VHF 68
Marina services: Water.
Power: 30 amps. Pumpout station.
Customer services: Garbage drop.
Nearby: Restaurants, accommodation.

Use chart 3311 and enter with great care during rough conditions and at low tide.

Port Stalashen makes a good stop en route off Sechelt when the weather becomes unsettled. The approximate dock layout has been superimposed over this photograph, taken while the marina was under construction.

Secret Cove
Chart 3535, 3311, 3512

Secret Cove Marina
Blaine Hagedorn
Box 1118 Sechelt,
BC, V0N 3A0.   VHF 68
Phone: (604) 885-3533 fax (604) 885-6037
email:info@secretcovemarina.com
www.secretcovemarina.com
Marina services:
Fuel: gas, diesel, oil, live bait, ice,
150 berth permanent and transient docks.
Water at dock. Many outlets.
Power at docks: 30, 15 amp.
Customer services:
Showers. Washrooms. Fish cleaning
tables, picnic tables, garbage disposal for
moorage customers only. Marine supplies
at chandlery. Fishing gear, licences,
charts, bait, ice, electronics, repair acces-
sories, books, gifts, arts and crafts, snacks.
Fax service. Cafe upstairs with patio.
General store. Liquor agency. Public pay
phone ashore.
Water Taxi available. Boat rentals.
Walking: Road access walking or cycling.
Cab or bus up to main shopping centres.
Entertainment.
Good fishing a short run from marina.
Hotels, restaurants and facilities nearby.
Adjacent facilities:
Golf. Swimming

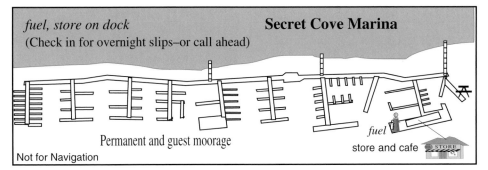

fuel, store on dock
Secret Cove Marina
(Check in for overnight slips–or call ahead)
Permanent and guest moorage
fuel
store and cafe
STORE
Not for Navigation

Buccaneer Marina

Bob, John, Gerry Mercer
RR 1 Halfmoon Bay
BC, V1Y0
Ph (604) 885-7888 Fax: (604) 885-7824
Chart 3311, 3535, 3512   VHF 68
Marina services:
Haulouts. **Fuel:** gas, diesel, oil, live and
frozen bait. Marine centre and store. Sales
& service. Parts and repairs. Mercury
Marine service. Permanent moorage and
repair dock. **Water** and **power** at dock.
Customer services:
Boat rentals. Fishing gear, licences, charts,
bait, ice, propane, groceries, snacks.
Hull repairs, steam cleaning, bottom
painting. Public pay phone ashore.
Walking: Road access walking.
Adjacent facilities:

Secret Cove,

Fisheries & Oceans dock
Chart   3311, 3535, 3512 Manager •
Float length 44 m • Lights • Power •
Public phone •
Adjacent marinas, lodges, provisions,
fuel, repairs, service.

Moorage, Secret Cove Marina. Accommodations, Lord Jim's Lodge (604) 885-7038,
and Jolly Roger Inn (604) 885-7184.
(Limited overnight guest moorage.)

Porpoise Bay, Sechelt

Fisheries & Oceans.   Bruce Haynes
 5397 Cowrie St, Sechelt, BC.
V0N 3A0 Phone (604) 885-1986
Fax 885-7591   Chart 3311, 3512
Manager • Float length 132 m• Launch
ramp • Grid • Aircraft float • Garbage •
Water • Lights • Power • Public phone
ashore • Adjacent restaurant, hotels,
nearby shops. Scuba diving in vicinity.
Charters. Rentals.

Halfmoon Bay,

Sunshine Coast
Transport Canada dock
Chart 3311, 3512
Float length 26 m • Lights •

Sechelt,

Sunshine Coast
Fisheries & Oceans dock
Chart 3311, 3512
Manager • Breakwater •

Above: The new harbour master's office at Madeira Park has washrooms and other facilities for transient mariners.
Right: Some vessels visit Princess Louisa early in the season to capture the loneliness and tranquillity of the place. Short days and long cool nights provide a brisk but refreshing atmosphere to this unique park.

Pender Harbour

The 32 miles of shoreline in Pender Harbour have long attracted holiday and permanent residents. The location of this sheltered inlet is central to many coastal areas, a favourite of which is Princess Louisa Inlet. As a base to launch from or cruise from, Pender Harbour has services and supplies to meet most needs of cruising mariners.

A short trip away is the famous Skookumchuck where the Sechelt Rapids tumble wildly over themselves during tidal changes in a display of unleashed fury that is practically without equal. A stop at Pender Harbour or Egmont is a staging area for viewing the magnificent sight.

Entering Pender Harbour use your chart and pass between Martin Island to port and Charles and William Islands to starboard.

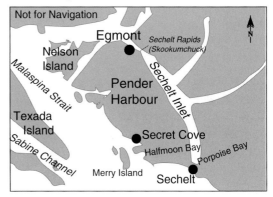

Garden Bay Hotel and Marina

Garden Bay Hotel and Marina (left and above) has a popular pub where meals are served at all hours.

Pender Harbour

Charts 3535, 3311, 3512

Coho Marina Resort

Gordie and Nichole Standal
P.O. Box 160 Madeira Park BC
V0N 2H0 Phone: (604) 883-2248
VHF call 68
Hazard: Rocks in bay–marked by beacons. Consult charts.
Marina services:
Moorage. Launch ramp.
Water at dock. Ice. **Showers.**
Power at docks: 15 amp.
Customer services:
Fishing tackle, licences. Marine hardware.
Washrooms. Campsites, trailers.
Nearby church/es: multi-denominational.
Public pay phone ashore.
Walking: Road access walking or cycling.
Entertainment.
Kayaking. Good scuba diving and fishing a short run from harbour.

Adjacent facilities:
Stores/shopping centre, marine service.

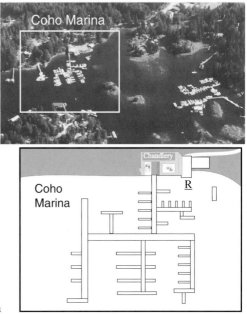

Overlooking Lowe's Marina with Coho Marina in the background. Coho Marina can be seen at left in the photo at top.

The one-time hospital at Hospital Bay is now a lodge and caters to dining and overnight guests. Yachts tying up at marinas in Hospital Bay will not be far from the facility. In Hospital Bay there should be ample dock space at the government float. Temporary tie up of a dinghy for the purpose of using adjacent restaurant or store facilities should be no problem at most marinas. Just advise them of your intentions and get their permission.

Garden Bay Hotel & Marina

Ted Meisinger and Heather Gratland
P.O. Box 90, Garden Bay,
BC, V0N 1S0
Phone/fax: (604) 883-2674
Marina services:
Moorage. Water at dock.
Power : 15, 30 amp.
Customer services:
Fine dining at pub, and waterfront restaurant.
Fishing charters. Air charters.
 Gift shop and art gallery.
Nearby church/es. Golf course.
Public pay phone ashore.
Entertainment. Live entertainment in pub.
Jazz Festival in September. Good fishing and
scuba diving a short run from the harbour.
Golfing, kayaking, hiking, easy walking or
cycling.

Nearby facilities:
Fuel: at John Henry's Marina in Hospital
Bay. Gas, diesel, stove oil, outboard fuel,
propane. Tackle.
Post Office, liquor agency, restaurants, an-
chorage.
Washrooms, laundry, showers.
Pumpout station.

Sportsman's Marina & Resort

Dennis Brown
P.O. Box 143, Garden Bay,
BC, V0N 1S0
Ph: (604) 883-2479
Marina services:
Visitor moorage.
Water at dock. **Power**: 15 amp.   Rental
cabins, **showers, laundry, washrooms.**
Open year round.

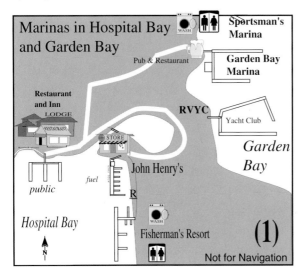

Marinas in Hospital Bay and Garden Bay

Not for Navigation

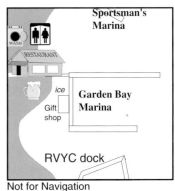

Not for Navigation

Fisherman's Resort
Hospital Bay
Yacht Club
Garden Bay

Chart 3535, 3311, 3512 VHF call 68

Fisherman's Resort & Marina

Wally and Susan Nowik
Box 68 Garden Bay
British Columbia, V0N 1S0
Phone/fax: (604) 883-2336
 Marina services:
Moorage. Launch ramp.
Power at docks: 30, 15 amp.
Water.
Customer services:
Laundry, showers, ice, bait.
Waterfront cottages. Public phone ashore.
Marine charts, books. Fishing gear, licences.
Nearby church/es: multi-denominational.
Scuba diving arrangements and charters
–ask marina for details.
Walking: Road access walking or cycling.
Entertainment:
Fishing is excellent in general area out of
Pender Harbour. Consult fishing guides.

Adjacent facilities:
Groceries at John Henry's general store.
Also, post office, liquor, restaurants.
Pharmacy and other necessities at store.
Sundowner Inn Restaurant. Phone: 883-9676.
Public marina. Anchorage (in Garden Bay).
Fuel at Irvine's Landing or John Henry's.

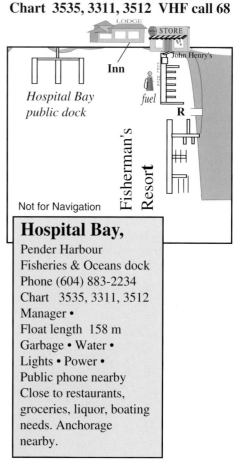

LODGE
STORE
Inn
John Henry's
Hospital Bay
public dock
fuel
R
Fisherman's Resort
Not for Navigation

Hospital Bay,
Pender Harbour
Fisheries & Oceans dock
Phone (604) 883-2234
Chart 3535, 3311, 3512
Manager •
Float length 158 m
Garbage • Water •
Lights • Power •
Public phone nearby
Close to restaurants,
groceries, liquor, boating
needs. Anchorage
nearby.

142

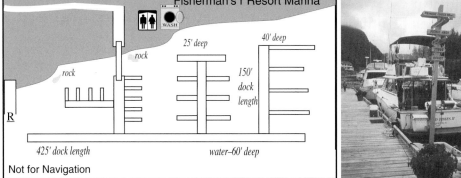

Fisherman's r Resort Marina

WASH

rock

rock

25' deep

40' deep

150' dock length

R

425' dock length

water–60' deep

Not for Navigation

Above: A view over the bay from Sundowner Inn includes John Henry's fuel dock in the foreground (photo below) and Fisherman's Resort beyond. The marina, busy in the early part of summer. The updated signpost showing some destinations and their distances.

The fuel dock at John Henry's.

Irvines Landing Marina & Pub

Lorna or Heather
**RR #1, Irvines Landing Road,
Garden Bay, B.C. V0N 1S0
Phone: (604) 883-2296
Fax(604) 883-2080
Phone: 883-1145 (Marina & Pub)
Chart 3535, 3311, 3512
Marina services:
Fuel:** gas, diesel, oil.
Transient moorage.
Power. 15 amps. **Water.**
Launch ramp.
Customer services:
Irvines Landing Pub dining.
Patio service. Tackle, live and
frozen bait, sundries.
Showers, washrooms.
Pay phones.
Good fishing nearby. Guides.
Fish freezing. Two fish cleaning
stations.
The marina is conveniently
located at the entrance to the harbour.

Irvines Landing,

This was the original Union Steamship stop
at Pender Harbour. View historic
phootographs from the 1920s in the pub.
It is located at the entrance to Pender Harbour and offers guests moorage, fuel, and
many of the needs of cruising mariners, as
well as the many sports fishing enthusiasts
who frequent the facility. It has a pub style
restaurant and patio service.

Entertainment.
Hiking, golfing nearby, mountain biking, fresh water lakes, animal and
marine life, fishing charters.

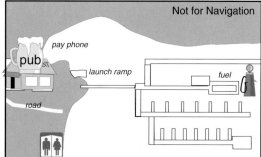

The dock at Fisherman's Resort.

John Henry's fuel stop with Fisherman's Resort beyond looking out over Pender Harbour.

PENDER

Farrington Cove
Sundowner Inn
Duncan Cove
Irvines Landing • *fuel*
R
Williams Island
Skardon Islands
Charles Island
fuel John Henry's Store
Fisherman's Resort
Garden Bay
Headwater Marina
R Sunshine Coast Resort
R Madeira Marina
R Coho Marina
Lowe's Resort
Francis
Gerrans Bay
Peninsula
HARBOUR

Not for Navigation

145

Madeira Marina

Karen Reid and Rick King
**P.O. Box 189 Madeira Park,
BC. V0N 2H0**
Phone: (604) 883-2266 Fax (604) 883-9250
Chart 3311, 3535, 3512
Location: next to Madeira Park public docks
and ramp.
Marina services:
Moorage.
Haulout to 50'. Marine repairs. Water taxi.
Water at dock. Ice. No power at docks.
Customer services:
Marine store. Saltwater licences, Ice, charts.
Walking: Road access walking or cycling.
Entertainment.
Scuba diving and fishing excellent
a short run from the harbour.
Adjacent facilities:
Public dock. Nearby supermarket, post of-
fice, bank, pharmacy, restaurant.

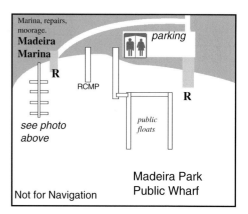

**Marina services: Showers, laundry,
washrooms**. Ice, **water, power**. Groceries, fishing tackle, licences, garbage
disposal, rental boats. Walking. Take care–
we have seen bears on the roads.

Duncan Cove Marina

Albert Hull. John MacLeod (mgr)
**4686 Sinclair Bay Road, Madeira Park,
BC. V0N 1S0**
Phone: (604) 883-2424
Fax: 883-2414
Chart 3512, 3535, 3311

Sunshine Coast Resort & Marina

Ralph Linnmann
**P.O. Box 213,
Madeira Park, BC, V0N 2H0**
Ph: (604) 883-9177 fax 883-9171
Marina services: VHF 16/69
Moorage. Water at dock. **Power** : 30, 15
amp. **Laundry, washrooms, showers.**
Boat rentals, live bait, accommodations.
Sundeck and spa. Nearby–shopping centre,
Launch ramp at Madeira Park.

Coho Marina

Lowe's Resort

Madeira Park Public Wharf. Pender Harbour Authority.

P.O. Box 118, Madeira park. V0N 2H0.
Fisheries & Oceans dock (right)
Phone Diana Pride Ph: (604) 883-2234
Fax (604) 883-2152. Charts 3535, 3311, 3512 • Float length 196 m • Launch ramp • Barbecue • Aircraft float • Garbage • Waste oil disposal • Washrooms • showers • Water • Lights • Power 30 amps • Pumpout • Nearby restaurants, supermarket, shops. See diagram opposite page, photograph page 139.

Top: Aerial photo shows Lowe's Resort to the right (Coho Marina to the left).

Headwater Marina Ltd

Wayne Bellavance
**P.O. Box 71 Madeira Park
BC V0N 2H0
Phone: (604) 883-2406 Fax: 883-2820
email:** *headwater@uniserve.com*
**Charts: 3535, 3311, 3512   VHF 73
Moorage:** Permanent and Transient to 45'.
Power, water. Launch Ramp.
Camp ground, RV park, **showers.**
Fishing and diving charters.
Adjacent facilities:
Kayaking, fishing, freshwater lakes, hiking, golfing, shopping, restaurants, pubs and bars.

Above: The docks at Maderia Park public wharf.

Lowe's Resorts

**Box 153, Madeira Park,
BC. V0N 2H0
Phone: (604) 883-2456 Fax (604) 883-2474
Chart 3535, 3512
Moorage.** Limited–primarily for lodge customers. Boats to 28/30 feet. **Water, Power.**
Manager–Larry Curtis.
**Customer services:
Showers, washroms**, tackle store, snacks. Accommodation. Scuba air station.
Entertainment:
Boat, mountain bike rentals. Kayaking, fishing, scuba diving. Shops nearby.

Note: *Moorage guests at Madeira Park or other transient boat crews are welcome to use coin operated laundry and showers at this marina. Access is by way of an easy walk from Madeira Park public docks.*

Chart 3512, 3535, 3514 VHF call 16. 68

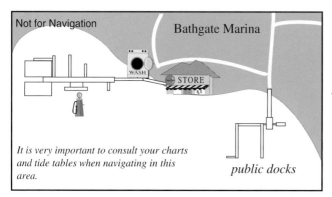

Not for Navigation

Bathgate Marina

WASH

STORE

It is very important to consult your charts and tide tables when navigating in this area.

public docks

Opposite: Bathgate Marina and public docks. Inset: Bathgate Marina docks and store with laundry and showers in building on left. Above: Docks and fuel float at Bathgate Marina. Below: Public docks at Egmont.

Public launch ramp nearby at Egmont.
Also gravel ramp at Egmont Marina.

Egmont

Bathgate General Store & Marina
Doug and Vicki Martin
Egmont BC V0N 1N0
Phone: (604) 883-2222 Fax 883-2750
email: *bathgate_egmont@sunshine.net*
Web: *www.bathgate.com*
Hazard: Drying reef in middle of bay on
approaches to fuel dock and another
off the government dock. Check your chart.

Marina services:
Fuel: Gas, diesel, propane, oils.
Moorage. Marine ways. Marine mechanic
on duty.
Water at dock. Ice.
Power at docks: 15, 20, 30 amp.

Customer services:
Liquor agency. Grocery store–fresh meat
and vegetables. Fishing tackle, licences.
Water taxi service. Washrooms for Bathgate
Marina customers**, showers, laundry.**
Boat, cabin, video rentals.
Public pay phone ashore.
Walking: Road access walking or cycling.

Nearby hiking trails. Trail to the
Sechelt Rapids viewpoint in
the Skookumchuck Provincial Park.

Entertainment.
Scuba diving and fishing in the immediate
vicinity is rated very highly. Kayaking.
Fishing and scuba diving charters.

Adjacent facilities:
Public dock. Base before trip
to Princess Louisa Inlet. Automobile fuel.

Egmont Public dock
Fisheries & Oceans dock
Phone (604) 883-9243
Chart 3512, 3514.
Manager • Float length 145 m
Aircraft Float • Garbage • Waste oil
service • Lights •

Egmont Marina at the Back Eddy Pub in Egmont. Opposite: Launching at the ramp adjacent to Royal Reach Marina.

Egmont Marina

John and Margaret Mills
**General Delivery,
Egmont, BC V0N 1N0
Phone/fax: (604) 883-2298
Tollfree 1 800 626-0599
Chart 3312, 3512 .**
email: *egmont_marina@sunshine.net*
Web: *www.egmont-marina.com*
Marina services
Moorage.
Fuel: gas diesel,oils, two stroke oil, live/ frozen bait at fuel dock.
Power 15, 30 amp.
Potable water. Ice, bait, tackle, fishing licences, book exchange, groceries.
Laundry, showers, washrooms. public phone ashore
rental boats available.
Entertainment.
Backeddy Marine Pub, summer long-week-end live entertainment.
Pool table. Nearby trails to Skookumchuck rapids.

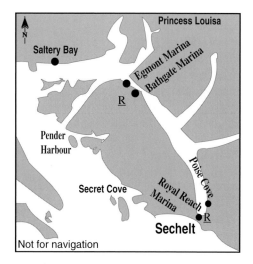

Not for navigation

Adjacent facilities:
Restaurant, store, scuba air station.
Dive and fishing charters.
Launch ramp. Campground–22 sites with power. View cabins. Hotel.
Kayak lessons and rentals.
Mountain bike rentals.

Sechelt Inlet

Royal Reach Marina & Motel
5758 Wharf Rd., Porpoise Bay BC. V0N
3A0. Phone: (604) 885-7844
fax (604)885-5969 Chart 3312, 3512
Marina services: Moorage.
Power 15 amp. **Water.**
Ice at marina and motel. **Laundry, showers,**
washrooms at motel and ashore.
Entertainment.
Sechelt nearby has numerous centres,
shops and facilities. Walk to Sechelt village.
Adjacent facilities: Pub, restaurant nearby.
Regular/scheduled flights.

Poise Cove Marina
RR #3, Plumridge Site. Site C. Sechelt
BC. V0N 3A0. Phone: (604) 885-2895
Chart 3311, 3512
Some visitor moorage available. Facilities
include launch ramp, power at dock.

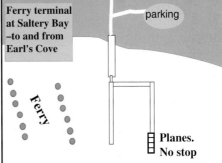

Not for Navigation

Saltery Bay,
Sunshine Coast
Fisheries & Oceans dock
Phone (604) 487-0663
Chart   3514
Manager • Float length 133 m
Garbage • Lights •
Adjacent ferry dock–Egmont,
Sunshine Coast.

If you travel down the Sechelt Inlet you will find a place to stop overnight at Poise Cove or
the docks at Royal Reach Marina. While few mariners venture all the way down the Inlet there
is a lot of activity there due to the substantial launching ramp and float plane base nearby. For
scuba divers, the artifical reef, *Chaudiere*, is a treat but, use a local dive charter vessel.

Westview–Powell River

Beach Gardens Marina

7074 Westminster Ave,
Powell River, BC. V8A 1C5
Phone: (604) 485-7734 Motel 485-6267
Fax (604) 485-2343 Ph: 1 800 663-7070
Chart 3563, 3311, 3513   VHF 68
email: bgardens@prcn.org
www.beachgardens.com
Marina Entrance.
At breakwater just south of Grief Point.

Marina services:
Fuel: Gas, diesel, oil. ice (in season).
Mechanic and services available from local
and nearby marine operators.
Moorage: Large permanent marina with
overnight moorage slips. Reserve.
Water at dock. Multiple outlets.
Power at docks: 30, 15 amp.
Laundry, showers, washrooms.

Customer services:
Motel with swaterfront accommodations.
Cold wine and beer store (pending).
Grocery store, post office nearby.
Church/es in town.

Walking trails or road access.
Some beachfront walks.
Fishing charters.
Scuba diving arrangements and charters–
ask hotel for details.
Public pay phones ashore.

Adjacent and nearby facilities:
Shuttle service to town in season, restau-
rants–pick up for dinner reservations.
Shopping, golf and hiking in the area.

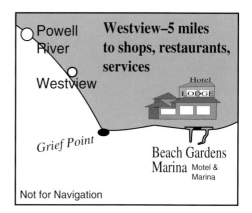

Powell River

Westview–5 miles to shops, restaurants, services

Westview

Grief Point

Hotel LODGE

Beach Gardens Marina Motel & Marina

Not for Navigation

152

Beach Gardens Resort is one of the most convenient stops on the Sunshine Coast.

The hotel/resort complex became a favoured stopover for cruising mariners in the mid 1970s when a breakwater was built in front of the hotel. The breakwater was later extended to accommodate resident boat owners in need of moorage. It became also a major stop for mariners en route to Desolation Sound. Monitoring the weather conditions at Grief Point has been made easy by the inclusion some years ago of Grief Point as a weather reporting station. The existence of Beach Gardens Resort at Grief Point provided the staffing required to observe and report up-to-the-minute conditions.

For years scores of boats have stopped over in search of recreation at the spa, the fine cuisine for which the hotel restaurant became famous. In the year 2000 the facility was operating as a motel, minus restaurant and other resort amenities. Despite this change the marina is still a favoured haven on the Sunshine Coast.

In summer time the fuel dock is usually located at the entrance to the marina and in winter it is moved closer towards the shore for protection from the swells that wash around the end of the breakwater. Some year-round marina tenants means that not all dock space is available for transient moorage and it is best to check with the dock manager before tying up. In boating season a full time staff working the docks will be awaiting your arrival. It is also best to check in by phone or call on VHF prior to your arrival. Reservations may be made well in advance or at the last moment depending on available space.

The next stop for fuel and moorage after Grief Point is Westview a few miles north en route to Powell River, Lund and Desolation Sound. Fuel is available south at Pender Harbour.

153

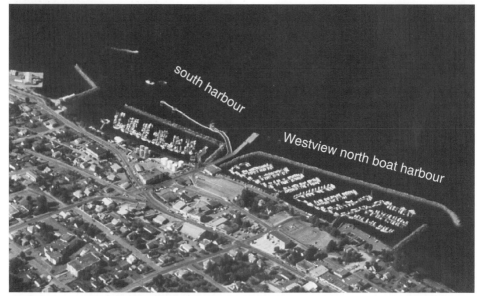

Powell River

Westview (north) Boat Harbour

Transport Canada dock/Boat Harbour
Ph (604) 485-5244 (no transient moorage)
Chart 3311, 3536, 3513
Breakwater and marina
Launch ramp • Water • Lights • Power •
Near ferry landing, city restaurants, shops.
Fuel dock nearby: Gas, diesel, outboard
mix, naptha, water, ice (in South harbour).

Fuel dock phone: (604) 485-2867
fax: (604) 485-7238

Powell River South Harbour

Charts 3311, 3563, 3513

Transient moorage
Fisheries & Oceans dock
Jim Parsons
(604) 485-5244 Fax 485-5286
• Float length 625 m • Tidal Grid •
Garbage • Waste oil disposal • Water •
Lights • Power • Public phone • Wash-
rooms • **Moorage:** no reservations. Near
city restaurants, shops, hotels. Enter south
marina via **Fuel dock**–Located inside
breakwater. Gas, diesel. Outboard mix.
Ice. Small boat rentals
Nearby: Laundry Showers, fresh &
frozen seafood, fishing tackle, marine
supplies. Free shopping
shuttle bus July, August.
Also Blackberry festival,
Seafair, Music FolkFest
(Sept).
Community events–phone:
Powell River Visitors Bureau
(604) 485-4701
Five flights daily Powell
River–Vancouver on Pacific
Coastal.
Ferries to Comox, Vancou-
ver Island and Texada Island.

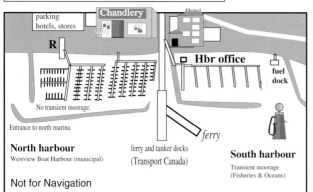

parking
hotels, stores

Chandlery

Hotel

R

Hbr office

fuel dock

No transient moorage.

Entrance to north marina

ferry

North harbour
Westview Boat Harbour (municipal)

ferry and tanker docks
(Transport Canada)

South harbour
Transient moorage
(Fisheries & Oceans)

Not for Navigation

Texada, Lasquiti

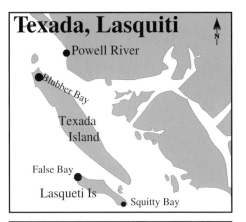

- Powell River
- Blubber Bay
- Texada Island
- False Bay
- Lasqueti Is
- Squitty Bay

N

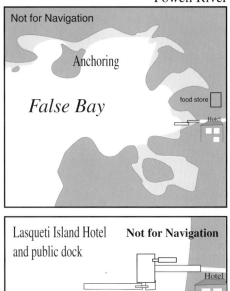

Not for Navigation

Anchoring

False Bay

food store

Hotel

Lasqueti Island Hotel and public dock   **Not for Navigation**

Hotel

False Bay

Not for Navigation

Blubber Bay

Texada Island
Transport Canada dock   Chart 3311
Float length 13 m • Limited facilities
and moorage. Best for overnight at
Westview on Sunshine Coast shore
opposite. Facilities also at Powell
River. Good moorage at the marina at
Beach Gardens (also for fuel).

Lasqueti Island

Hotel and Resort

see False Bay public dock)
Lasqueti Island, BC,
V0R 2J0
Phone: (250) 333-8846 Fax (250) 333-8897
Chart 3312, 3512, 3513
Local services:
Ice at hotel/store. **Moorage** (limited) at
public dock. No facilities. No fuel.
Customer services:
Hotel with facilities including convenience
store, showers, public phone.   Washrooms.
Restaurant–licensed, pub.
Walking road access. Fishing. Good scuba
diving nearby. Public pay phone.
Poor dock space for overnight.
Entertainment.
Bike rentals. Kayaking
Adjacent facilities:
Anchoring at end of bay–see local chart.
Bakery, Post office, whole food store.

False Bay

False Bay public dock
Lasqueti Island (adjacent hotel)
Transport Canada–Bruce Bird
Chart   3536, 3512, 3513
Float length 36 m • Aircraft Float •
No facilities at dock.

Squitty Bay
Lasqueti Island
Fisheries & Oceans dock   Chart 3512
Float length 47 m • Walking, trails,
island roads.

Lund

Lund Public Marina

Rosemarie O'Neil
Phone: (604) 483-4711
Chart 3311, 3538, 3513 VHF call 73
Marina services:
Moorage – over 500 feet for transient use.
Launch ramp. **Water.** Lights. **Power**–20
amp. Public phone.
Adjacent Lund Hotel, restaurants, shops.
Launch ramp and access upgraded.

**Fuel dock service to mariners provided by
the Lund Hotel and local store.**
Steve & Kathy Tipton
(604) 414-0474 fax (604) 414-0476
Fuel: Gas, diesel, **showers, laundry,** ice,
propane. Paid garbage drop. Restaurant, pub–
open 7 days a week.
General store, groceries, tackle, marine
supplies. Charts. Some hardware.
Liquor agency. Nearby church/es.
Walking trails or road access.
Some beachfront walks. Boardwalk.

Fishing charters. Dive shop, air, rentals.
Scuba diving arrangements and charters–see
dive/kayak shop adjacent to hotel. Kayak
rentals, water taxi service. Post Office.

Adjacent facilities:
Stores, coffee house, arts and gifts.
Restaurants. Ice cream, pizza. Bakery. Fresh,
live seafood. Fish and Chips and breakfast
kiosk. Farm market Sundays 10:30 to 2 pm.

Composite photograph above shows a view of the Lund waterfront looking south. The hotel on the left overlooks the wharf and fuel dock. Lower opposite photo shows the Copeland Islands dock now at Lund.

Public docks

Okeover Inlet (Arm)
Fisheries & Oceans dock
Phone (604) 483-2218
Chart   3512, 3514, 3312
Manager • Float length 35 m
Breakwater • Lights • Power •
Public phone ashore •
Near restaurant.

Finn Bay, Lund
Fisheries & Oceans dock
Phone (604) 483-4478
Chart 3311, 3513, 3538
Manager • Float length 49 m

Savary Island
Transport Canada dock
Chart   3311, 3538, 3513
Float length 11 m

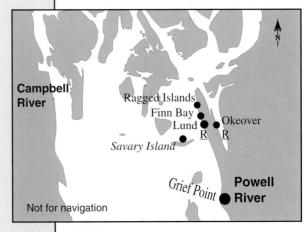

The Lund Hotel is a landmark on the Sunshine Coast where it sits at the northern end of Highway 99, an extension of the US I-5 freeway.

Lund is an interesting place, existing as the northernmost town on the Sunshine Coast road. It has an historic hotel and numerous facilities including antique store, watersport and dive shop, grocery store selling a fair selection of marine hardware, fishing gear, books and charts, a fresh seafood shop and an adjacent marine service centre and chandlery catering year round to the local community. It's also a busy fuel stop before entering Desolation Sound.

Ragged Islands Marine closed down their facility in Thulin Passage just north of Lund after the 1999 season and the fuel dock was relocated to Lund.

157

After Lund pay a visit to Okeover where the cuisine at the restaurant is exceptional. Most wisened mariners anchor in Grace Harbour and dinghy down to Okeover for dinner at the Laughing Oyster. The docks (left) accommodate dinghies or a few small boats.

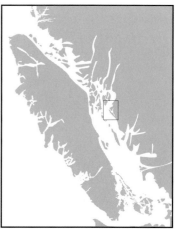

Ragged Islands Marine's Wendy Cox has retired and is living at her home in the cove where mariners stopped for decades to fuel up and enjoy a friendly visit with her.

The launching ramp at the Lund public marina.

The Copeland Islands (top) provide a protected waterway from Lund to the entrance of Desolation Sound. Not far into Desolation Sound is Refuge Cove (above), a centre of activity for fuel and supplies.

Vancouver Island

Central east coast

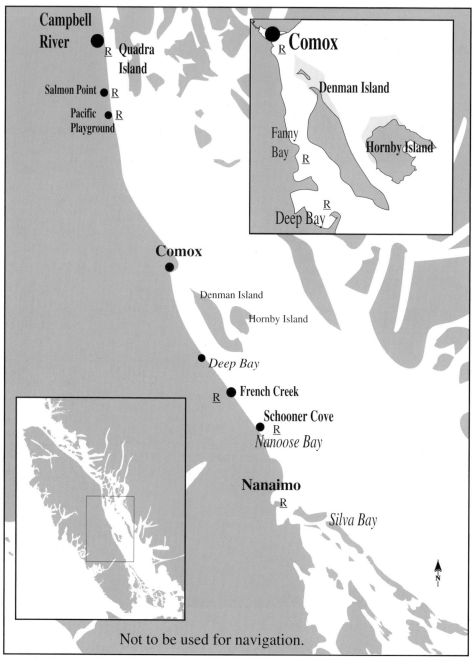

Campbell River ● R Quadra Island

Salmon Point ● R

Pacific Playground ● R

Comox ●

Denman Island

Hornby Island

● Deep Bay

R ● French Creek

Schooner Cove
● R
Nanoose Bay

Nanaimo
R

Silva Bay

(Inset, top right)

● R Comox

Denman Island

Fanny Bay

Hornby Island

R

R
Deep Bay

N

Not to be used for navigation.

Above and Left: Snaw-Naw-As Marina, a local aboriginal band facility in Nanoose Bay, welcomes all transient boats.

Nanoose Bay area

Snaw-Naw-As Marina

(Located at entrance to Nanoose Bay)
209 Mallard Street,
Lantzville, B.C. V0R 2H0
Phone/Fax: (250) 390-2616
Fax (250) 390-3365
Chart 3459, 3512

Marina services:

Fuel: gas, diesel.
Water. Power. Showers.
Tidal grid, launch ramp, coffee shop.
Telephone ashore. Garbage disposal.
Fish cleaning. Porta Potti toilets ashore.
Camping.

From Nanaimo go along the coast to Campbell River with a stop possible at Nanoose Bay or at Schooner Cove, one of the largest and finest facilities anywhere with hotel and all amenities including golfing nearby, good fishing and good scuba diving. Farther north up Vancouver Island's east coast is Comox with a vast set of docks, private and public. Comox Marina or Blackfin next door, with lots of transient moorage and restaurants ashore, a park and nearby stores and other facilities along with events such as Nautical Days each August will keep you entertained and enthused about the stop-over. En route to Campbell River you will find sheltered facilities at Deep Bay or French Creek.

Schooner Cove

Schooner Cove Resort Hotel & Marina

Dock managed by hotel
**Box 12, Schooner House,
3521 Dolphin Drive,
Nanoose Bay, BC, V9P 9J7
Phone: Marina (250)468-5364
Hotel (250) 468-7691 Fax: (250) 468-5744**
email: *info@fairwinds.bc.ca*
Web: *fairwinds.bc.ca*
*Hazard: Drying rock in entrance to marina.
Pass marker to port and keep close to floats.*
Marina services:
Fuel: Gas, diesel, oils, service available–
can be arranged at dock.
400 permanent and transient berths.
Water at dock. All berths.
Power at docks: 30, 50, 15 amp. All slips.

Chart 3512, 3459, VHF call 16 & 73

Customer services:
Hotel, accommodation, restaurant, lounge,
pub. Fine dining. Coffee shop. Full fitness
centre and spa.
Laundry, Showers, Washrooms.
Outdoor pool, hot tub. Public phones.
Marine supplies, fishing gear, licences,
charts, bait, **ice,** books, gifts, snacks.
Cold beer and wine store. Bakery.
Nearby church/es: multi-denominational.
Post Office:
Courtesy shuttle to post office, banks,
groceries. Scuba diving arrangements and
charters–ask marina for details.
Walking: Road access walking or cycling.
Nearby parks.

Part of the marina at Schooner Cove.

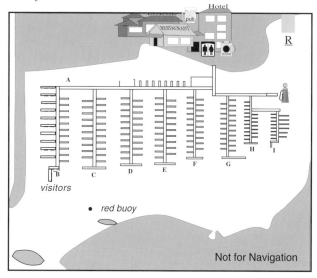

Schooner Cove is in one of the most beautiful settings on the coast. Nearby golf courses and developments have turned the area into a prized piece of real estate and the adjacent waters into prime fishing and scuba diving destinations. The hotel marina office (below) is adjacent to restaurants and other facilities, including marine supplies.

Entertainment.
Fishing excellent near marina. Rental bicycles. Horseback riding, nature walks.

Adjacent facilities:
Courtesy shuttle to golf at Fairwinds 18 hole course, bare boat charters and fishing charters. Group facilities. **Launch ramp**. Picnic area overlooking marina.

Above: A wide, segmented view of Schooner Cove Marina.

Schooner Cove to Comox

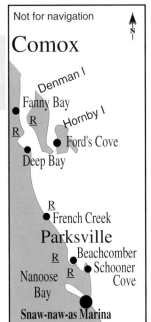

Not for navigation

Comox

Denman I

Fanny Bay
R
R
Hornby I
Ford's Cove

Deep Bay

R
French Creek

Parksville

R   Beachcomber
Nanoose   R   Schooner
Bay   Cove

Snaw-naw-as Marina

Beachcomber Marina

(Located in Northwest Bay)
Bill Loewen
**RR #1 Box 21, Beachcomber Nanoose Bay, BC, V0N 3A0
Phone/Fax: (250) 468-7222
Chart 3459, 3512.** *Refer charts for reefs–enter between red and black buoys.*

Marina services:
Fuel: gas, diesel, ice
(in summer).
Permanent and very limited visitor docks.
Water at dock.
Power at docks: 30 amp.
Launch ramp.
Anchorage across bay behind log booms.

Deep Bay

Large, protected marina near Hornby and Denman Islands.
Chart 3513
Launch ramp.
Trailerable–**fuel**.
Coffee.

Ford's Cove, Hornby Island

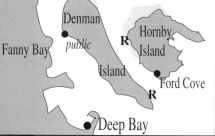

Left: Deep Bay. Use caution in adjacent shallow waters. Launch ramp access with store and fuel for trailerable boats. Public dock is near the ramp.
Lower: Ford Cove on Hornby Island.

Denman Island

Fisheries & Oceans dock
Chart 3527, 3513
Float length 24 m
Launch ramp • Breakwater •
Ralph Walton
fax (250) 335-2510

Fanny Bay

Fisheries & Oceans dock
Phone (250) 335-2513
Charts 3513, 3527 • Manager •
Float length 42 m • Breakwater • Grid • Power • Yacht sales

Ford's Cove, Hornby Is

Photograph—above and right

Fisheries & Oceans dock
Phone (250) 335-2169 Fax (250) 335-2312
Chart 3527, 3513
Manager • Float length 86 m
Breakwater • Grid • Garbage • Waste oil disposal •
Water • Lights • Power • Public phone
• Washrooms • arts and crafts • convenience store
• Scuba diving resort adjacent.

165

Charts 3512, 3513

Photograph above: French Creek.
Bottom: A view of the French
Creek docks.

French Creek

11055 Lee Rd
Parksville, BC,
V9P 2E1
Phone: (250) 248-5051
1 977-4725 toll free
FAX (250) 248-5123 (pub)
Fisheries & Oceans dock

Chart 3512, 3513

Manager • Float length
804 m • Ramp • Break-
water • Grid • Garbage •
Waste oil disposal •
Water • Lights • Power •
dry storage • rentals •
repairs • moorage •
public phone • ice • gas •
adjacent restaurants,
shops. Seafood store–
prawns, crabs. Foot ferry
to Lasqueti. Coast Guard
station. **Launch ramp.**

Comox

Denman I

Hornby I

Strait of Georgia

N

Fanny Bay R

Ford Cove

Deep Bay R

French Creek R

Parksville

R Schooner Cove

R

Nanoose
Bay

Nanaimo

VANCOUVER
ISLAND

166

View over Comox Municipal marina from the tide grid in the foreground.

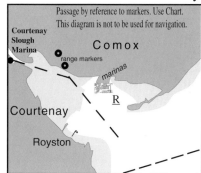

Passage by reference to markers. Use Chart. This diagram is not to be used for navigation.

Courtenay Slough Marina

C o m o x

range markers

marinas

R

Courtenay

Royston

Comox–Courtenay

The Black Fin Pub & Marina

Sharlene Bentley (marina)
132 Port Augusta St,
Comox, BC, V9N 3N7
Phone: (250) 339-5030 (pub)
Phone: (250) 339-4664 (marina)
Fax: 339-3022
Charts 3527, 3513   VHF call 68

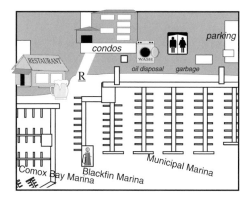

Marina services:
Fuel: Gas. Diesel. oils, outboard mix. Ice.
Moorage: Boats up to about 45 feet.
Water at dock.
Power at docks 15, 30 amps.
Customer services:
Laundry, Showers, Washrooms.
Restaurant and pub.
Scuba diving arrangements and charters–

Public pay phone.
Entertainment.
Town pier–pleasant for walking.
Nautical Days and Filberg Arts & Crafts Festival celebrated every August.
Picnic facilities at Marina Park.
Rental vehicles.
Adjacent facilities:
Boat charters. Golf, Shopping centre, liquor store, post office. Public dock. Garbage disposal.
Canadian Armed Forces base. HMCS Quadra camp at Goose Point. Filberg Lodge.

Comox Bay Marina

1805 Beaufort Ave.,
Comox, BC, V9N 1R9
Phone: (250) 339-2930
Charts 3527, 3513

Marina services:
Moorage: Transient and permanent. Boats to all sizes.
Water at dock.
Power at docks: 50, 30, 15 amp.
Hydro-hoist available. Tidal grids.

Customer services:
Laundry, Showers, Washrooms. Ice.
Restaurant. Lunch, dinner. Plus breakfast at new motel.
Walking: Road access, nearby park. Town

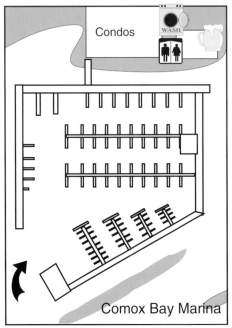

Condos

Comox Bay Marina

View over Comox Bay Marina looking west.

Comox Bay Marina (continued)

of Comox.   Public pay phone.
Entertainment.
Town pier–walk.
Nautical Days celebrated every August.
Picnic facilities at Marina Park.
Rental vehicles available.

Adjacent facilities:
Charters. Golf, shopping centre,
liquor store, post office. Motel suites and
condos.
Yacht club. Good view and location. Public
dock. Garbage disposal.
Canadian Armed Forces base. HMCS
Quadra camp at Goose Point.
Ferry to Powell River departs Comox.

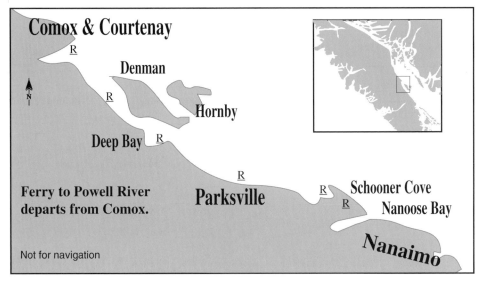

Comox & Courtenay

Denman

Hornby

Deep Bay

Parksville

Schooner Cove

Nanoose Bay

Nanaimo

Ferry to Powell River
departs from Comox.

Not for navigation

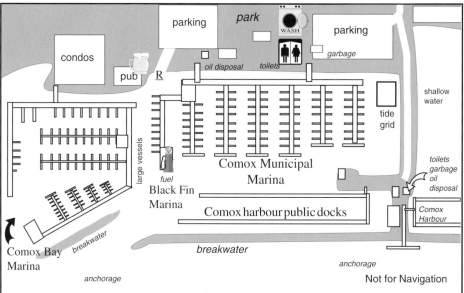

parking | *park* | WASH | parking

condos | garbage

pub | R | oil disposal | toilets

shallow water

tide grid

large vessels

fuel | Black Fin Marina

Comox Municipal Marina

Comox harbour public docks

toilets garbage oil disposal

Comox Harbour

Comox Bay Marina | breakwater | breakwater

anchorage | anchorage

Not for Navigation

Courtenay Slough

Fisheries & Oceans dock
Chart   3527, 3513
Manager • Float length 210 m
Garbage • Waste oil service •
Water • Lights • Power •

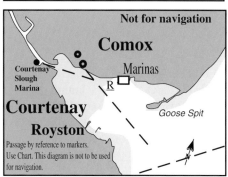

Not for navigation

Comox

Courtenay Slough Marina

R

Marinas

Courtenay

Goose Spit

Royston

Passage by reference to markers.
Use Chart. This diagram is not to be used
for navigation.

Courtenay Slough Marina

Limited moorage for small boats.
Water, power, public phone.
*Hazard: Shallow river. Depths allow boat
with shallow draft only– about 4 feet. Check
chart 3527.*
Walking: Uptown Courtenay.
Public pay phone.

Comox Valley   VHF 68
Harbour Authority

Fisheries and Oceans dock
Phone (250) 339-6041
Fax 339-6057
Chart 3513, 3527
Manager • Float length 340 m •
Breakwater • Grid • Garbage • Waste oil
service • Water • Lights • Power • Public
phone • Washrooms • **Pumpout.**
Washrooms.
Fish sales.
Popular fish and chips restaurant. Many
facilities and services in the vicinity.

Comox Municipal Marina

Richard Kanigan.
Ph: (250) 339-3141. Town of Comox (250) 339-2202
Fax 250 339-7110 Chart 3527, 3513.
Water, power, garbage disposal.
Moorage for small boats & a few large slips.
Public phone. Used oil disposal. Tidal grid.
Fishing pier and promenade. Adjacent an-
chorage.
Hazard: drying flats near Goose Spit.

169

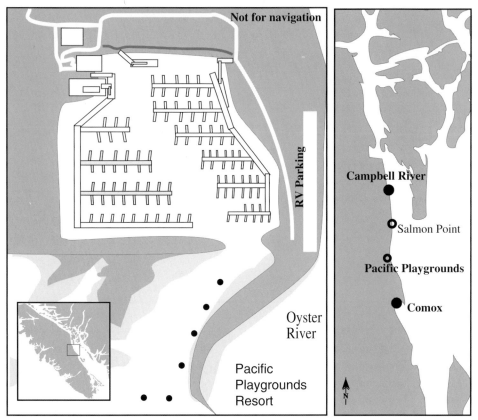

Not for navigation

RV Parking

Oyster
River

Pacific
Playgrounds
Resort

Campbell River

Salmon Point

Pacific Playgrounds

Comox

N

Comox to Campbell River

Pacific Playgrounds Resort

Walt Lengerke
9082 Clarkson Drive,
Black Creek, BC. V9J 1B3
Ph (250) 337-5600. Fax (250) 337-5979
Chart 3527, 3513 (Alongside Oyster
River Mouth.)
Hazard–Channel may be entered at 4 foot
(plus) tides. Follow pilings.
Marina:
Moorage. Sheltered basin. Numerous slips
to 40 feet.
Fuel: Gas, diesel. **Water.**
Power–30 amp.
Services:
Marine store: Supplies, tackle, charts,
fishing licenses, groceries. public phone.

Resort facilities including heated pool,
grassy play area. **Showers, laundry,**
washrooms. Garbage disposal.
Entertainment and nearby facilities:
Golf, mini-golf, driving range, tennis,
hiking roads and trails. Stores and
restaurants. Scenery, sunsets and eagles.
Nearby beach walks, bird watching.
Fishing: guides available.

Diagram: Pacific Playgrounds Resort with its
open water entrance. Its approaches are shallow
but are clearly marked.

Salmon Point Resort & Marina

2176 Salmon Point Road,
Campbell River, BC. V9H 1E5
Phone (250) 923-6605 Fax (250) 923-7572
Chart 3527, 5313

Hazard: Narrow channel into marina. Shallow. Proceed between floats off breakwater. Call–ask marina for entrance guidance.

Marina:
Sheltered moorage for up to 200 small boats (to 26 ft.). Limited transient moorage.
Fuel: Gas, limited water, power. Phone.
Services:
Resort with many amenities–for resort, moorage and RV guests. Restaurant.
Hot tub, heated pool.
Nature trails, tenting. Laundromat. Restrooms, showers.
Fishing guides and charters. Garbage disposal. Fish freezing and packaging.
Entertainment and nearby facilities:
Golf, mini-golf, driving range, tennis, hiking roads and trails. Stores.
Scenery, sunsets and eagles.
Nearby beach walks, bird watching. Fishing.

Make certain your children are wearing life jackets around the water, and particularly on marina docks.

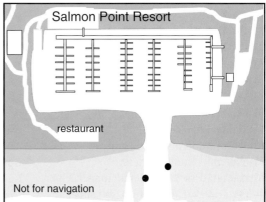

Salmon Point Resort

restaurant

Not for navigation

Vancouver Island

After putting into Campbell River for supplies and perhaps a break from solitude, many visiting boats head for the marina tucked into Quadra Island on the other side of Discovery Passage. It is located beyond the resort at April Point.

Campbell River

April Point
Resort & Marina

Dock manager
P.O. Box 248, Campbell River,
BC. V9W 4Z9
Phone: (250) 285-2222 (Marina)
Fax (250) 285-2016
Charts 3312, 3540, 3539   VHF 10
Moorage. Large permanent marina with overnight or extended moorage available. Reservations recommended in mid summer. **Marina services:** Cable TV. **Laundry, showers, washrooms. Garbage drop. Launch ramp. Water** at dock–multiple outlets. Ice. **Power** at docks: 15, 30, 50 amp.
Customer services:
Lodge with full numerous amenities.
Fishing guides and charters.
Restaurant. Breakfast, lunch, dinner. Open 7 days a week. Coffee shop. gift shop.

Conference rooms.
Nearby church/es.
Walking trails or road access.
Some beachfront walks. Horseback riding.
Scuba diving arrangements and charters–ask lodge for details.
Public pay phones ashore.
Scooter rentals. Kayak rentals, eco-tours.
Accommodations at lodge and bungalows.
Transport to golf courses. Airport limo.
Free water shuttle to and from Painters Lodge in Campbell River and access to their facilities including dining room, pub, swimming pool, exercise room.
Adjacent facilities:
Kenmore Air regular flights.
Liquor, grocery, arts and crafts and other stores including post office nearby.

172

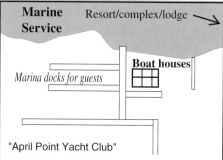

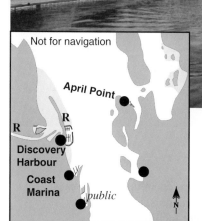

Approaching marina, pass red buoy to your right. Consult your chart.

April Point 'Yacht Club' docks

The April Point Lodge with its fishing lodge floats out front. Restaurant service at the lodge. Inset: Farther in the cove is the 'Yacht Club' moorage for overnight guests.

Hiking trails at Rebecca Spit Provincial Park on Quadra Island.

Also walk island roads, trails and beaches. Visit the Native Museum and Cultural Centre on the island.

There is a large public marina at Quathiaski Cove.

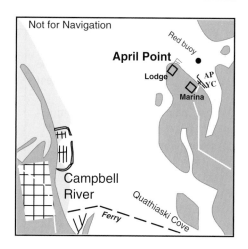

Photograph: Osvaldo Brasca

1. The Coast Marina

Osvaldo Brasca

975 Shopper Row, Campbell River, BC. V9W 2C5. Phone: (250) 287-7155
Fax (250) 287-2213
Chart 3540, 3539, 3312   VHF call 73
Marina Services
Moorage. 2700 feet docks.
Power: 15, 20, 30, 50 amp/220 volt.
Water. Garbage disposal.
Dockside marine services.
Customer services:
Laundry, showers, ice, bait.
Public phone ashore.
Marine charts, books, fishing gear,
licences, boat supplies, CNG, kerosene and stove fuels.   Light refreshment (snacks).
Nearby church/es: multi-denominational.
Walking: Foreshore Park with walkway to scenic downtown Campbell River.
Entertainment:
Scuba diving arrangements and charters–ask marina for details.

Fishing excellent in general area .
Fishing charters, boat rentals.
Adjacent facilities
Ferry adjacent. Restaurants and all services–located in centre of town.
There is a large, modern shopping centre in Campbell River just north of this marina. Adjacent to the marina is the ferry landing for Quadra Island and opposite is the Coast Hotel and adjacent downtown shopping centre. Nearby are marine stores and services.

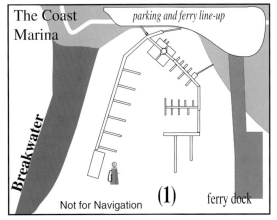

The Coast Marina

parking and ferry line-up

Breakwater

Not for Navigation   (1)   ferry dock

174

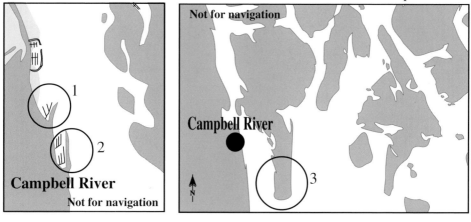

Not for navigation

Campbell River

Campbell River

Not for navigation

2. Campbell River

Fisheries & Oceans
Phone 287-7931
Chart   3540, 3539, 3312
Manager • Float length 1033 m
Breakwater • Grid • Garbage •
Waste oil service • Water • Lights •
Power •
Public phone • Washrooms •
Showers •
Fuel • Gas, diesel, CNG, stove oil.
Ice, bait, tackle, charts.
Campbell River town adjacent.
Also ferry to Quadra Island.

3. Cape Mudge

Fisheries & Oceans dock
Phone 285-3622
Chart   3540, 3539
Manager • Float length 60 m • Breakwater
• Marine Ways • *The float is to the left of Cape Mudge–
shown on a calm day in the photograph below.*

Campbell River is a busy place. There are resorts at this international sportfishing
playground that cater solely to fishermen, offering guided salmon fishing and tourna-
ments. Some offer no transient moorage while others have an open door to overnight
boating stops. The velocity of water surging through Seymour Narrows just north of the
town makes for interesting navigation, even dangerous so be mindful of tides and
current, especially when venturing through the narrows or around the bottom of Quadra
Island and its infamous Cape Mudge during gusty winds and swift moving waters.

Fuel up at Campbell River or across the way at Quathiaski Cove, or just beyond
Seymour Narrows at Brown's Bay, because you may not find fuel too conveniently for a
while if you are going north up Johnstone Strait, unless you turn off to Blind Channel or
head into Desolation Sound. Blind Channel not only has fuel but also a fine restaurant,
general store and other facilities including a liquor agency. Fuel is available also at
Heriot Bay on the east side of Quadra Island as well as at Gorge Harbour and Refuge
Cove.

This area has been developed into a large, busy shopping centre with stores, restaurants and services.

Discovery Harbour Marina

1400 Weiwakum Road,
Campbell River BC. V9W 5W8
Phone: (250) 287-2614
Fax: (250) 287-8939
Chart 3540, 3539, 3312
VHF call 73
ask for Discovery Harbour Marina

Marina services:
Fuel: At Esso dock. Gas, diesel, oils.
Moorage: 150 berths for transient moorage. Boats to 100 feet and over.
Power at docks: 15, 20, 30, 50, 100 amp.
Water.
Dockside marine service can be arranged.

Customer services:
Laundry, showers, ice, bait.
Public phone ashore.
Nearby churches: multi-denominational in Campbell River.
Walking: Road access walking or cycling. Vehicle rentals in town.

Entertainment:
Scuba diving excellent in the area. There are

Dock A is for 18 foot boats, B is for 20, C & D for 24, E & F for 30, H is for 36, I and J are for 40 and K for 100 footers.

strong tidal currents and it is suggested that divers use local dive operators as guides. Fishing excellent in general area.

Quathiaski Cove

Quadra Island.
Fisheries & Oceans dock
Phone (250) 624-2244
Fuel dock: (250) 285-3212
Chart   3540, 3539, 3312
Manager • Float length 195 m
Launch ramp • Garbage • Waste oil disposal •
Lights • Power • Public phone •
Adjacent–Shipyard, ***Fuel dock**: Diesel, gas, outboard mix, water, propane, oil. Shops nearby. Adjacent ferry to Campbell River.

*Coastal Mountain Fuels

Fuel. Bait, snacks, fishing gear.

Quathiaski Cove

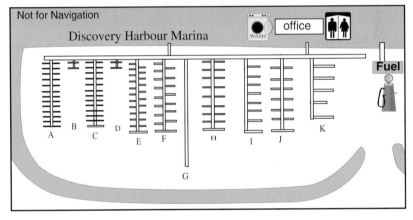

Not for Navigation

Discovery Harbour Marina

WASH office

Fuel

A B C D E F H I J K G

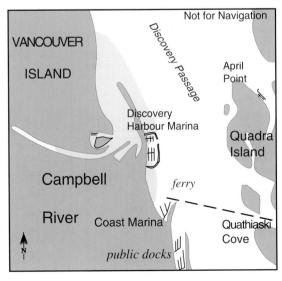

Discovery Harbour Marina is a large marina with a vast breakwater. It is on aboriginal native land and is operated by the local native Indian band. A new shopping complex has been built adjacent to it. Opposite Campbell River is Quadra Island with its Quathiaski Cove serving as the ferry landing.

Not for Navigation

VANCOUVER

ISLAND

Discovery Passage

April Point

Discovery Harbour Marina

Quadra Island

Campbell

River   Coast Marina

ferry

Quathiaski Cove

N

public docks

Brown's Bay Marina

Jim and Julie Camp
Box 668, Campbell River
BC, V9W 6J3
Phone: (250) 286-3135 Fax 286-0951
Chart 3539, 3513, 3312

Marina services:
Fuel: Gas, diesel, oils.
Propane. Oil change facility.
Moorage. 1800 feet transient dock.
Boats to over 100 feet.
Power at docks: 30, 20, 15 amp.
Water. Ice. Garbage disposal.
Customer services:
Bed and breakfast accommodation.
Laundry, showers, ice, bait.
Public phone ashore.
Store. Marine charts, tackle, licences, foul
weather gear. Fish cleaning. **Launch ramp.**
Floating restaurant/cafe.
Boat rentals. Fishing. Wildlife viewing.
Guides available. Charters.
Walking: Road access walking or cycling.
Entertainment:
Fishing superior in general area near
harbour. Outstanding scuba diving at
Campbell River and vicinity.
Adjacent facilities:
Ripple Rock RV Park–many facilities.

Not for navigation

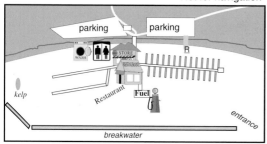

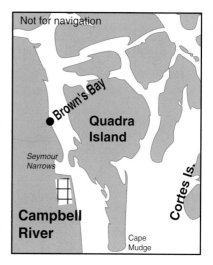

178

Desolation Sound

Central Coast Playground

Once in Desolation Sound you will not be stuck for fuel because there is a full service fuel stop at Refuge Cove. This facility is a centre for all boating needs to serve the cruising mariner. It has liquor, fresh produce, groceries, frozen foods, books, charts and more. The crafts shop, coffee bar and hamburger stand on the property above the marina make an ideal place to wander or sit in the sun and enjoy the ambience of being out boating.

Desolation Sound is a popular place to anchor for days on end in the summertime. From the many coves and bays of Grace Harbour or Prideaux Haven to Pendrell Sound and Walsh Cove, or Roscoe Bay, Theodosia Inlet, Van Donop Inlet and Squirrel Cove to name a few,

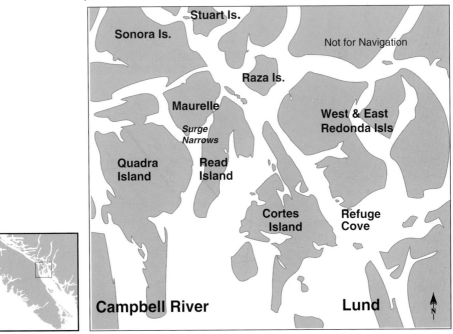

one can find the ideal place to set up home aboard for a few days or play musical moorages and move from one to the next as one spends a summer vacation in this warm water oasis in BC. Move early in the day to avoid difficulty in finding a place to drop anchor in some of the busier bays.

To the west is Heriot Bay for moorage and fuel and Drew Harbour with its anchorage behind Rebecca Spit. Kayaking is drawing increasing number to this area each year. Go to Surge Narrows from Heriot Bay, or cross over and spend the rest of your vacation at Gorge Harbour, one of the most sheltered large bays in the area, with a fine marina and restaurant to keep you in comfort for your stay. There is fuel at Gorge Harbour, a store, all facilities plus petroglyphs on the sheer rock face at the entrance. In the vicinity you may want to stop in for a stroll at nearby Whaletown. Dock space is limited. *See* **Anchorages and Marine Parks** *for more information on Desolation Sound.*

Gorge Harbour

1. Gorge Harbour Marina & Resort

Glen and Verlie Carleton
**P.O. Box 89 Whaletown,
Cortes Island BC. V0P 1Z0
Phone: (250) 935-6433 fax 935-6402
Charts 3538, 3312, 3311 VHF 73 CB 18**

Marina services:
Fuel: Gas, diesel, oil.
Moorage: Guest moorage.
Water at dock. Multiple outlets.
Power at docks: 30, 15 amp.
Multiple outlets.

Customer services:
Grocery store. Coffee counter.
Fishing licences, bait, tackle.
Ice, books, gifts, charts, propane, postage
stamps. **Laundry, showers, washrooms.**
Public pay phones ashore. Boat rentals.
Private rooms with showers and baths.
Good scuba diving nearby.

Charters. Fish cleaning station on docks.

Entertainment.
Adjoining campground with good facilities.
Trail to roadway. Walk to rustic Whaletown.
Art Gallery *en route*. Video rentals. Restaurant dining. Tooker Library at Whaletown.

Adjacent facilities:
Licenced restaurant on property–breakfast,
lunch and dinner (May 1–September 30).
Arts and crafts and museum on island.
Campground. RVs. Scooter, car and kayak
rentals.

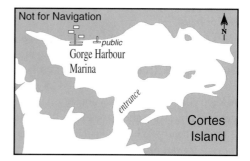

180

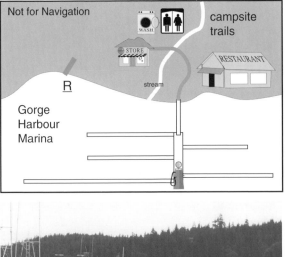

Not for Navigation

WASH

campsite trails

STORE

stream

RESTAURANT

R

Gorge
Harbour
Marina

Below: The entrance to Gorge Harbour is narrow and subject to current. There are petroglyphs on the rock face to port. Opposite: Gorge Harbour Marina. Lower left and right: Manson's Landing and Whaletown.

Quadra
Island

Cortes
Island

3 1
2

2. Manson's Landing

public dock and marine park
Chart 3311, 3538 VHF 73
Hazard: Exposed to westerly winds.
Shallows on north approaches.
Moorage
Limited moorage at small government dock.
See *Anchorages and Marine Parks.*
Alternative services:
Groceries nearby at Gorge Harbour.
Road to store and cafe.
Entertainment.
Walking on island roads. Beaches. Lagoon.
Adjacent facilities:
Marine Park, toilets

Cortes Island. (store at Squirrel Cove)
(250) 935-6361
Irvine and Doreen Redel
Joanne Prestley

3. Whaletown

Cortes Island, BC V0P 1Z0
(250) 935-6562 fax 935-6624
George Frost
Charts 3538, 3311
Hazard: Rock near government dock.
See chart 3538.
Marina services: *No garbage.*
Transient, limited moorage at public dock.
Dock space no charge (1998). Rafting likely.
Customer services:
Post office (Mon, Wed, Fri). Store: groceries, bakery goods, fresh produce, ice cream cones, milk, frozen foods, ice, water, tackle, bait, charts, novelties, gifts. Video rentals.
Entertainment.
Walking on island roads, swimming, scuba diving, fishing, kayaking, bird watching.
Adjacent facilities:
Ferry to/from Quadra. Public phone.
Dentist office afloat at foot of ramp.
Library nearby.

Heriot Bay Inn caters to boating. It has lodging, restaurant, marine bar, a spacious marina, store and fuel.

Heriot Bay

Heriot Bay Inn

Julia and Tom Pearson
P.O. Box 100, Heriot Bay,
Quadra Island, BC V0P 1H0
Phone: (250) 285-3322 Fax 285-2708
Chart 3538/9, 3312   VHF 73
email: *marina@heriotbayinn.com*
www.heriotbayinn.com
Marina services:
Fuel: Gas. Diesel. Oil. Propane.
Moorage, repairs, service available nearby.
Water at dock.
Power at docks: 30, 15 amp.
Fish cleaning station. Boat rentals.
Customer services:
Restaurant–patio service (seasonal), pub (all year)–The Logger & The Fisherman. Kayak rentals. Fishing licences, bait, tackle.
Store: Ice, books, gifts, charts.
Laundry, showers, washrooms.
Public pay phones ashore. Boat rentals.
Private rooms at Inn. Cottages. RV Park (cable TV). Hook-ups, tents.
Fishing, sight-seeing charters. Good scuba diving nearby. Bicycle rentals at marina.
Entertainment.
Historic Heriot Bay Inn and its classic pub. Walking–roadway and some beach access. Also at Nearby Rebecca Spit. Kayaking, adventure packages (ask for information at office). Internet connection.

Adjacent and nearby facilities:
Heriot Bay Store, liquor store and mini shopping centre–delivery to boats–Phone (250) 285-2436. fax: (250) 285-2430.
Post Office, Arts and crafts store at centre.
Campground. RVs. Government dock.
Anchorage at Drew Harbour inside Rebecca Spit at Rebecca Spit Marine Park.

Opposite: The public dock in Cortes Bay. No private marinas are open to public use. Yacht clubs own two major marina in the bay. They are for the exclusive use of members and reciprocal guests.

Heriot Bay
Quadra Island Harbour Authority
Lisa Leippi dock manager
Phone (250) 285-3555
Chart 3538, 3539, 3312
Manager • Float length 204 m
Launch ramp • Garbage • Lights •
Power • Public phone • Near marina
and inn, ferry to Cortes Island, park,
shops. Heriot Bay store nearby.

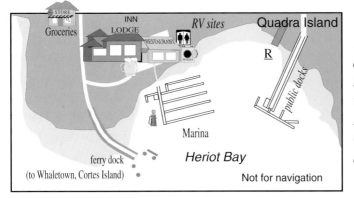

Groceries
STORE
INN
LODGE
RESTAURANT
RV sites
Quadra Island
R
public docks
Marina
ferry dock
(to Whaletown, Cortes Island)
Heriot Bay
Not for navigation

Below: Cortes Bay public dock, where wharfinger Bill Brown (lower) gives regular visitors a warm welcome. Bottom: Aerial view of Cortes Bay shows public dock to left, entrance to right.

Cortes Bay

The dock is wide and sturdy although not anchored at the deep end. It is controlled by a wharfinger and shared with local residents owning pleasure and commercial craft. Space is limited and many yachtsmen favour anchoring out in the bay. Cortes Bay is windy and often appears to be more wind-swept than the waters outside. In recent years boat owners walked up the road to tour Wolf's Bluff Castle, a fairytale structure with an old Europe rustic atmosphere complete with dungeon, built by the owner Karl Triller, on a secluded two-and-a-half acre homestead property. No pets or smoking allowed inside the castle. Check with the wharfinger whether tours are still available. You will find him in his house at the public dock. Ask about the craft stores nearby. There are two yacht club outstations in the bay which do not permit non-member moorage.

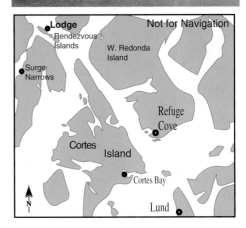

Lodge
Rendezvous Islands
W. Redonda Island
Not for Navigation
Surge Narrows
Refuge Cove
Cortes Island
Cortes Bay
N
Lund

183

Desolation Sound

Left: The dock at North Rendezvous Island and the lodge (below) with a view towards Raza Island. It is located 25 miles south of Big Bay near Surge Narrows or Refuge Cove. Bottom: The store on the wharf at Surge Narrows.

Surge Narrows

Doug and Teresa Beyerstein
P.O. Box 31, Surge Narrows
Reid Island, BC V0P 1W0
Phone: (250) 285-3643 Cell 285-6962
Charts 3312, 3537, 3539

Moorage limited. Small dock with aircraft float. Post Office on dock. Open Mon, Wed, Fri 1 to 4 pm.
General store: Island fresh produce, baked goods and provisions. Coffee. Snacks. Some hardware and marine supplies. Limited water available.
This is a public dock. Additional private docks adjoining store are planned.
Passage through Whiterock Pass to Rendezvous Islands is always possible.

Rendezvous Lodge

Roy and Darlene Bugeaud
P.O. Box 309, Quathiaski Cove
BC. V0P 1N0 (Rendezvous Is)
Cell phone: (250) 287-0318 Fax 203-1123
Charts 3539, 3541, 3312   VHF 12
email: *rbugeaud@oberon.ark.com*
Web: *www.rendezvouslodge.com*
Moorage. Toilets.
240' of useable dock, used mostly by transient boats with lunch or dinner reservations at lodge. Use of hot tub included. Meals include wine. Rooms available.
Entertainment: Hiking trails, coves, beaches, oysters. Kayaks available.

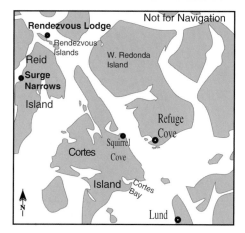

184

*Dock at Squirrel Cove
and inside the cove.*

Squirrel Cove (Cortes Is)

Irvine and Doreen Redel
Ph (250) 935-6327 Fax (250) 935-6327
Charts 3555, 3538, 3312 VHF 73
Fisheries & Oceans public dock
Manager • Float length 60 m
Garbage • Lights • Power •
Marina services:
Temporary moorage at government dock.
Garbage drop.
Customer services:
Showers, laundry. Groceries. Public phone.
Baked goods and fresh produce, milk, frozen foods, ice, water, tackle, bait, charts.
Propane. Liquor. Gifts. Marine supplies.
Entertainment.
Hiking. Island roads. Beaches. Lagoon.
Adjacent/nearby facilities:
Squirrel Cove Marine Park. Anchorage.
Arts and crafts shop.

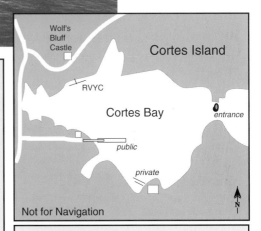

Not for Navigation

Cortes Government Dock

Cortes Island
Bill Brown (Wharfinger)
Charts 3555, 3538, 3312
Cortes Bay photopgraph left
Hazard: Entering bay–keep rock and day marker at entrance to starboard (passage south of marker).
Marina services:
Moorage at government dock.
About 200 feet of dock, wide and solid.
Windy at times in bay.
Power at dock: 15, 20 amp.
Customer services:
Public phone. Arts and crafts available.
Entertainment.
Hiking. Island roads. Possible tour of Wolf's Bluff Castle–Information from wharfinger.
Adjacent facilities:
Yacht club station. Anchorage.
Restaurant nearby–ask wharfinger.

Cortes Bay–
note: passage south of
reef at entrance

Refuge Cove

Chart 3555, 3538, 3312   VHF 73

Refuge Cove
Colin Robertson & Norm Dowler
Refuge Cove, BC
V0P 1P0
crobert@oberon.ark.com
web: www.boattravel.com/refuge

Marina services:
Fuel: Gas. Diesel, oil, propane.
Moorage: Government dock and private.
Overnight moorage. 2000 feet of docks.
Water at dock–multiple outlets.
Power at docks: 15 amp.

Customer services:
Laundry, showers, washrooms.
Propane, ice, books, gifts charts,
Grocery store, post office. Liquor.
Public pay phone on shore.

Adjacent facilities:
Gifts, arts and crafts, coffee bar,
hamburger kiosk.

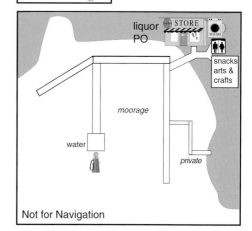

Not for Navigation

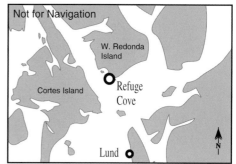

186

Above: The docks at Refuge Cove from the patio of the coffee bar next to the general store. Left: Refuge Cove Store is a busy place in summer.

Oasis in Desolation Sound

En route to all parts of Desolation Sound, Refuge Cove is a busy stop during the brief summer season. It affords replenishment of everything from fuels and fresh water to liquor, fresh produce, bread, meat and groceries. Charts, books and a limited selection of clothing are also sold at the store, as well as ice and fishing supplies. The store is built on a barge and positioned high and dry above the high-water mark. It and the fuel dock are run effectively to accommodate the heavy traffic of the short summer season and survive the balance of the year.

One of the burdens of summer is the threat of fire when forest conditions are very dry. Water shortages are sometimes threatened but seldom occur. The lake that drains into Refuge Cove supplies domestic water and the local population sometimes finds it difficult to prevent visitors from misusing it. The dock does, however, have adequate water for conservative use with outlets at various points for mooring customers.

The south docks at Big Bay Marina. Boats to 130 feet can be accommodated on these and the adjoining dock. Right: The restaurant and store are just up the path.

Stuart Island

Big Bay Marina Resort

Bruce and Kay Knierim
**Big Bay P.O. Stuart Island,
BC V0P 1V0
Phone: (250) 830-7524
Charts 3543, 3312**

Hazard: Shoal in centre of Bay especially near public dock. Currents.

Marina services:
Fuel: Gas. diesel, oil.

Moorage, outboard motor repairs & service. Honda dealer.
Water at dock.
Power at docks: Limited: 15 amp.
Power at marina is being upgraded.
Fish cleaning station.
Customer services:
Restaurant, pub. Breakfast, lunch, dinner. Patio tables. Liquor store.
Store. Fishing licences, bait, tackle, ice, groceries, frozen foods, fresh bread, books, charts, gifts, video movie rental. Coffee,

Toba Wildernest

Ed and Mary Schlote
**Mouth of Toba Inlet at Double Island
Desolation Sound.
Ph (250) 286-8507 Chart 3312
Surrey contact: (604) 576-1079 ph/fax**

Dock available for overnight–350 feet.
Facilities: Toilet, showers, cabins, ice.
This is a fishing resort offering resort amenities for fly-in guests. Also available for transient mariners when space is available. It is located near Walsh Cove.

Big Bay lodge, marina and fishing camp, a place to stay on Stuart Island, refuel, replenish supplies, charter a fishing guide and much more.

There is moorage also at the nearby Wheelhouse pub or at the adjacent public dock.

expresso, latte.
Laundry, Showers, Washrooms.
Public pay phones. Cottages.
Fishing charters. Guides. Good fishing.
Scuba diving nearby. Beware of currents.
Entertainment.
Walk in coastal trails. Games room at resort.
Adjacent facilities:
Pub, restaurant. Government dock.
Post office. Seaplane landing and mooring.

Dent Island Resort

Stuart Island BC. V0P 1V0
Charts 3312, 3543
Ph (250) 203-2553
Fax (250) 203-1041
Visitors dock–800 feet.
Facilities: Lodge with overnight accommodation and full service. Restaurant.
Power: 30, 50 amp. **Water.**
Hot tub and sauna. Fishing guides. Scheduled seaplane.
Water taxi service.
www.dentisland.com

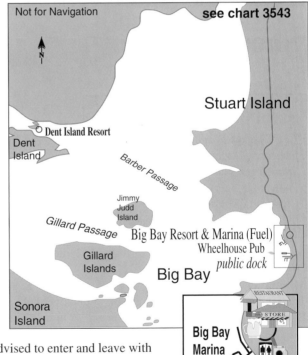

Not for Navigation   see chart 3543

N

Stuart Island

Dent Island Resort
Dent Island

Barber Passage

Jimmy Judd Island

Gillard Passage   Big Bay Resort & Marina (Fuel)
                  Wheelhouse Pub
Gillard   public dock
Islands
                  Big Bay

Sonora Island

RESTAURANT
STORE
Big Bay Marina
fuel
kelp reef
public

In Big Bay mariners are advised to enter and leave with caution, noting the shallows near the shore facilities. Consult your chart and watch for kelp–a summertime marker for the reef. The perfect way to end your busy day in Big Bay is dining at the Eagle's Wing restaurant in the main building of the lodge. On cool days find a table near the warmth of the large wood-burning fireplace.

Shoal Bay

Shoal Bay.

East Thurlow Island
Fisheries & Oceans dock
Wharfinger: Nancy (& Chris) Carson
Phone: "Loggers Dream" N114672
Channel E. Thurlow 23.
Float length 76 m. Charts 3543, 3312

Shoal Bay Lodge

Marina services:
Transient moorage. Government dock.
Pay moorage to wharfinger Nancy Carson

Hiking trails. Logging roads. View points
along a network of paths. Animal and marine
life. Eagles.
Nearby: Canoeing. Kayaking. Day trips in
adjacent waterways. Includes Thurston Bay
Marine Park. Rentals. Picnic area.

The lodge was destroyed by fire during
the 2000 summer season. This was an historic old building and attempts over the past
few years to turn it into a successful summer
destination were never quite realised.

However, some outstanding meals were
prepared and served to passing boaters and
fishermen as well as logging crews. It will be
missed. The marina stands and is serviced by
the wharfinger,
Nancy Carson.
It is a good
overnight spot
in calm condi-
tions.

Usually it
is only winter-
time when one
has to be mind-
ful of adverse
winds.

Owen Bay

Transport Canada dock
Charts 3537, 3539, 3312
Manager •
Float length 9 m

Evans Bay

Read Island
Transport Canada dock
Charts 3538, 3539, 3312
Float length 18 m

At Shoal Bay a government dock with fairly generous moorage provides overnight accommodation for several large or additional smaller boats. The grounds of the old lodge are pleasant for walking.

The floating lodge pictured below is in Cordero Channel–known internationally for fine dining and successful fishing charters.

Chart 3543

Cordero Lodge

Doris & Kellie Kuppers
General Delivery
Blind Channel P.O.
BC. V0P 1B0
Phone (250) 286-8404
Chart 3543, 3312
Marina services:
Transient moorage.
Customer services:
Restaurant–Fine dining.
Lodging–up to eight guests.
Fishing: Boats–guided or unguided.
Entertainment.
Sunsets and views. Animal and marine life. Bears and eagles.
Adjacent facilities:
Cordero Islands anchoring.

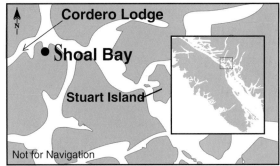

N

Cordero Lodge

●Shoal Bay

Stuart Island

Not for Navigation

Blind Channel

Charts 3544, 3543   VHF 73
Blind Channel Resort

Philip Richter
Blind Channel BC
V0P 1B0
Ph (250) 949-1420 Fax (250) 830-8620
email: *info@blindchannel.com*
www:*blindchannel.com*
Marina services:
Moorage: Transient moorage.
Fuel: Gas, diesel, propane.
Water at dock. Ice.
Power at docks: 20 amp
Customer services:
Restaurant open June—Labour Day.
Lunch, fine dining-excellent cuisine.
Patio.
Groceries. Post Office. Public
phone. Baked goods, bread,
fresh produce, milk, frozen foods, ice,
tackle, bait, charts. Fax service.
Laundry, showers, washrooms.
Liquor. Arts and crafts. Gifts.
Excellent fishing and prawning nearby.

Scheduled flights.
Entertainment.
Hiking trails. Logging roads. Several
view points along a network of paths. See
the huge "Thurlow" Cedar tree. Incredible sunsets and views. Animal and marine
life. Eagles. Dock are wide and embellishments are fascinating.
Adjacent facilities:
Picnic area.

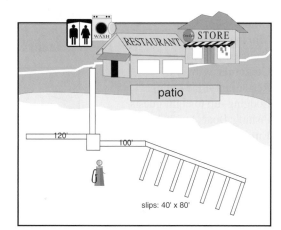

Blind Channel Fine Dining and good facilities

Three generations of Richters are busy around Blind Channel when guests are moored at their docks. This long-established marina in one of the coast's busy waterways has evolved over the years to become a well maintained and contemporary facility for cruising yachtsmen. Philip's parents, who established the marina still live and work at the property. Annemarie usually finds time to chat with guests in the restaurant while Edgar continues to be involved with planning and preparing further additions on the property. Philip does stints in the store while his wife, Jennifer, can be found preparing bread and other baked delectables for the store and restaurant. The marina offers moorage, fuel, water, propane and 110 volt shore power at the dock. The services include showers, laundry, ice, liquor agency, store and post office.

Nature lovers and hikers will be kept busy for days hiking trails that have been established by a large logging and sawmill company on West Thurlow Island. These trails are designed to show the features of a second growth forest and it just happens that they begin about 300 meters from Blind Channel Marina. There are three different trails, one to a spectacular viewpoint overlooking

The stop at Blind Channel has been a favourite among mariners for many decades and the Richter family continues to cater to their needs with fresh produce, baked goods and gourmet cuisine in a fine waterfront restaurant.

Mayne Passage and East Thurlow Island, a second to the Big Cedar, a tree with a diameter of 16 feet, via a forest of 80 year old second growth and the third through a thinned western hemlock stand that was naturally established in 1964. The final segment of this trail descends through 100 year old second growth.

Across Cordero Channel, a few miles from Blind Channel is Cordero Lodge which also offers fine dining. Guests stop overnight but there is limited space usually requiring advance reservations for moorage and dinner. Owned and operated by Reinhart and Doris Kuppers, this popular facility has been a stopping place for those in the know for many years.

Johnstone Strait
South section to Port Hardy

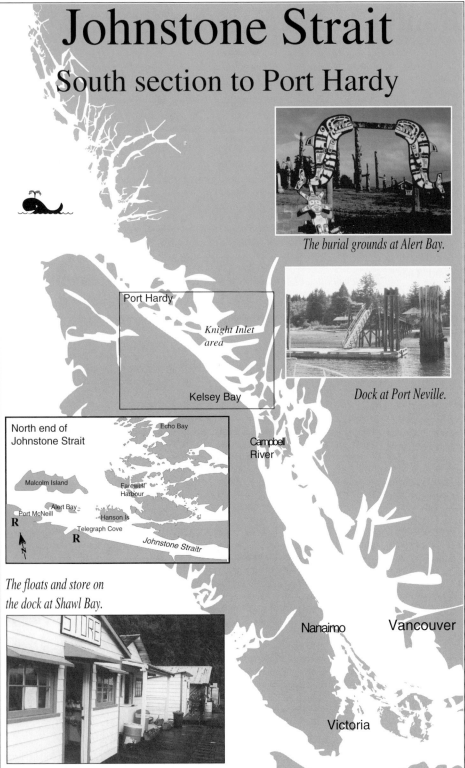

The burial grounds at Alert Bay.

Dock at Port Neville.

Port Hardy

Knight Inlet area

Kelsey Bay

North end of
Johnstone Strait

Echo Bay

Campbell
River

Malcolm Island

Farewell
Harbour

Alert Bay
Port McNeill

Hanson Is

Telegraph Cove

R

R

Johnstone Straitr

*The floats and store on
the dock at Shawl Bay.*

Nanaimo

Vancouver

Victoria

The dock and old store at Port Neville.
There is a post office ashore and an art gallery and
gift shop on the opposite shore. Left: Port Neville.

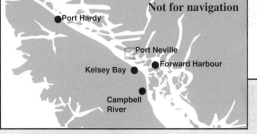

Not for navigation

Port Hardy
Port Neville
Kelsey Bay
Forward Harbour
Campbell River

Kelsey Bay

Vancouver Island
Fisheries & Oceans dock
Phone (250) 282-3465
Chart 3544
Manager • Float length 177 m
Breakwater • Garbage • Water • Lights •
Power •

Kelsey Bay

Vancouver Island
Transport Canada dock
Chart 3544
Manager • Float length 31 m
Breakwater • Water • Lights • Power •

Forward Harbour

Off Wellbore Channel (Whirlpool Rapids)
Chart 3544. Anchorage–good weather.

Photo left: The late Olaf Hansen, his family settled at Port Neville in 1891.

Port Neville Historic settlement.

Johnstone Strait
Transport Canada dock
Chart 3564, 3545
Address: Port Neville, BC. V0P 1M0
Call: *Sea Scout III.* VHF 6.
Float length 34 m • Managed by Lorna
Chesluk Hansen (and Erica)–also post office
manager. P.O open Mon, Wed, Fri.
Forwarded mail held for arriving boats.
Art gallery and gift store nearby.

Minstrel Island

Minstrel Island Resort

Grant Douglas and Sylvia Douglas
Minstrel Island P.O. 69,
B.C. V0P 1L0
Phone & fax (250) 949-0215
Chart 3564, 3545, 3515 VHF 73
Marina services:
Moorage: Transient moorage. (public)
Fuel: Gas, diesel, stove oil, propane, aviation
fuel. **Water** at dock. Ice. **Power.**
12,000 lb dry dock–tidal grid.
Customer services:
Restaurant. Full menu. Speciality–Fish and
Chips (reportedly "*awesome*").
Homemade bread, pies, jams. Pub. Accom-
modation in resort rooms and cottages.
Groceries. Postal drop. Post office located
nearby in Chatham Channel.
Cold beer. Bakery goods and fresh produce,
milk, frozen foods, ice, tackle, bait, charts.
Boat rentals.
Laundry, Showers, Washrooms.
Good fishing and prawning nearby.

Entertainment.
Hiking trails. Incredible sunsets and views.
Animal and marine life. Bears and eagles.
Adjacent facilities:
Regular scheduled flights. Boardwalk.
Wheelchair access up ramp. Hiking trails.
Picnic area.

Fishdance Lodge Resort

Dick and Elaine Boss
**Located in Soderman Cove, East Cracroft Is-
land, Call Inlet near Minstrel Island at 50 33
3'N 126 13 2' W. Chart 3564.**
**Contact 15035 73A Avenue, Surrey,
B.C. V3S 7H5. Ph (604) 591-7661.**
Services: Marina moorage. Gourmet home
cooked meals. Luxury accommodations.
To do: Excursions, tours, sea kayaking.
Local interest: Visiting abandoned Indian
villages. **Fuel, water.**

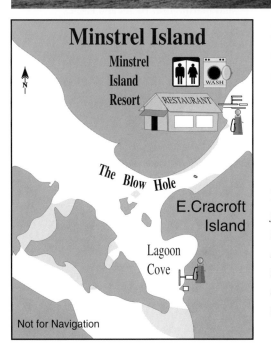

Minstrel Island

Minstrel
Island
Resort

RESTAURANT

WASH

The Blow Hole

E.Cracroft
Island

Lagoon
Cove

N

Not for Navigation

Minstrel Island

Fisheries & Oceans dock
Chart   3564, 3545, 3515
Manager • Float length 135 m
Aircraft float • Lights •
Managed by Minstrel Is Resort.
Adjacent facilities include: Fuel,
restaurant, lodge, store.

*The marina at Minstrel Island is protected
from most wind and weather. The public dock
is adjacent to the private property of Minstrel
Island Resort and is subject to government
maintenance and regulations. They provide
access to the shore where fish and chips are
the speciality at the full menu restaurant.*

Lagoon Cove

Lagoon Cove Marina

Bill and Jean Barber
c/o Minstrel Island P.O.
British Columbia. V0P 1L0
Charts 3545, 3564. VHF 73
post office now located in Chatham
Channel

Marina services:
Moorage: Transient moorage.
Fuel: Gas, diesel, propane. Oils.
Some repairs subject to available help.
Haulouts. Charts, books.
Water at dock. **Power:** 30 amps.

Customer services:
Coffee kiosk. Fishing licences, ice, tackle,
bait, sodas, candies. Crab and prawn traps.
Showers, washrooms.
Boat rentals.
Excellent fishing and prawning nearby.
Cabin and boat available to fly-in guests.

Entertainment.
Hiking trails. Sunsets and views. Animal
and marine life. Bears and eagles.
Join in group barbecues.

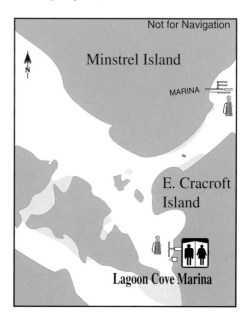

Many people have chosen to anchor in Lagoon Cove over the past, but with secure docking and the associated peace of mind when the wind is up it is worth while stopping at the marina. There are showers, washrooms, additional accommodation and the friendly greeting of owners, Bill and Jean Barber.

Former owners accumulated an incredible collection of marine and other hardware, enough for a museum. Some items have been discarded but many remain in a work shed display area and patio coffee nook.

Attend the barbecues and other group get-togethers in summer.

199

Hanson Island

Double Bay Resort

Murray, Cheri and Shawna Gardham
371 McCarthy Street,
Campbell River BC. V9W 2R7
Phone: (250) 949-1911
Fax (250) 286-1937
Chart 3546 VHF 73
Web: *www.doublebayresort.com*
Moorage available on 700 foot dock.
No dock services. **Showers, washrooms**.
bait, ice, tackle. Restaurant 8am to 8pm–
home cooked meals. Fishing resort offers
fishing charters. Rental boats.
Open May–September.
View eagles, whales, dolphins.

Photo above: Double Bay Resort on Hanson Island. Below: Aerial photo shows the resort tucked inside Double Bay.

Telegraph Cove Marina

Clyde Wagner
PO Box 2-8, Telegraph Cove,
BC. V0N 3J0   VHF 73
Ph (250) 928-3161 Fax (250) 928-3162
email: tcv@island.net   **Chart 3546**
Moorage for visitors. Also commercial
dock for loading. **Pumpout, Power,**
water. Laundry, washrooms, showers.
50' wide launching ramp.
Nearby: Fuel: gas, oil. Restaurant.
Scuba diving and whale watching–Also
marine and bird life.
Contact Stubbs Island Charters on the
boardwalk via the fuel dock ramp at
the entrance to Telegraph Cove.

Telegraph Cove Resort

Moorage reserved for resort clients and
small launch ramp (below).

Photo above: Fuel dock at Telegraph Cove.
Inset: Restaurant and boardwalk.

Stubbs Island Charters

Jim and Mary Borrowman,
P.O. Box 7, Telegraph Cove,
BC. V0N 3J0
Phone: (250) 928-3185 Fax 928-3102
Chart 3546 VHF 10
email: *stubbs@island.net*
Web: *www.stubbs-island.com*
Customer Services:
Gifts. Fine art. Arts and crafts. Whale
watching, day trips. Scuba diving charters.
Accommodation. Cabins on boardwalk.

Stop briefly at the fuel dock and visit the
craft shop on the wharf. The fuel dock
does not belong to the store on the wharf.
It is operated by Telegraph Cove Resort.

There is fuel also at Alert Bay and Port
McNeill. Telegraph Cove **Resort** accommodates resort guest boats only.

Telegraph
Cove
Marina
offers
overnight
visitor
moorage.

The public dock at the far end of Alert Bay

Above: Remnants of bygone activity and population in Bones Bay near Minstrel Island.
Left: A quiet anchorage in a corner of Potts Lagoon.

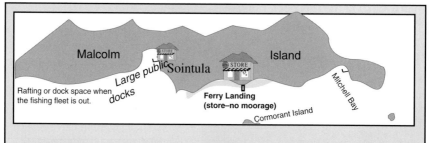

Malcolm   Island

Large public Sointula

STORE

Rafting or dock space when
the fishing fleet is out.   docks

Ferry Landing
(store–no moorage)

Mitchell Bay

Cormorant Island

Sointula

Malcolm Island Lions Club
Harbour Authority
Phone (250) 973-6544
Chart   3546
Manager • Float length 745 m
Breakwater • Aircraft float

Malcolm Island Beachcombers Inn

Phone: (250) 973-6366
• Rooms • Showers • Garbage •
Water • Lights • Power • Public
phone • Store
Nearby facilities. Road access to
ferry to Port McNeill, Alert Bay.

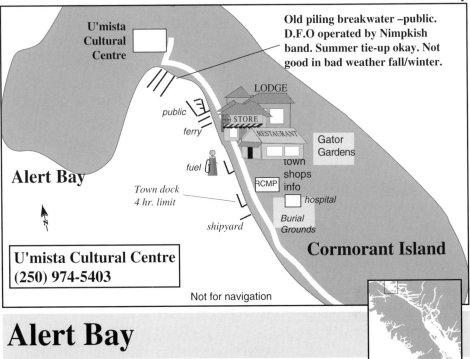

Old piling breakwater –public. D.F.O operated by Nimpkish band. Summer tie-up okay. Not good in bad weather fall/winter.

U'mista Cultural Centre

LODGE

STORE

RESTAURANT

public

ferry

fuel

Gator Gardens

town shops

RCMP

info

hospital

Alert Bay

Town dock 4 hr. limit

shipyard

Burial Grounds

Cormorant Island

U'mista Cultural Centre (250) 974-5403

Not for navigation

Alert Bay

Alert Bay Boat Harbour

(250) 974-5251 res. 974-5727 office.
Government dock.
Chart 3546   VHF 73
DFO (Fisheries) VHF 78
Marina services:
Transient moorage.
Power. Water.
Customer services:
Restaurants. Dining.
Groceries. Tackle, bait, charts.
Garbage disposal.
All services at village of Alert Bay.
Accommodations, meals.
Credit Union (bank machine). 974-5527.
Entertainment.
Hiking trails and roads. **Gator Gardens**, an anachronism–Florida's Everglades come to BC. On the hill above the town. Animal and marine life. Prime scuba diving nearby.
U'mista Cultural Centre. Visit this outstanding display of native history.

Nearby facilities:
Paved airstrip (2800 feet).
Marine services: Alert Bay Save On Fuels: (250) 974-5411. Alert Bay Shipyards: (250) 974-5446. Alert Bay Travel Info Centre: (250) 974-5213

Alert Bay

Fisheries & Oceans dock
Phone (250) 974-5727 res: 974-5251.
Chart   3546
Manager • Float length 533 m
Breakwater • Aircraft Float • Garbage
Water • Waste oil service *Best to return used oil to fuel stations* • Lights • Power • Public phone • Walking–*Gator Gardens* on the hill. Visit *U'mista Centre.*

Transport Canada dock
Chart   3546
Manager • Float length 61 m
Launch ramp •
Garbage • Water (on wharf only) •
Lights •

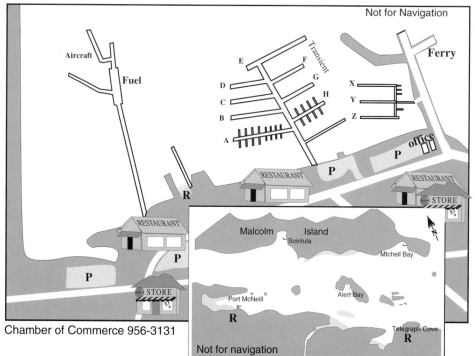

Chamber of Commerce 956-3131

Port McNeill Boat Harbour

**P.O. Box 1389, Port McNeill, BC.
V0N 2R0**
Ph (250) 956-3881 fax (250) 956-2897
Harbour Manager
Chart 3546, 3548 VHF 73
Moorage: Extensive sheltered docks.
Outer floats for transient moorage.
Oil disposal. **Water. Power**: 50, 30, 20
amps. **Fuel** (adjacent)**:** Gas, diesel.
Propane. Oils. Aviation fuels. **Launch
Ramp** adjacent.

Services:
Garbage disposal. Tidal grid. Fish cleaning
station.
Entertainment:
Walk along shore and sea wall. Uptown
facilities–hotels, restaurants, shops,
Heritage buildings. Flights.
Grocery stores deliver to dock.
Adjacent facilities:
Ferry to Sointula, Alert Bay.
Marine repairs–adjacent and nearby
Marinas/fuel barge. Also offering ice,
showers, snacks and pop, hospital nearby.

| R = Launch ramp |
| P = Parking lot |

Opposite, top: Port McNeill. Inset: Well known gateway to burial ground at Alert Bay. Bottom: The lesser-known Gator Gardens on the hill near the radio tower.

Alert Bay

Alert Bay attracts mariners as a stop for replenishment and an opportunity to go ashore for some exercise as they travel en route to points north or home again. For many Alert Bay is a final destination on their northward travels. Whatever the reason for stopping at Alert Bay surprisingly few people seem to know of the existence of Gator Gardens. This very name may well indicate that this attraction is somewhat misplaced here in British Columbia. In name and character it is more like something you would expect to stumble across on a tour of Florida. It is a marshy, swampy

glade complete with large still pools of water afloat with
the massive leaves of various forms of vegetation and
sprouting large sprays of skunk cabbage. Wooden
walkways have been erected across the park to allow
access for easy walking and viewing. The most promi-
nent feature of the park is its
incredible trees which appear to
have been struck by lightning at one
time. These massive trees are broad
and tall and mostly scarred and
craggy with eerie looking branches
and cracks and splits appearing as
though they were the inspiration for
the tale of Sleepy Hollow. And the
surprising thing is that the entire
park is not where you would expect
to find it, down near sea level, but
rather up on top of the hill overlooking Alert Bay. From the government
marinas of Alert Bay to Gator
Gardens is a good uphill walk to the

back of the residential area overlooking the bay. There are several routes, marked here and there by
signs indicating the way. All routes end up alongside or near the transmitter station and entrances to
the Gardens, although not well marked, will eventually lead you to the wooden planked walk
through the glades.

Alert Bay boasts the once tallest totem pole in the world. It is located a short walk up the hill
behind the U'umista Native Cultural Centre which is on the shore adjacent to the government docks
north of town.The museum at the cultural centre is well worth a visit. Among other interesting
items it has on display segments of the exhibits that were shown at Expo 86 in Vancouver.

You may be lucky when visiting Alert Bay and experience some rare calm, sunny weather. If
not you should watch the currents and sea conditions that sweep around the northern channel en
route to Port Hardy or the open northern reaches of Johnstone Strait. In windy conditions it is
usually possible to sneak around the bottom end of Malcolm Island and through the rocky channels
and islets in the area. We once took shelter for two days in the Plumper Islets while the wind raged.
It is not really a suitable anchorage for more than a temporary stop because the current rips through
quite fast especially at high tides.

205

Echo Bay

Echo Bay Resort

Bob & Nancy Richter
Simoom Sound P.O.
B.C. V0P 1S0
Phone and fax (250) 956-2121
email: echobay@island.net
website: www.echobayresort.com

Marina services:

Transient moorage. Reserve in peak season–July, August. Open three days per week in winter.

Fuel: Gas, diesel, kerosene, oils, propane. **Water** at dock. Ice. **Power**: 30, 15 amps. 12,000 lb dry dock. Can haul out boats to about 23 feet.

Laundry, showers, washrooms (for overnight guests.)

Customer services:

Use Interac/Debit card.

Check your email at office. Groceries. Post office. Public phone. Bakery goods and fresh produce, milk, frozen foods, ice, tackle, books, charts, film, and gifts.

Charts 3515   VHF Ch 73

Eight lodging units. Hotel for groups of six or more. Boat and motor rentals.
Popular fishing and prawning nearby
Block and party ice.

Entertainment.

The main dock is a part of the former Lake Washington floating bridge. Hiking trail and park access. Incredible sunsets and views. Animal and marine life. July 8 to August 23– Wednesday nights: Potluck dinners. Resort supplies fish or ribs. Covered 40'x50' float with picnic tables and barbecue. Available for use by overnight moorage guests.

Adjacent facilities:

Regular scheduled flights. Local arts and crafts shops and artists. Nearby anchorage and public float. Marine park.

Note: Docks have had an upgrade to supplied electrical power. Other improvements include new dock ramp to land.

206

Above: View looking out of Echo Bay with Echo Bay Marina on the left, the public dock in the foreground. The marine park and public dock are located alongside a delightful, white, sandy beach.
The aerial photograph opposite shows Echo Bay Resort on the right of the bay.

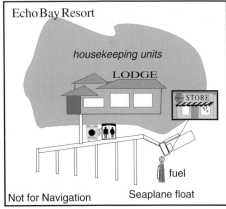

Echo Bay Resort

housekeeping units

LODGE

STORE

fuel

Not for Navigation   Seaplane float

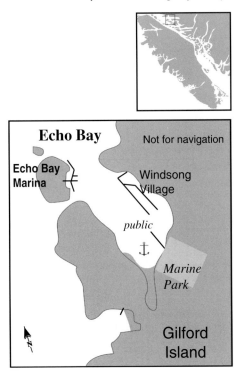

Echo Bay   Not for navigation

Echo Bay Marina

Windsong Village

public

⚓

Marine Park

Gilford Island

Echo Bay

History and commerce converge at Echo Bay. It is a hub of activity drawing summertime travelling boaters, whale watching tourists out of Telegraph Cove, sportfishing groups from near and far and a constant flow of local people from neighbouring logging camps and fish farms to pick up and drop off their mail and replenish some of their grocery needs. The lodge on the island at the entrance to the cove, for that's all that Echo Bay is—a tiny sheltered cove, caters to a steady flow of itinerant visitors in for a few days of fishing or stopping by in their boats for a spell in the area. Fuel and moorage with

207

Brou...

...Canada
...515
...gth 55 m
...y and exposed.

...ilford Island

Fisheries & Oceans
Chart 3515
Float length 60 m
Aircraft float •

Echo Bay
(Marine Park)

All weather anchorage
Boat dock, camping
sites, water, toilets..
Waddington Bay Part
of Broughton Archi-
pelago (Park)
See *Anchorages and
Marine Parks*

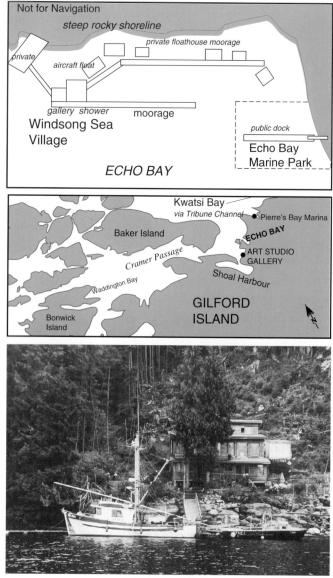

Not for Navigation

steep rocky shoreline

private floathouse moorage

private

aircraft float

gallery shower   moorage

Windsong Sea
Village

public dock

Echo Bay
Marine Park

ECHO BAY

Kwatsi Bay
via Tribune Channel   Pierre's Bay Marina

Baker Island   ECHO BAY

Cramer Passage   ART STUDIO
                        GALLERY

Waddington Bay   Shoal Harbour

GILFORD
ISLAND

Bonwick
Island

*Right: Maximchuk gallery
and art studio just outside
Shoal Harbour entrance.
Above right: Diagram and
photograph (opposite page)
show the Windsong Sea
Village with its spacious
docks, rental cottages and
arts and crafts shop.*

power and water are available from Echo Bay Marina which also serves as post office
and store.

A marina on the opposite shore, Windsong Sea Village Resort, has large floats which
will accommodate a good number of boats and offers moorage for seaplanes too. This
marina offers no fuel or dockside electricity but has a delightful craft shop representing
works of local artists such as Alexandra Morton, Yvonne Maximchuk, natives from the
nearby Gilford Island Village and the proprietor herself, Christine O'Donnell.

Yvonne Maximchuk has a house just outside the entrance to Shoal Harbour and
provides an opportunity for artists or tyros to brush up on their skills. Here, in her gallery
studio, she conducts instruction and classes in art, water colour, acrylics and oils, available to people on visiting boats. She also has a fine selection of works for sale and can be
reached by calling her at *Sea Rose* on channel 16.

Windsong Sea Village Echo Bay.

James O'Donnell
Box 1487, Port McNeill
B.C. V0N 2R0
Phone: (250) 974-5004
Ph/Fax (250) 974-3009

Marina services:
Moorage: Transient moorage. Float planes. Showers.

Customer services:
Arts and crafts store. Fine art. Floating cabin rentals. Floathouse moorage available.

Entertainment.
Hiking trail and marine park access.
Incredible sunsets and views.
Animal and marine life.

Adjacent facilities:
Regular scheduled flights. Marine park and trail.
Local artists live in vicinity.
Corky's Bakery moored at marina during season.
Some overnight space also, subject to space availability, at nearby public dock.

Chart 3515   VHF Ch 73

Pierre's Bay Lodge & Marina

Pierre and Tove Landry
c/o Box 257, Gabriola Island
B.C. V0R 1X0   Fax (250) 247-9551
Phone (250) 247-9704 (250) 949-2503

Marina services:
Moorage: Transient moorage.
Showers, laundry, washrooms. No power at the docks. Limited water.

Customer services:
Self-contained ental suites. Restaurant, gift shop, arts and crafts.
Use large scale chart 3515.
Avoid Powell Rock at the entrance to Scott Cove.

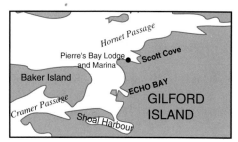

Shawl Bay

Chart 3515   VHF 73

This photo shows Kwatsi Bay Marina beneath towering coastal mountains off Tribune Channel.

Shawl Bay Marina

Lorne and Shawn Brown
**General Delivery, Simoom Sound P.O.
BC, V0P 1S0. (250) 974-8334**
Marina services:
Moorage: Transient moorage.
Store. Some provisions. Rental cabins.
Power, water. Extended dock.
Entertainment.
Animal and marine life. Picnic float.
Pancake breakfast included with moorage
(inset photograph above, top right).
Visit Kingcome native village nearby.
Adjacent facilities:
Water in good supply but use sparingly
during summer.
Daily scheduled flights to Port McNeil and
Campbell River.
*Look for the turquoise docks to locate the
marina in the bay.*

Kwatsi Bay

Doug Knierim and Anca Fraser
Simoom Sound, V0P 1S0   VHF 73
Cell (250) 949-1384 Chart 3515
Moorage. Floats. Wilderness facilities.
Peaceful and quiet. Anchorage nearby.
Water (plentiful, good).
Nearest fuel at Minstrel Island, Lagoon
Cove, Echo Bay or Sullivan Bay.
This is a small marina at remote Kwatsi
Bay off Tribune Channel. Cruise from
Echo Bay or from Minstrel Island via
beautiful scenery in Tribune Channel area.

Shawl Bay is a busy place during the summer season. Many regular boating friends and customers of the people who own and operate the cosy marina at the southern corner of the bay return each year or periodically to tie up at the spacious docks. These docks and the structures on them comprise Shawl Bay Marina operated until 1994/5 by the late Edna Brown and her sister Johanne along with Edna's son Gary. Brother Alf Didriksen ran a logging camp in the bay for many years and the family's hospitality is legendary among fishermen, loggers and pleasure boats alike. It is now being run by Lorne Brown his wife Shawn and aunt Jo. Lorne Browne reports possible moorage at **Jennis Bay.**

Inset, opposite: Photo shows pancake breakfast at Shawl Bay Marina—comes with the moorage compliments of the owners.

Aerial photo shows location of Brown's Marina at the far corner of Shawl Bay

On to Greenway Sound

Not for Navigation

In 1985 Tom and Ann Taylor opened their floating resort at nearby Greenway Sound. The bay where their lodge is located is large and the docks extensive totalling one half kilometer in total length. They are laid out in a wide square 'u' with a finger pointing into the square near the far corner where the facilities are located. These facilities set the floating resort apart from others in the area. The store is part of a restaurant with an airy, clean kitchen that serves up mouth-watering dinners, wholesome lunches—hamburgers, chili, sandwiches, salads, excellent clam chowder and ice cream in waffle cones— and splendid breakfasts.

The moorage is typically busy with large visiting yachts, especially from the USA, some of which remain during summer and have owners and their friends fly in for brief or extended visits. The resort literally gives arriving boats the red carpet treatment, from the smiling attendance of young dock helpers to the full length coverage of the floats with red indoor/ outdoor carpet. It is not unusual to see boat crews walking the docks for their daily exercise. Walk the length of the floats twice and you have walked a mile. Another walk that is being favoured nearby is an area ashore that has been designated as parkland by the Ministry of Forests. A dinghy float and ramp are being installed jointly by the Taylors and the Ministry Moorage customers or anyone who calls in the area will have access to the park. A path from the ramp leads to the lake a short distance up the mountainside.

The resort offers fly in service from points south including Seattle (Tacoma, Renton, Anacortes), Campbell River and Vancouver. The store carries produce including fresh and frozen foods, books, charts, tee-shirts and hats. In separate buildings attached to the adjacent docks are laundry and shower facilities as well as a hair and beauty salon and a book exchange library. The docks are serviced with water and 120/208 volt shore power. The resort stands by on channel 73 and is equipped with regular telephone service. It is possible to reach Alert Bay on VHF 86 for BC Tel radio operated service, and cellular is within close reach with the likelihood that it will provide full coverage at the dock soon.

Greenway Sound

Charts 3547, 3515   VHF Ch 73

Greenway Sound
Marine Resort

Tom and Ann Taylor
P.O. Box 759 Port McNeill, BC.
V0N 2R0 (Also at 19924 Aurora Ave.
North #54 Seattle Wa. 98133–off season)
Ph (360) 466-4751. 1 800-800-2080 Ch 73
(250) 949-2525 (Port Hardy)
Marina services:
Moorage: Large permanent marina with plenty of transient moorage at up to 2,700 feet of red carpeted dock. Good for power walking. Reserve dock space in peak season. **Garbage** disposal (for mooring customers).
Water at dock.
Power at docks: 50, 30, 15 amp. 120/208 shore power available.
Facilities:
Restaurant. (Reservations essential). All meals. Breakfast at 11 am (lunch), dinner

6:30-8 pm. Licenced. Food and beverages. Groceries. Baked goods and fresh produce, milk, frozen foods, ice, tackle, books, charts, film, and gifts. Video movie rentals.
Laundry, showers, washrooms.
Postal service and phone available.
Boat sitting.
Excellent fishing and prawning nearby.
Block and party ice.
Hair/beauty salon, barber shop.
Entertainment.
Take-out food–pizzas, baked goods, snacks.
Book exchange. Hiking trail and lake access.
Incredible sunsets and views. Animal and marine life.
Customer services:
Regular scheduled flights. Assisted travel arrangements. Tacoma, Renton,(Sea-Tac) Anacortes departures. *Greenway Sounder.*
Plus Kenmore Air and Air Rainbow.

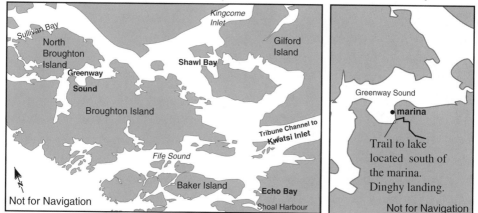

Not for Navigation

Greenway Sound

• marina

Trail to lake
located south of
the marina.
Dinghy landing.

Not for Navigation

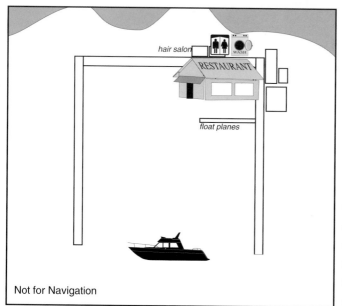

hair salon

RESTAURANT

float planes

Not for Navigation

The restaurant is on a float
alongside the dock. It also
houses a small store as well
as the marina office. An
aircraft float has been added
to the far dock since the
aerial photograph was taken.

*Opposite: An aerial view of
Greenway Sound Marine
Resort. Nearby, a hiking
trail leading to a lake has
been established. It is being
maintained by the resort in
conjunction with the BC
Forest Service that
provided the trail.
Right: Restaurant and
marina.*

Sullivan Bay

Sullivan Bay Marine Resort

Pat Finnerty and Lynn Whitehead
Sullivan Bay, BC. V0N 3H0
Phone: (250) 949-2550

Marina services:
Fuel: Gas, diesel, oil, ice, bait.
Mechanic and services at Vancouver Island towns and ports. Some repairs possible.
Moorage: Large permanent marina with plenty of transient moorage at up to 4,000 feet of dock. Reserve in peak season.
Water at dock. Plentiful.
Power at docks: 50, 30, 15 amp.
110 plus 220 shore power available.
Laundry, showers, washrooms.

Customer services:
Liquor store. Groceries. Post office. Fresh produce, dairy products, frozen foods, ice, tackle, and souvenirs. Video movie rentals.
Smokehouse.
Boat sitting.
Fishing and prawning in vicinity.

Chart 3547 VHF Ch 73 and 16

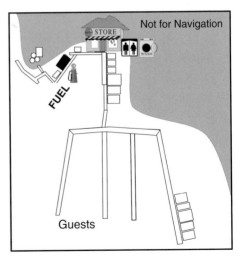

Entertainment.
Library, TV lounge. Novel building structures, street names on docks.
Adjacent facilities:
Regular scheduled flights. Private floating homes village.
Flying activity. This facility has long been a seaplane refuelling stop. It has an interesting aviation history.

Views of Sullivan Bay Marine Resort with its floating sidewalks, permanent moorage, client residences and itinerant visitors.

Sullivan Bay has long been known for its remote but popular location on the BC coast. It has served for many years as an air traveller's focal point and as a final destination or layover point for mariners.

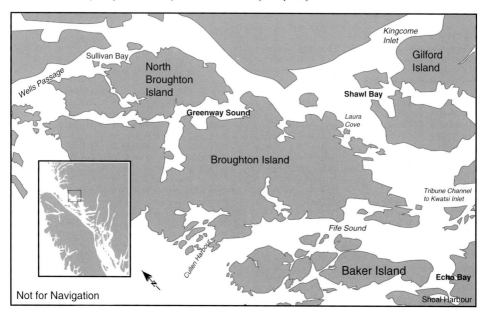

215

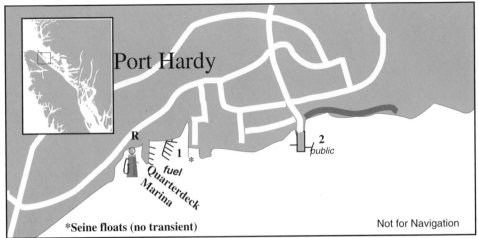

Port Hardy

R

1

fuel

Quarterdeck Marina

2
public

*Seine floats (no transient)

Not for Navigation

Quarterdeck Inn & Marina Resort

Box 910, 6555, Hardy Bay Road, Port Hardy, BC. V0N 2P0
Phone: (250) 949-6551 Fax 949-7777
Chart 3548, 3605 VHF 73
email: *info@quarterdeckresort.net*
Marina:
Moorage to 150 feet. 40 room Motor Inn.
Reservations required from June 15th on.
Power 15, 30, 50 amp. **Water.**
60 ton travel lift. Full repairs available.
Pressure wash. Marine store, Charts, ice, dry ice, propane,natural gas, fishing tackle.
Services:
Fuel. Showers, laundry. Launch ramp.
Flights, bus service, ferry nearby.
Pub restaurant ashore.
Taxi and limo service to airport,
BC Ferries and shopping.

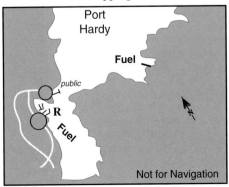

Port Hardy

Fuel

public

R

Fuel

Not for Navigation

1. Port Hardy (Public)

(Inside breakwater–Fisherman's Wharf)
Port Hardy Harbour Authority,
P.O. Box 68, Port Hardy, V0N 2P0.
Phone (250) 949-6332 Fax 949-7433
Chart   3548, 3605
Manager - Rick Davidge. Also Seagate.
• Float length 574 m
Launch ramp • Breakwater • Grid •
Garbage • Waste oil disposal • **Water** •
Lights • **Power**–15, 20 amp • Public phone
• **Washrooms** • Customs • **Fuel** nearby •
Near city restaurants, services, shops.
All services and facilities in Port Hardy
and local marina. Ferries nearby for
northern route.

2. Port Hardy (Public)

Transport Canada–Seagate Pier
Phone (250) 949-6332
Charts 3548, 3605
• Float length 250 m • **Garbage** • Waste
oil disposal • **Water** • **Power** • **Moorage**–
Commercial but some transient when
space available. Floats in place May to
September only. Excellent scuba diving
nearby. Enquire at dive facilities in town.
Nearby departure for Ferries north.
Coast Guard station adjacent.
Downtown Port Hardy location with
access to shops and services.

Hurst Island

God's Pocket

Bill Weeks & Annie Geschi
P.O. Box 471, Port Hardy,
BC. V0N 2P0
Phone: (250) 949-9221
Charts 3921, 3549, 3605 VHF 73

Marina:
Moorage: Limited, sheltered docks.
Washrooms, laundry. Some accommodation on availability.

Services:
Cabins, excellent meals. Scuba diving.
Kayaking.
Some provisions, gifts, arts and crafts.
Coffee shop, lunches, pies.

Entertainment:
Walking trails on island. Hiking.

Bull Harbour

Hope Island
Fisheries & Oceans dock
Refer to charts 3921, 3549
Float length 35 m
Anchor in bay. Use dinghy.

Not for Navigation

God's Pocket
Bull Harbour
Goletas Channel
Queen
Charlotte
Strait
Vancouver
Hardy
Bay
Port Hardy
Island

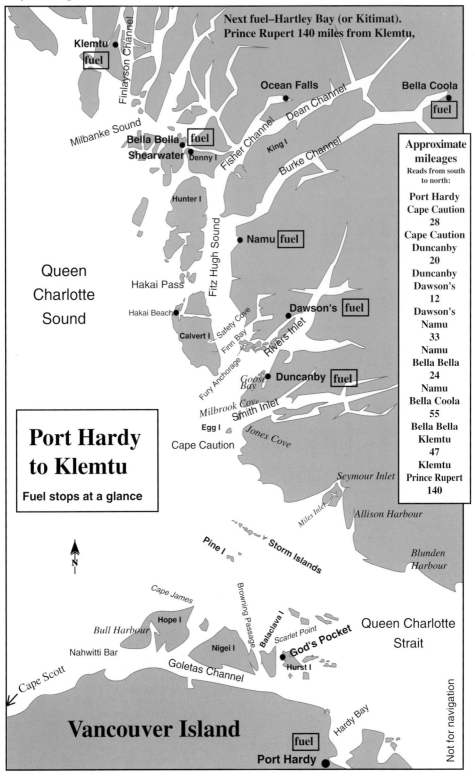

Next fuel–Hartley Bay (or Kitimat).
Prince Rupert 140 miles from Klemtu,

Klemtu •
fuel

Finlayson Channel

Ocean Falls •

Bella Coola •
fuel

Dean Channel

Milbanke Sound

Bella Bella • fuel
Shearwater
Denny I

Fisher Channel

King I

Burke Channel

Hunter I

Fitz Hugh Sound

Namu • fuel

Queen
Charlotte
Sound

Hakai Pass

Hakai Beach •

Calvert I

Safety Cove

Finn Bay

Dawson's • fuel

Rivers Inlet

Fury Anchorage

Goose Bay

Duncanby • fuel

Milbrook Cove

Smith Inlet

Egg I •

Jones Cove

Cape Caution

Seymour Inlet

**Approximate
mileages**
Reads from south
to north:

**Port Hardy
Cape Caution
28
Cape Caution
Duncanby
20
Duncanby
Dawson's
12
Dawson's
Namu
33
Namu
Bella Bella
24
Namu
Bella Coola
55
Bella Bella
Klemtu
47
Klemtu
Prince Rupert
140**

Port Hardy
to Klemtu

Fuel stops at a glance

Miles Inlet

Allison Harbour

Blunden
Harbour

N

Pine I •

Storm Islands

Cape James

Browning Passage

Balaclava I

Scarlet Point

God's Pocket

Queen Charlotte
Strait

Hope I

Bull Harbour

Nigei I

Nahwitti Bar

Goletas Channel

Hurst I

Cape Scott

Hardy Bay

Not for navigation

Vancouver Island

fuel

Port Hardy •

Section 6

The North Coast

Beyond Cape Caution

To reach Rivers Inlet from Port Hardy it is necessary to round Cape Caution and pass the entrance to Smith Inlet. There are no facilities between God's Pocket just out of Port Hardy, and Rivers Inlet. If weather is a deterrent temporary anchorage is possible off Hurst Island or moorage at God's Pocket dock if space is available. Bull Harbour, slightly out of the way for a passage around Cape Caution is a good anchorage. It is shallow off Cape Caution and many yachtsmen round the Cape about five miles off. Local mariners cut close to the Cape and take passage behind the islands, rocks and islets off Smith Inlet to slide around into Rivers Inlet off Goose Bay. Choose to round Cape Caution in gentle wind and sea conditions and be wary of fog. On the passage around Cape Caution one can find temporary and some good protected overnight anchorages at places such as Blunden Harbour, Allison Harbour, Miles Inlet, Seymour Inlet, Jones Cove and Milbrook Cove. Please refer to **Anchorages and Marine Parks**.

The first fuel stop is at Goose Bay–Duncanby Landing or farther up Rivers Inlet at Dawson's Landing. Some mariners travel past Rivers Inlet, stopping, if necessary for overnight anchorage, at Safety Cove on Calvert Island, or at Fury Anchorage at the entrance to Rivers Inlet.

Located at Goose Bay, Rivers Inlet.

Rivers Inlet

Duncanby Store & Marina

Ken Gillis
Rivers Inlet P.O. BC. V0N 1M0.
Phone: (250) 949-2101
Chart 3934 VHF 6
Marina services:
Moorage. Water, power–15 amp.
Fuel: gas diesel, propane.
Facilities: Pub, food.
Showers, laundry, washrooms.

Store: charts, books, tackle, bait, fishing licences, groceries. Ice subject to availability. Liquor store. Accommodations.

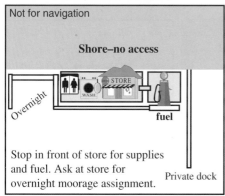

Not for navigation

Shore–no access

STORE
WASH.
Overnight
fuel

Stop in front of store for supplies
and fuel. Ask at store for
overnight moorage assignment.

Private dock

Tied up to the fuel and store dock at Dawson's Landing. Inside the store there is always a warm welcome.
Opposite page: The dock at Hakai Pass Resort looking down Pruth Harbour.

Dawson's Landing
and General Store

Robert and Nola Bachen
Dawson's Landing, BC. V0N 1M0
Phone/Fax 949-2111
Autotel 250-949-2111
Chart 3934, 3932 VHF 6, 85
Marina services: Moorage. Water.
Fuel: gas, diesel, oils.
Customer Services: Showers, laundry.
General store: tackle, fishing licences, bait,

Approximate milages
Cape Caution to Duncanby
20 miles
Duncanby to Dawson's
12 miles
Dawson's to Namu
33 miles

groceries, liquor agency.
Post office, gifts, toys, souvenirs,
books, charts, supplies for marine
maintenance and repairs.

Note: No power at docks.
Excellent anchorages in nearby islands.

Fitzhugh Sound

Finn Bay Retreat

Pete and Rene Darwin
Finn Bay
General Delivery, Dawson's Landing
BC. V0N 1M0 VHF 06
Chart 3934
Moorage: Overnight. 270' dock.
New marina in 1999, on the north side of
Penrose Island. Down Darby Channel from
Dawson's Landing. Limited facilities.

Hakai Beach Resort

Dock manager
Pruth Harbour, Calvert Island
P.O. Box 3819, Smithers, BC. V0J 2N0
Phone (250) 847-9300
Charts 3784, 3727.
Anchor in bay. This is not a public dock
or marina. Shore access–tie up small
dinghies under ramp inside marina.

Resort offers restaurant and
accommodations when
available. Store–gifts, film,
snacks, cappuccino. Walk to
white, sandy beach on open
Pacific.
Anchorage–Pruth Bay.
Boats at anchor receive
welcome flyer.
Guided fishing excursions
available.

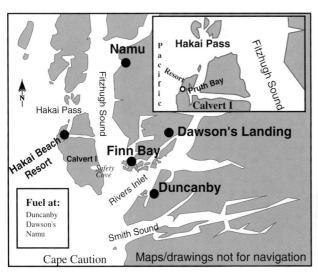

Namu to
Bella Coola
55 miles
Bella Bella to
Ocean Falls
30 miles
Bella Bella
to Klemtu
47 miles

Namu

Caution: Beware of unmarked rocks in the bay. See chart 3785 for Loo Rock.

Namu

Bob Gardiner
Namu, BC. V0N 1M0
(604) 857-5455   VHF 6
Charts 3785, 3727, 3784
Marina services:
Moorage. No power at docks.
Water at main dock.
Fuel dock nearby: gas, diesel, oils.
Customer services: (Subject to changes)
Historically the store offered tackle, fishing licences, bait, ice, groceries, post office, gifts, charts, books and marine supplies. There was also a ways, and marine repairs were available. Constant changes are in place. Expect only what

you find on arrival. Check our website for updates at *www.marineguides.com.*
This is a popular area for kayaking.
Activities: Hiking trails. Trout fishing in Namu Lake. This stop is an interesting historic and archaeological site. Fuel and supplies availability (subject to confirmation, please phone to verify).

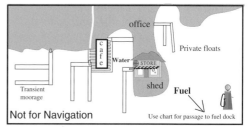

Not for Navigation

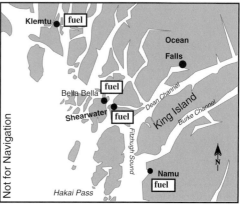

Shearwater

Shearwater Marine

Al Tite
P.O. Box 68, Shearwater,
Bella Bella, BC. V0T 1B0
Phone: (250) 957-2305 Fax 957-2422
Vancouver (604) 270-6204 Fax 270-4974
Charts 3720, 3785, 3787
Web: *www.shearwater.ca*
Marina services: Fuel. Gas, Diesel.
Marine service. Avgas. Lubricants.
Moorage. 2000 feet of docks (1,000 of
concrete dock) **Water, Power** 15, 30, 50
amps. **Laundry, showers, washrooms.**
Propane. Public phones. 100 ton haul outs.
Boat and engine repairs. 70 tonne travel
lift. Boat launch.

The restaurant at Shearwater, since photo above.

Customer services:
Electronics shop. Store: tackle, fishing
licences, bait, groceries, gifts. Charts,
marine supplies. Pub. Off-sales.
Restaurant. (250) 957-2366
40 room hotel. 3,000 foot airstrip. Yacht
charters. Fishing charters, boat rentals.
Scuba air station. Daily plane service
nearby. B.C. Ferry terminal.

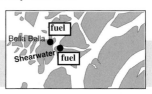

Bella Bella

Bella Bella

Bella Bella, BC. V0T 1B0
Campbell Island
(250) 957-2440
Chart 3720, 3785, 3787
Marina:
Fuel: gas, diesel, stove oil, lubricants.

Customer services:
Moorage. Water, Store. Public phones,
showers, pub, coffee shop. BC ferry stops
weekly. RCMP station. Hospital. Liquor.
Repairs, haul out facility. Short distance to
Shearwater Marine Group. Bella Bella is a
native village.

Ocean Falls

Namu to
Bella Coola
55 miles

Namu to
Bella Bella
24 miles

Bella Bella to
Ocean Falls
30 miles

Bella Bella to
Klemtu
47 miles

Ocean Falls to
Bella Coola
50 miles

Namu to Kitimat
181 miles

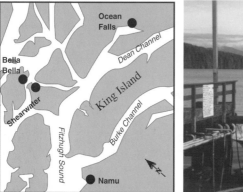

Ocean Falls

Dean Channel

Bella Bella

Shearwater

King Island

Burke Channel

Fitzhugh Sound

Namu

Docks at Bella Bella

Ocean Falls

Ocean Falls

Ocean Falls

Herb Carpenter, Greg Ingram
(Ocean Falls Yacht Club)
Ocean Falls, BC. V0T 1P0
Chart 3781, 3720, 3729.

Marina:
Moorage. Power 20 amps. **Water,** Fish
cleaning station. Floating fish and chips
restaurant on docks. Delivery service
groceries to your boat. (250) 289-3333.
Also fishing tackle, licences, bait, supplies. Phone at head of dock. Post office
and town administration offices in old
courthouse.
Marine ways, repairs available. Power-
boats to about 45 feet.
No cellular reception.
Walking old roads and roadway to lake.
Old powerhouse and mill barricaded for
safety.

Not for navigation

Ocean Falls docks

Moorage on outside of floats
okay–some wind conditions may
cause minor discomfort

Breakwater

Entrance to inner moorage

Fish &
chips

Public
phone

Fuel at:
Namu
Bella Coola
Bella Bella
Klemtu

Float plane dock

road

Marine ways

BC Ferries slip

Admin offices

Old hotel

*Top and bottom opposite page: Ocean Falls
docks. Above: An old house at Ocean Falls.
Below: The floats include a small fish and chips/
restaurant which is open several days a week.*

Bella Coola main street.

Bella Coola

Bella Coola

Kevin O'Neill
Bella Coola, BC.
V0T 1B0
Charts 3730, 3729

Marina:
Fuel, (closed week-ends).
gas, diesel. **Power** 20
amps. **Water.** Garbage
disposal. On site **showers,**
washrooms, public
phones. One and a half miles to uptown
laundry, showers, washrooms.
Stores, restaurants, co-op, museum,
motels, taxi, car rentals. Tackle, fishing
licences, bait, groceries, liquor, gifts.
Charts, marine supplies.
Cedar Inn Restaurant. Kopas Store.
No food services at marina.
Rafting necessary at pleasure boat moorage near shore on east side of marina.
No VHF radio reception. Wharfinger
available 9-11am only (weekdays).

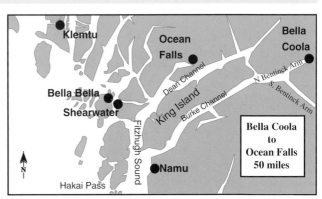

Bella Coola
to
Ocean Falls
50 miles

If you ask the townsfolk at Bella Coola
where their favourite hot springs is located,
they may tell you. Just down North
Bentinck Arm to South Bentinck Arm and
turn south. Several miles down the arm just
beyond Bensins Island and on the opposite
shore is Talheo hot springs at the mouth of
Hotsprings Creek. Anchor off and row
ashore for a hot soak in the sulphur waters
of this delightful pool. It has been improved
by the local people of Bella Coola so please
respect it and leave it clean.

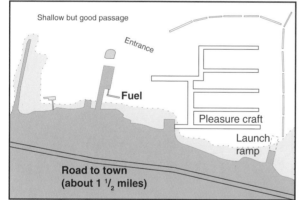

Shallow but good passage

Entrance

Fuel

Pleasure craft

Launch ramp

Road to town (about 1 ¹/₂ miles)

fuel dock

Above, centre and top: Views of Bella Coola harbour and dock plan.

Bella Coola may be reached overland but it is far easier by water. And the town is worth a visit. The walk into town from the harbour is pleasant, about one and a half miles, with magnificent views over the delta and the high adjacent mountains. History was made in this area with the arrival of Alexander McKenzie in July, 1793 when he completed the first recorded crossing of North America–even before Lewis and Clark, by some 13 years. He was not far behind Captain Vancouver who had passed through the area only seven weeks previously.

In Bella Coola visit the museum where the curator may have some surprise information in store for you. She is Rene, daughter of Cliff Kopas, early settler and author of the book *Bella Coola* as well as founder of Kopas General Store.

In summer months the town is busy with festivities ranging from an indigenous canoe festival, to a rodeo, theatre, music festival and a fall fair and parade.

227

Klemtu

Hartley Bay

Klemtu

Klemtu

Klemtu Marine Station

Steve Robinson
Klemtu, BC. V0T 1L0
Phone (250) 839-1255
Charts 3711, 3734, 3902 (3728 enroute)
CB   Call sign 44
Marina:
Fuel: gas, diesel, stove oil. Ice. **Water.**
Store at fuel dock open 6 days a week:

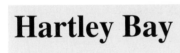

Hartley Bay

Hartley Bay (Public)
Ed Robinson
Hartley Bay, BC. V0T 1L0
BC Tel 60.   Chart 3711, 3742
Phone (250) 841-2500
Marina: Moorage at public docks behind breakwater.
Fuel. Power 20 amps**. Water**. Groceries. Post office. General store. Emergency helipad. Nearby mooring buoys in Stewart Channel. Smaller gas boats top up at Hartley Bay during the 150 mile trip from Klemtu to Prince Rupert.

> **Klemtu is the last significant stop before Prince Rupert or Kitimat.**
> Butedale has some fuel (reported summer 1998) but don't rely on it as a stop unless you check first.
> Fuel at Hartley Bay–call to confirm.
> **Distance Klemtu to Prince Rupert 150 miles.**

Mon–Sat 8.30 to 12 noon. 1–5pm. Coffee shop. Public phone.
Moorage nearby at Klemtu public dock.
Up town store: Propane. Groceries—open 9am to 12 noon. 1-5pm. 6.30-10pm.

Klemtu to Hartley Bay 65 miles

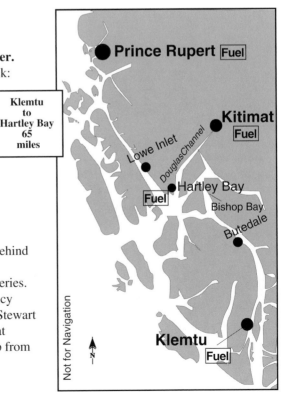

Not for Navigation

228

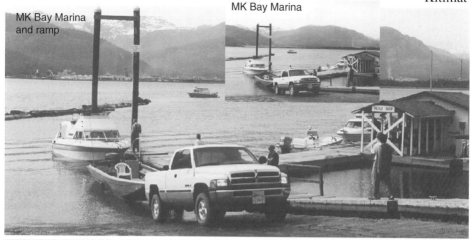

MK Bay Marina and ramp

MK Bay Marina

Kitimat

M.K. Bay Marina

Brenda Bourzane, Richard Small
P.O. Box 220, Kitimat, BC. V2C 2G7.
Phone (250) 632-6401
Fax: (250) 632-6889 VHF 68
Web: www.mkbaymarina.com **email:** *mkbay@sno.net*
Chart 3743, 3736   Launch ramp
Marina: Fuel: **gas**, diesel, oils. Water.
Moorage: Power 15, 20, 30 amp. **Laundry, showers, washrooms.** Repairs.
Haulouts to 25 tons. Public phone. Fishing licences, tackle, bait. Campground adjacent. Taxi to Stores–11 kilometers to town. Liquor, post office, hospital.

Moon Bay Marina

Moon Bay Marina

Peter Jensen
P.O. Box 196, Kitimat, BC. V8C 2G7
Phone (250) 632-4655. Monitors Channel 16–Call vessel Moon Bay.
Fuel. Water. Power can be made available. Marine repairs and service. Rental fishing boats. Owner Don Pearson operates a tug with supplies and some **fuel** in Douglas Channel/Bishop Bay area in summer. The tug is a base station for small boats wanting to join group excursions: it offers showers and other amenities at sea.

MK Bay Marina

Left: photo shows the docks at Hartley Bay. Above, left: MK Bay Marina, Kitimat. Above, right, Moon Bay Marina. Top: at the MK Bay launch ramp. Opposite top, right: the church at Hartley Bay. Top left, opposite page: the fuel dock at Klemtu.

Prince Rupert

Prince Rupert, BC is a fishing town. Its docks in season are brimming with commercial vessels rafted as many as six deep at the town's two major public docks. Moorage overnight for pleasure craft is best at the Prince Rupert Yacht Club where the spaces are tight and subject to being available only if members are away temporarily. It is necessary to call ahead to reserve space, although frequently boats arriving early in the day will be allocated a slip immediately or later in the day.

Directly above the marina there are friendly services for the transient mariner, from laundry and showers to nearby restaurants, pubs, shopping and marine repairs. Arts and craft of local people can be found in stores up town. A good hotel with restaurant and pub sit atop the cliff overlooking the harbour.

Fuel is available at a number of fuel docks along the waterfront. Prince Rupert is the final major stop before continuing to Alaska. Mariners learn while talking to other yachtsmen during stops along the British Columbia coast that entering Alaska may not always be straight forward. Wind can prevent vessels, especially slow cruising yachts, from making the Rupert to Ketchikan run all in one stretch. And the reason

most skippers plan it in one step is the belief that one has to do so as a customs clearing requirement. What one learns is that it is possible to stop en route, either on the Canadian side at Dundas Island or on the Alaskan side several miles up channel from Cape Fox at Foggy Bay. If there is any doubt whatever that you can make the run in one leg, it is best to call Alaska customs and ask for permission to stop at a specific place en route. Remember also that Alaska, unlike BC, remains on Standard Time all year.

Once in Ketchikan there is much to do and see, from a visit to the Totem Heritage Center to walking the old town with its infamous Creek Street, once the place of bawdy houses and frontier life at its most colourful.

It's a tourist town with several large cruise ships at a time lining the docks right alongside the downtown main streets. And it's a town which will prompt you to stay a while, test the delights of fine cuisine and then go on deeper into the Alaskan South West or Panhandle, whichever you prefer to call it. There are numerous books and guides on cruising Alaska. Once in the State you will find easy access to lots of cruising options with the easy availability of fuel and services along the way.

The Prince Rupert Yacht Club. It is located in the distance on the east shore of the harbour in the photo on the opposite page.

Prince Rupert Yacht Club

121 George Hills Way
Prince Rupert, BC. V8J 1A3
Phone (250) 624-4317
Chart 3964, 3957, 3958, 3955 VHF 72

Marina services:
Moorage. Power 15 & 20 amps. **Water.**
Shower, ice, bait, tidal grid, power wash available. No reciprocal club moorage. All visitors pay moorage fee towards upkeep.
Adjacent facilities:
 Fuel, Esso (628-6277), Petro Canada (624-4106), Chevron (624-3316)–next to PRYC–Gas, diesel, stove oil, water, **showers, laundry,** ice. Snacks.
Up town Prince Rupert is five minutes walk. Also restaurants (Smiles, Breakers Pub, Crest Hotel).

Anchorages at Pilsbury Cove and Tuck Inlet.
Public docks nearby–busy during fishing season: Rafting. Fishing openings usually begin 6pm Sundays.

Note: Five miles an hour speed limit strictly enforced in Prince Rupert Harbour. Boats are monitored by radar and any one caught exceeding the limit will be fined $300 by ticket in the mail.

Prince Rupert Public docks:

Rushbrooke Harbour
Robert Small
P.O. Box 1026, Prince Rupert,
BC. V8J 4B7. Chart 3958 VHF 10
Phone (250) 624-9400
Marina services:
Large marina with about 400 slips.
Power 15 amps. **Water,** portable toilet, public phone, free launch ramp adjacent. Garbage disposal. 20 minutes walk into town.

Cow Bay
Robert Small
P.O. Box 1026, Prince Rupert,
BC. V8J 4B7. Chart 3958 VHF 10
Phone (250) 624-9400
(minimal space for brief stops)

Fairview Harbour
Robert Small
P.O. Box 1026, Prince Rupert,
BC. V8J 4B7. VHF 10 Chart 3958
Phone (250) 627-3127
Marina Services: Fishing harbour with limited moorage when available.

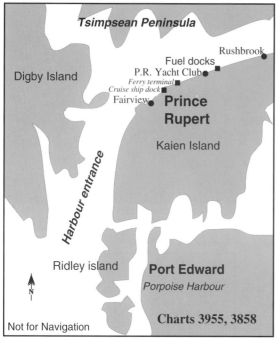

Check in with the Prince Rupert Yacht Club.
Call on channel 72 for moorage reservations.

Prince Rupert
alternative moorage
Porpoise Harbour Marina
Rick Hill
email: *peharbor@citytel.net*
P.O. Box 1820, Port Edward, BC. V0V 1G0
Phone (250) 628-3211
Charts 3955, 3958 VHF 79A

Marina services: Fishing harbour–public moorage. **Fuel. Power** 20 amps. **Water, laundry, washrooms,** public phone. Travel lift.
Adjacent facilities: Cab service to Prince Rupert–Skeena Taxi 624-2185. Convenience store. North Pacific Museum.

The Queen Charlottes
Charts 3890,3894

For those crossing to the Queen Charlottes there are a few marinas available for transient moorage. There is a large marina at Sandspit and several public marinas in other parts of the islands as listed below and on the following page.

Sandspit Harbour Marina
Brenda McIntosh
email:*harbour@sandspitqci.com*
www.sandspitqci.com/harbour
P.O. Box 477, Sandspit, BC. V0T 1T0
Phone (250) 637-5700 fax 637-5369
Chart 3890, 3894 VHF 72A
Marina services: Moorage up to 100'. Power. Water, **showers, washrooms,** public phone. Launch ramp.
Adjacent facilities: Car rentals, shops and city services and amenities.

232

The Queen Charlottes

QC Small Craft Harbour

Bob Olson
P.O. Box 68, Queen
Charlotte V0T 1S0
BC. V0V 1G0
Phone (250) 559-4650
Charts 3890,3894
Marina services: Public
dock moorage
Water, garbage, **power,**

Port Clements Small Craft Harbour

Chris Marrs
P.O. Box 198, Port
Clements V0T 1R0 BC.
Phone (250) 557-4295
fax (250) 557-4574
email: *portclem@qcislands.net*
Chart 3893
*caution: shallow at low
tide.*

Delkatla Slough

Dale Otto
P.O. Box 35, Masset, BC
V0T 1M0
Phone (250) 626-5487
fax 626-5193
Charts 3892,3895
VHF 06
Marina services: Fuel.
Power 20, 30 amp. Water.
Tidal grid.
Shower, laundry. Shops

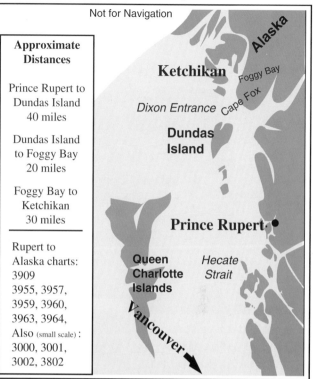

Not for Navigation

Approximate Distances

Prince Rupert to
Dundas Island
40 miles

Dundas Island
to Foggy Bay
20 miles

Foggy Bay to
Ketchikan
30 miles

Rupert to
Alaska charts:
3909
3955, 3957,
3959, 3960,
3963, 3964,
Also (small scale) :
3000, 3001,
3002, 3802

Next stop—Alaska:

If you are proceeding to Alaska, your fist stop will be Ketchikan, probably via a short stop at Foggy Bay. This protected bay is a short distance beyond Cape Fox which you pass as you venture across Dixon Entrance into Alaskan waters. If you are planning to stop in American territory before reaching Ketchikan, official customs port of entry, you must obtain permission from customs in Ketchikan first. This can be done by calling (907) 225-2254 and advising customs that you will need to stop at Foggy Bay. Ask for permission to do so rather than telling the customs officer that you are going to stop there. And if the weather permits a straight, uninterrupted run into Ketchikan simply dock at a convenient slip and call customs. They may ask you to walk up town to their offices to clear. Note: It is important to read the customs document you are issued, as it instructs you to notify customs at certain other Alaska points as you proceed farther along the coast. This is the case, even though you have cleared at Ketchikan (or elsewhere in Alaska). Customs hours are office hours, week-days only. Special arrangements are required for clearing at weekends.

A safe harbour to spend time waiting for suitable wind and sea conditions to cross Dixon Entrance is at Goose Bay on the north end of Dundas Island. If you set out from Prince Rupert in calm seas but the wind picks up and dictates a rough passage beyond Dundas stop a while and do some fishing, reading and relaxing. Then travel when conditions improve. At Dundas you are about 20 miles from Foggy Bay or about 70 from Ketchikan. Rupert to Ketchikan is 90 miles.

Above: The docks at Moon Bay Marina in Kitimat looking up Kitimat Inlet towards the town. This marina has limited amenities but is popular among visitors and permanent tenants. It is located on the southwest side of the inlet.. Excellent facilities at MK Marina.

Inset: Infamous Creek Street, Ketchikan. Above: City docks in downtown Ketchikan. First stop en route to Alaska cruising destinations.

South Bound
on the West Coast of
Vancouver Island

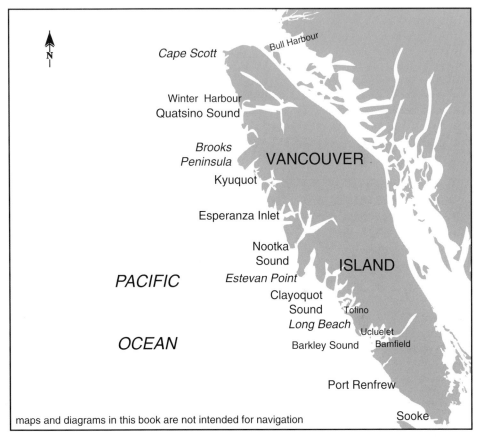

The west coast of Vancouver Island enjoys a short summer season of recreational boating. All year around, however, there is maritime activity catered to by a small number of marine facilities. These are scattered among the inlets and coves that indent the rugged coast and serve as a home away from home to those out working the coast. They serve also as havens of safety and replenishment for those seeking to extend their pleasure boating experiences in British Columbia. It is possible to travel along the Pacific west coast of Vancouver Island yet remain in sheltered waters a good deal of the time. The open coast is broken up by numerous islands, large and small, forming inlets and protected waterways. One can travel along these waterways, poking out into the open Pacific during calm conditions and moving along to the next inlet which in some cases is no more than about 25 miles distant. The longest stretches of open water are between Juan de Fuca Strait and Barkley Sound in the south and between Quatsino Sound and Bull Harbour to the north.

Winter Harbour

Winter Harbour

Fisheries & Oceans dock
Charts 3686, 3679
Manager • Float length 171 metres •
96 m wharf • Garbage disposal • Derrick • Water •
Plus: Showers, (Laundry for commercial boats—
pleasure boat owners should ask permission).
Public phone ashore. General store nearby.

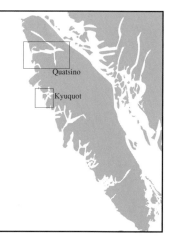

The photograph above was taken some years ago at Winter Harbour.

Wildlife presence and the "main road" walkway have not changed.

BC Packers
Winter Harbour, BC.
Services:
Fuel–gas, diesel.

Quatsino

Transport Canada dock
Charts 3681, 3679
Manager • Float length
31 metres •
30 m wharf • Aircraft
float • Sheds

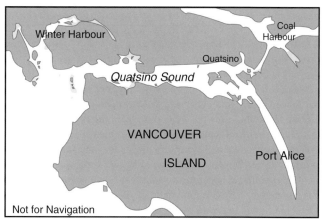

Not for Navigation

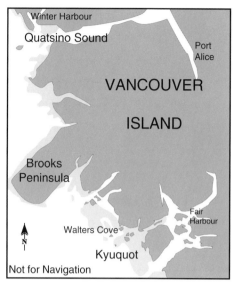

Coal Harbour
Anchor Petroleum
VHF 10
Charts 3681, 3679 VHF 10
Marina services:
Moorage–no moorage. **Fuel** dock for commercial trade but pleasure craft are welcome.

Coal Harbour.
Transport Canada dock
Charts 3681, 3617
Float length 94 metres • Garbage/waste oil disposal • Derrick • Lights • Power •

Quatsino Boatyards and Marina
Chris and Debbie Bradley
General Delivery, Quatsino BC.
V0N 2V0
Phone (250) 949-6651
Charts 3681, 3679 VHF 10
Marina services:
Moorage–summer transient available at times. **Power** 110/220.
Boatyard haulouts and repairs.
Nearby:
Walk the roads around Quatsino. The Narrows just beyond this point leads on to Coal Harbour, an historic whaling station. Down Neroutsos Inlet you will find Port Alice, where the only possibility of a casual stop is at the yacht club.

Port Alice
Yacht Club
Charts 3681, 3679
Temporary mooring (unofficial) at club docks. It's a pleasant cruise down the inlet but if it is windy there is not much protection. The marina, which is remote from the nearby settlement, provides shelter.

Kyuquot

Walters Cove
Susan Bostrom
P.O. Kyuquot, BC.
Chart 3651, 3682, 3683, 3623
Marina services:
Moorage–public dock. Post office and store at head of dock. Cafe adjacent to post office.

Kyuquot (Houpsitas)
Fisheries & Oceans dock
Charts 3651, 3682, 3683, 3623
Float length 82 m •

Kyuquot Transport Canada dock
Charts 3651, 3682, 3683
Float length 103 metres •
30 m wharf • Derrick • Sheds

Fair Harbour
Transport Canada dock
Charts 3682, 3623
Manager • Float length 28 metres • 24 m wharf • Derrick • Sheds
Launch Ramp adjacent.

Tahsis

Westview Marina

Mike and Cathy Daynes
P.O. Box 481, Tahsis, BC. V0P 1X0
Phone (250) 934-7622 1-800-992-3262
Fax: 934-6445. Chart 3676 VHF 73, 06
Moorage–year round. Summer transient
available. Reservations recommended.
Fuel-gas, diesel. **Power** 15, 30 amp.
Water. Store–groceries. Licenced restaurant. Patio. **Laundry, showers.** Quarter
mile to Tahsis for **launch ramp**, pool,
restaurants, supermarket, RCMP,
Info Centre and Museum.
Beware of logs in harbour as you approach
Tahsis and the marina.

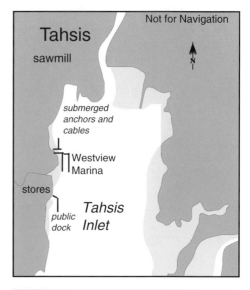

Tahsis

Transport Canada dock
Charts 3676, 3604
Manager • Float length 30 metres •
42 m wharf • Garbage disposal •
Derrick • Lights • Sheds • Public
phone ashore • General store •
liquor agency • Post Office • shops
and accommodations nearby.

Esperanza

Box 398, Tahsis, BC. V0P 1X0
Phone (250) 949-6651
Chart 3676, 3604 VHF 06, 17

Transport Canada (Hospital Floats)
Manager • Float length 42 metres •
Water • Lights • **Moorage**–summer
transient space available.

Esperanza Public dock/fuel dock.
Float length 15 m • Wharf 29 m •
Derrick • Lights. **Fuel–**gas, diesel,
stove oil, naptha, kerosene • **Water.**
Mini store • Showers. Laundry.
Phone ashore (emergency use only).
Food available at Nootka Mission camp.

Zeballos

Weston Enterprises

Tom and Alice Weston
Box 100, Zeballos, BC. V0P 2A0
Phone (250) 761-4201
Fax (250) 761-4618
Chart 3676, 3664 VHF 68
Fuel gas, diesel, propane, ice.
Seaplane landing and fuel dock
Moorage at nearby public docks.
Water, garbage drop, public phone.
Nearby: Village recreational dock, general
store, liquor agency, museum, information
centre, clinic laundromats, restaurants,
post office. washrooms, showers.

Zeballos Small Craft Harbour Authority Dock

A. Coburn
P.O. Box 99, Zeballos, BC. V0P 2A0
Phone/fax (250) 761-4333
Chart 3676, 3604. VHF 68
Float length 191 metres •
96 m wharf • Garbage/oil disposal •
Water • Lights • **Power** 15 amp. Fuel
adjacent (at Weston) Launch ramp—all
tides. Available free. Nearby–as above.

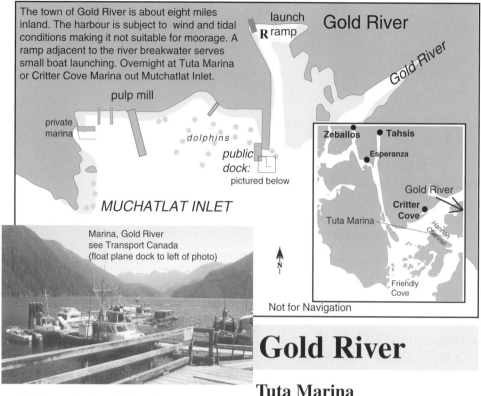

The town of Gold River is about eight miles inland. The harbour is subject to wind and tidal conditions making it not suitable for moorage. A ramp adjacent to the river breakwater serves small boat launching. Overnight at Tuta Marina or Critter Cove Marina out Mutchatlat Inlet.

launch
R ramp

Gold River

Gold River

pulp mill

private marina

dolphins

public dock:
pictured below

MUCHATLAT INLET

Zeballos • Tahsis
Esperanza
Gold River
Critter Cove
Tuta Marina
Hannah Channel
Friendly Cove

Not for Navigation

Marina, Gold River
see Transport Canada
(float plane dock to left of photo)

N

Gold River

Critter Cove Marina

Cameron and Dean Forbes
**Box 1118, Gold River,
BC. V0P 1G0
Phone (250) 283-7364 (604) 886-7667
Chart 3675, 3603 VHF 07
Moorage** on 1000 feet of dock space as available in summer May 16 to September 15. Call for reservations. Anchoring nearby. Rental cabins and suites available.
Fuel–gas. Store, licences, bait.
Coffee House. Known for their chowder and home-made pies.
Showers, washrooms, water.
Launch ramp at Gold River.

Tuta Marina

Larry and Shirley Andrews
**Box 765, Gold River, BC. V0P 1G0
Phone (250) 283-7550
Chart 3675** Located in Hanna Channel, Nootka Sound. Open summer only Victoria Day to Labour Day.
Fuel–gas, oil. Boat launch.
Store, licences, bait.
Showers, laundry.

Gold River

Transport Canada dock
Charts 3675, 3603
Manager • Float length 47 metres •
wharf • Aircraft float • Garbage disposal • Water •
Lights • Power • Telephone • Sheds • **Launch Ramp**

Fourth St. Docks at Tofino

Not for Navigation

Hot Springs Cove

Ahousat

Meares Island

Clayoquot Sound

Tofino

Hot Springs Cove

public dock
Chart 3674, 3603
VHF 10   Marine Park

Photograph above: Fourth Street public dock at Tofino. Fuel is available at Method Marine (opposite). The service station, part of the marina complex, is a major fuel stop on the west coast.

Below: Weigh West Resort docks. This is a lodge that attracts longer term small boats. If there is space overnight moorage is provided. Larger boats check out the long floats on the outside. There is an adjacent restaurant and other facilities.

Ahousat Matilda Inlet

Marktosis–Fisheries & Oceans
Hugh Clarke
Charts 3673, 3674, 3603
Float length 232 metres • 21 m wharf •
Derrick • Lights • Sheds • Public phone.
General store. Cafe. Post Office. **Fuel.**
Marine Ways. **Water.** Nearby is the
Gibson Marine Park and Hot Springs.
See **Anchorages and Marine Parks.**

Armitage Point dock at Tofino

Tofino

Method Marine Supply

Steve Bernard
Box 219, 380 Main Street, Tofino. BC, V0R 2Z0.
Phone (250) 725-3251 Fax 725-2111
VHF 06 *(formerly Ocean West)*
Charts 3685, 3673, 3603.
Moorage–summer transient at adjacent marina docks. Reservations recommended in summer. **Power** 20 amp. **Fuel**: gas, diesel, stove oil. **Water**, ice, propane, **laundry, showers, toilets.**
Chandlery, marine service station–parts and accessories. Tackle shop–snacks, coffee. Scuba air fills. Charts, bait.
Nearby
Launch ramp, accommodations, art gallery, restaurant, liquor, bakery, super-market and other stores.

Weigh West Marine Resort

Box 69, 385 Campbell St, Tofino.
Phone (250) 725-3277

Guest moorage, charters, marina and pub.

Tofino
Fourth Street, Tofino
Fisheries & Oceans dock
Charts 3685, 3673, 3603
Manager • Float length 444 metres •
15 m wharf • Breakwater • Grid •
Garbage/oil disposal • Derrick • Water •
Lights • Power • Sheds • **Launch ramp.**
Public phone ashore. General stores, liquor agency, Post Office, shops, laundry and accommodations nearby.

Armitage Point, Tofino
Fisheries & Oceans dock
Charts 3685, 3673, 3603
Manager • Float length 121 metres •
30 m wharf • Garbage disposal •
Derrick • Lights. Public phone ashore. General stores, liquor agency, Post Office, shops, laundry and accommodations in town, nearby.

Above: Method Marine docks. Note the native village of Opitsat across the harbour.
Inset: Armitage Point public docks.

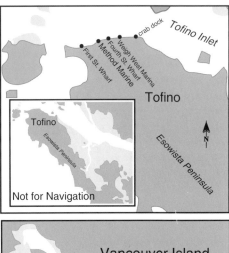

Ucluelet Boat Harbour docks–the entrance from shore in photo at top, entrance passage from the inlet in the photo above.

Diagrams show–Tofino on the Esowista Peninsula. Note the shallows throughout the harbour. Use a large scale chart for safe navigation. Ucluelet and Ucluth Peninsula. Note approximate location of primary marinas. Barkley Sound with Ucluelet and Bamfield locations.

Ucluelet

Island West Resort

P.O. Box 32 Ucluelet, BC. V0R 3A0
Phone (250) 726-7515 Fax 726-4414
Chart 3646, 3671, 3603 VHF 69
email: *fish@islandwestresort.com*
Web: *www.islandwest.com*
Marina services:
Moorage–summer transient available at
times. **Power** 15 amp.
Launch ramp. Water, ice, tackle shop,
laundry, showers, toilets. Chandlery.
Deli. Accommodations (resort), RV park.
Fishing gear and charters.
Nearby: Fuel: gas, diesel, stove oil.
Restaurant, pub, bakery and other stores.

Ucluelet Public Docks

Boat Harbour– (inner harbour)
Box 910, Hemlock Street, Ucluelet,
BC. V0R 3A0.
(250) 726-4241 Fax (250) 726-7335.
Charts 3679, 3681
Fisheries & Oceans dock
Charts 3646, 3671, 3603
Manager • Float length 820 metres •
Breakwater • Garbage/oil disposal •
Derrick • Water • Lights • Power •
Phone • Toilets • Showers • Near
general stores, restaurants, Post Office,
shops, laundry, accommodations, pool.
Other public docks (outer hbr)
Otter Street–
Fisheries and Oceans dock
Manager • Float length 150 m •
Garbage disposal • Lights • Phone.
Itatsoo–Fisheries and Oceans dock
Manager • Float length 64 m • Wharf
36 m • Aircraft dock •
Main Street–Transport Canada dock
Manager • Float length 36 m • Wharf
42 m • Aircraft dock • Garbage
disposal • Derrick • Lights • Power.
East–Fisheries and Oceans dock
Float length 49 m.

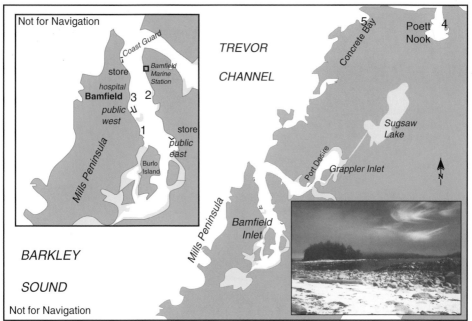

Bamfield

1. McKay Bay Lodge

Brian and Cheryl McKay
P.O. Box 116, Bamfield, BC.
V0R 1B0. Phone (250) 728-3323
Fax 728-3255
Chart 3646, 3671, 3602
Moorage–summer transient available.
Fishing gear and charters. Fast-freeze.
Accommodations (resort), restaurant, pub,
bakery and other stores.

2. Bamfield Kingfisher Marina

Peter and Carol Brown
P.O. Box 38, Ucluelet, BC. V0R 1B0
Phone (250) 728-3228
Charts 3646, 3671, 3602
Fuel: diesel, gas. **Water.** Ice. Limited
visitor moorage.

Bamfield Public Docks

East–Transport Canada dock
Charts 3646, 3671, 3602
Manager • Float length 128 metres •
Wharf 18 m • Breakwater • Garbage
disposal • Derrick • Lights • Phone •
Sheds. Near general store.
Port Désiré–
Fisheries & Oceans dock
Manager • Float length 22 m •
Launch ramp.
West–Fisheries and Oceans dock
Manager • Float length 154 m •
Garbage
West–Transport Canada dock
Manager • Float length 24 m •
Wharf 18 m • Garbage disposal •
Derrick.

Barkley Sound is known for its fishing and scuba diving.
The town of Bamfield is a good base for reaching some
of the beautiful waters and beaches strewn throughout
the Sound, especially in the islands of the nearby
Broken Group. Photo above: Turret Island.

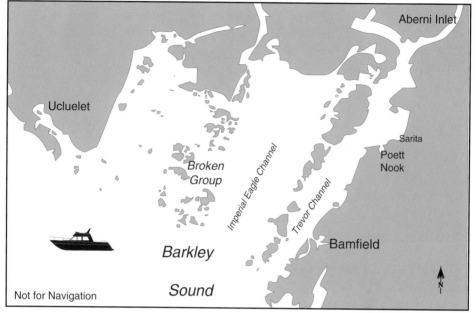

Not for Navigation

3. Bamfield Lodge and Cottages

Barry Otterson
**P.O. Box 23, Bamfield,
BC. V0R 1B0   VHF 06
Phone (250) 728-3419 Fax 728-3417
Chart Charts 3646, 3671, 3602.**
Email: *barry@bamfieldlodge.com*
Website: *www.bamfieldlodge.com*
Moorage–summer transient when available. **Power. Water.** Ice. Fish freezers.
Cappuccino bar.
Facilities–Accommodations (resort), cottages, charters, tours, marine field trips, kayaking, whale watching.

4. Poett Nook Marina

Stan and Flo Salmon
**2178 Cameron Drive, Port Alberni, BC.
V9Y 1B2.   Charts 3671, 3688, 3602
Phone (250) 724-8525
Marina:** Moorage. Boats to 26 feet.
Fuel: gas.
Washrooms, showers.

5. Barkley Sound Resort

Craig Filipchuk
**5425 Argyle Street, Port Alberni, BC.
VV9Y 1T6
Phone (250) 723-7462 Fax 723-3422
Chart 3671, 3668, 3602
Moorage**, Accommodations, meals.
Power. Water. Showers.
Comfortable fishing boats are available
22–43 feet for charter.
Nearby
Accommodations (resort), restaurant, pub,
RV park, bakery and other stores.
In Concrete Bay near Sarita and Poett Nook.

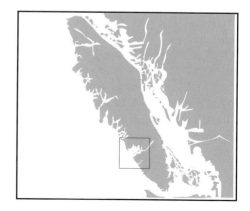

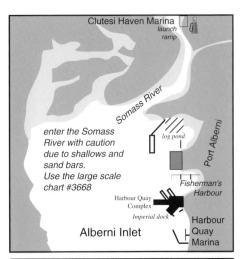

Port Alberni

Clutesi Haven

Tom McMillan
**5104 River Road, Port Alberni,
BC. V9Y 6Z2   VHF 68
Phone (250) 724-6837 Fax 723-1114
Chart 3668** (up Somass River)
Moorage–summer transient available at
times. **Water. Power** 30 amp.
Fuel: gas. Sani-dump. Phone.
Launch ramp. Ice, **laundry, showers,
toilets**. Chandlery. Fishing gear and
charters.
Nearby: Port Alberni: Grocery, hardware,
propane, marine supplies, restaurants,
bakery, liquor store and other facilities.

Haggard Cove Resort

Ron Clark
**P.O. Box 396, Port Alberni,
BC. V9Y 7M9**
Located near entrance to Alberni Canal.
**Phone (250) 723-8457 Fax 723-5657
Chart 3668, VHF 27 (MV Our Way)
Moorage**–Occasional summer transient
available June to September.
Fishing Lodge. Fishing gear and charters.
Water. Accommodations, meals.

Fisherman's Harbour

3140 Harbour Rd. Port Alberni.
Fisheries and Oceans dock
Chart 3668
Managed by Port Alberni Harbour
Commission–Mark Braithwaite
(wharfinger) • Float length 825 metres
• Breakwater– 70 m wharf • Garbage
disposal • Derrick • Water • Lights •
Power • Phone. (250) 723-2533

China Creek Marina

Bruce Kramer
**P.O. Box 575, Port Alberni,
BC. V9Y 7M9   VHF 16, 18A
Phone (250) 723-9812 Fax 723-9842
Chart 3668
Moorage**–summer transient moorage if
space available.
**Fuel: diesel, gas. Water.
Power:** 30 amps.
**Customer Services:
Laundry. Showers. Washrooms.**
Launch ramp adjacent. Ministore–fishing
gear and supplies, cafe.
Campsite, sani-dump.

246

Harbour Quay Marina

Colleen Schiller
Richard Hartigan–Harbour Master
2900 Harbour Rd
Port Alberni V9Y 7X2, BC.
(250) 723-1413 Fax (250) 723-1114
cellular (250) 720-6256. Chart 3668
Moorage: Harbour–breakwater and
retaining shoreline with primary docks.
116 resident slips with power, water and
nearby shore facilities.
Visitor moorage.
Moorage is also available at the nearby
Fishermen's Harbour.
Visit the quay at Fisherman's Harbour for
restaurants, gift and craft shops. The
Boathouse chandlery and marine service
are nearby.
The local Marine Historical Society and
the Port Alberni Museum plan to mount
the former Chrome Island lighthouse on
top of the Discovery Centre which is to be
constructed on the pier.

*Inset above, left: The lauch ramp on the Somass River
at Clutesi Haven in Port Alberni extends in the river
(above). Fuel is available at China Creek Marina,
below, and at Clutesi haven (bottom).*

*Inset above, right: At the Harbour Quay complex in
Port Alberni.*

Port Alberni Harbour Authority

Port Renfrew

Port Renfrew Marina

Rex Colburn
**Gordon River Rd, Port Renfrew,
BC. V0R 1B0 fax 478-3696
Phone (250) 478-3674 or 474-2643
Chart 3647, 3606 VHF 06**
*www.portrenfrewmarina.com
email:cactusdevelopments@home.com*
Marina: Bait, tackle and fishing
licences . **Fuel:** Gasoline, oil. RV
park. Campground. **Launch ramp**.

Port Renfrew
Public Docks
On east side–Transport Canada dock
Manager • Float length • Wharf 33 m
(Breakwater) • Derrick • Lights • Phone
ashore • Pub. Restaurant nearby.

Open May through September.
*Enter up river on instructions from marina.
Larger boats require high tide.*

*Photo above: The launch ramp at Port Renfrew is
located on the Gordon River.*
*Opposite: The public docks at Sooke are located on the
west shore of the harbour just after entering past
Whiffen Spit. Exercise great caution entering Sooke,
using the channel markers to avoid hazards at the
entrance.*

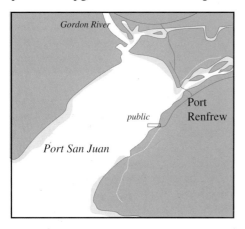

Sooke Harbour Marina

Sooke

Sooke Harbour Marina VHF 16 &68

Larry and Darlene Doucette
6971 West Coast Road,
Sooke, BC. V0S 1N0
Phone (250) 642-3236
Charts 3410, 3411, 3461, 3606
Marina: Power 15 amp. **Water. Ice.**
Laundry. Showers. Washrooms.
Moorage–limited summer transient.
Phone, Camping. Launch Ramp.
Fuel–2 km by road, also stores and
restaurants.

Beware of sand bank out in channel.
Follow markers and use marine chart.

Sunny Shores Marina

Andrew Planeta
5621 Sooke Road, Sooke,
BC. V0S 1N0   Ph: 1-888-805-3932
Phone (250) 642-5731 Fax 642-5737
email: *sunnyshores@sookenet.com*
Charts 3410, 3411, 3461, 3606
(Enter from Eliza Point favouring the
eastern shore)
Fuel gas, diesel, oil. **Power. Water.**
Launch Ramp. Fishing licences.
Moorage–some summer transient slips.
Showers. Washrooms. Laundry.
Mechanical service. Ministore–groceries.
Hotel and camping. Nearby restaurants
and bus service to Sooke and Victoria.

Sooke Public Docks

Fisheries and Oceans dock
Chart 3641
Manager • Float length 243 metres •
Wharf 34 m • Garbage disposal •
Derrick • Water • Lights • Power •
Easy walk up into town for all shops
and services.

Sunny Shores Marina

Cheanuh Marina

Stan Chipps
**Box 4, 4901 East Sooke Road,
RR#1 Sooke, BC. V0S 1N0
Phone (250) 478-4880 Fax 478-3585
Chart 3410, 3461, 3606 Located in
Becher Bay (Enter with caution)
Fuel** gas only. **Moorage**–some summer transient available–call for reservations. Boat rentals. Fishing and camping.

Not for Navigation

Pedder Bay Marina

Sean Moore
**925 Pedder Bay Drive, No 12
Metchosin, Victoria, BC. V9Z 4H1
Phone (250) 478-1771 Fax (250) 478-2695
Fax (250) 728-3255
Chart 3410, 3461, 3606   VHF 68
Moorage**–some summer transient. Fishing licences. Phone, washrooms, showers, laundry. Rental boats and fishing guides available. Camping, mini chandlery. **Launch Ramp.**
Beware of the reef at entrance to marina.

Top:A view of Cheanuh Marina in Becher Bay. Right: Pedder Bay Marina

Skyline Marina

Southbound to Olympia

Most vessels returning from a cruise in British Columbia or the San Juans to their home ports in Puget Sound are probably familiar with much of the following information.

Hopefully there are some docks in this section that you have not yet discovered and will experience pleasure in visiting them. The information relating to the marinas is intended to provide input for the mariner to check into the most suitable overnight facilities.

For those mariners who have spent all or most of their boating years in British Columbia waters, a pleasant surprise is in store for you when you travel south. There are destination marinas that are well equipped to cater to visiting boats. And there are surroundings that will make you want to stay longer than intended and return again soon.

Many Canadians are inclined to think of Puget Sound as a busy, commercial and built-up residential-lined waterway. But there are passages, bays and coves that compare with some of the most remote wilderness areas of northern British Columbia. In the following pages I have included those marinas which offer overnight moorage. Most have special visitor moorage, some have visitor docks and additional space available for guests while others offer space as available. This latter type of marina has been included only where I consider there to be adequate visitor moorage. There are other marinas I have not included. This is because they either do not offer visitor moorage, or do so on a very limited basis.

Whether returning home from northern destinations or just going south for a change, plan a visit to Admiralty Inlet, Puget Sound or Hood Canal and check out some of the outstanding facilities for yourself.

Right: Diagram shows where the primary overnight moorage marinas are located.
Top: Skyline Marina at Anacortes, where resident boats occupy hundreds of slips and special docks are set aside for visitors, is one of the largest in the region–see page 259.

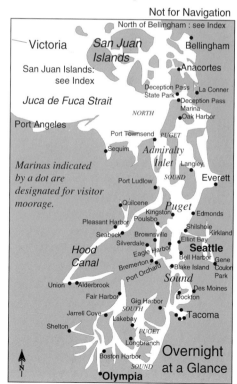

Not for Navigation

North of Bellingham : see Index

Victoria   San Juan   Bellingham
            Islands
San Juan Islands: Anacortes
   see Index
                    Deception Pass   La Conner
                    State Park   Deception Pass
Juca de Fuca Strait   Marina
                    NORTH   Oak Harbor
Port Angeles
              Port Townsend   PUGET
         Sequim   Admiralty
Marinas indicated   Inlet   Langley
by a dot are   SOUND   Everett
designated for visitor   Port Ludlow
moorage.   Quilcene   Puget
              Kingston   Edmonds
    Pleasant Harbor   Poulsbo
         Seabeck   Brownsville   Shilshole
Hood   Silverdale   Elliot Bay   Kirkland
Canal   Eagle Harbor   Seattle
         Bremerton   Bell Harbor   Gene
              Blake Island   Coulon
              Port Orchard   Sound   Park
   Union   Alderbrook   Des Moines
      Fair Harbor   Gig Harbor   Dockton
   Jarrell Cove   SOUTH
         Lakebay   Tacoma
   Shelton   PUGET
         Longbranch
      Boston Harbor   Overnight
         SOUND   at a Glance
      Olympia

View towards Juan de Fuca Strait from John Wayne Marina

Blaine

San Juan Islands

La Conner

Neah Bay

Sekiu

Clallam Bay

Juan de Fuca Strait

Dungeness Bay

Whidbey Island

Port Angeles

Port Townsend

Sequim Bay

OLYMPIC PENINSULA

Not for Navigation

Juan de Fuca Strait

Makah Marina Neah Bay

P.O. Box 137 Neah Bay, WA, 98357
Phone: (360) 645-3015 fax (360) 645-3016
email: mtcport@olypen.com
Charts 18485, 18484 **VHF 66**
Moorage. Water. Power 30, 50 amps.
Fuel: gas, diesel.
Showers, Laundry, Washrooms.
Pumpout. Portadump.
Nearby: Accommodations, shops,
museum, culture center. **Launch ramp.**

Big Salmon Resort

P.O. Box 204 Neah Bay, WA, 98357
Phone: (360) 645-2374 fax (360) 645-3016
email: mtcport@olypen.com
Charts 118485, 18484 **VHF 68**
Moorage at Makah Marina. Seasonal.
Boats to 60 feet. **Water. Power** 30, amps.
Fuel: gas, diesel. **Washrooms.** Pumpout.
Adjacent: Launch ramp. Store. Some
supplies. Accommodations, services
nearby.

Snow Creek Resort

P.O. Box 248 Neah Bay, WA, 98357
Phone: (360) 645-2284 (fax) (360) 645-2997

Chart 18460 **VHF 16, 17**
Moorage at Makah Marina. Water.
Showers, Washrooms. Portadump.
Nearby: Launch ramp, scuba air fills,
camping, RV park.

Van Riper's Resort

P.O. Box 246 280 Front Street,
Sekiu, WA, 98381
Phone: (360) 963-2334
Chart 18460   CB 14
Moorage nearby. 3000' dock. **Water.**
Showers, Washrooms. Portadump. Rental
boats. Groceries, charts, books, ice.
Nearby: Restaurant, marine store. **Launch ramp.**

Olson's Resort

P.O. Box 216, 444 Front Street,
Sekiu, WA, 98381
Phone: (360) 963-2311 fax (360) 963-2928
Charts 18460 CB 14, 21
Fuel: gas. diesel. **Moorage. Water.**
Showers, Laundry, Washrooms.
Portadump. Rental boats.
Fishing charters. Busy in summer.
Nearby: Launch ramp.

John Wayne Marina

Ron Amundsen
2577 W. Sequim Bay Road,
Sequim, WA, 98382
Phone: (360) 417-3440 fax: (360) 417-3442
Chart 18471
Fuel: gas, diesel. **Moorage:** Visitor dock at marina inside breakwater. Power 20, 30 amp. **Washrooms, laundry, showers.** Pumpout. Portadump.
Adjacent: Restaurant. Store, books, marine supplies.
Nearby: Beach, picnic area, grocery store.

Sequim Bay State Marine Park, Sequim Bay 420 foot guest dock. Washrooms, showers, Portadump. Park, picnic sites, scuba diving, launch ramp. Mooring buoys. Shallow at low tide.

Curley's Resort (Clallam)

P.O. Box 265,
Sekiu, WA, 98381
Phone: (360) 963-2281 1 (800) 9542-9680
Fax (360) 963-2291 Chart 18460
Moorage: Seasonal. Boats to 30 feet.
Motel. Rooms and cabins to rent.

Coho Resort Clallam

P.O. Box 265,
Sekiu, WA, 98381
Phone: 1 (800) 9542-9680
Chart 18460
Moorage: Seasonal. Boats to 25 feet.
Washrooms, laundry, showers.

John Wayne Marina. Left photo shows entrance.

Thunderbird Boathouse

826 Boat Haven Drive,
Port Angeles, WA, 98362
Phone: (360) 457-4274
Chart 18465
Fuel: gas. **Moorage:** Visitor dock, boats to 30 feet. Seasonal. **Washrooms. Pumpout.** Near city amenities.

Port Angeles City Pier

312 E 5th,
Port Angeles, WA, 98362
Phone: (360) 457-0411 (Port Angeles Utilities)
Chart 18465
Moorage: Visitor dock, seasonal.
Washrooms.
Access to city and amenities. Public aquatic centre (showers), nearby stores, restaurants.

Port Angeles Boat Haven

Harbor Manager: Chuck Ferris.
832 Boat Haven Drive,
Port Angeles, WA, 98362
Phone: (360) 457-4505
Fax (360) 457-4921 Chart 18465
Fuel: gas, diesel. **Moorage:** Visitor dock, boats to 120 feet. **Power** 15 amp.
Washrooms, showers.
Pumpout. Portadump. Customs.
Adjacent: Haulouts, repairs, service, marine supplies, charts, stove oil, kerosene. Cafe. Laundry nearby.

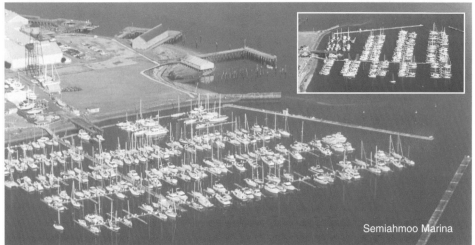

Semiahmoo Marina

Blaine

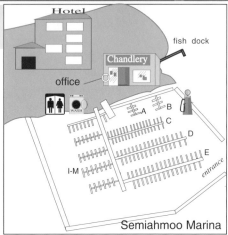

Semiahmoo Marina

Semiahmoo Marina

Bill Tetreault
9540 Semiahmoo Parkway,
Blaine, WA. 98230
Phone (360) 371-5700 fax (360) 371-2422
VHF 68 Chart 18421
Email: *marina@semiahmoo.com*
Moorage: 500 feet, plus slips.
Fuel: gas, diesel, propane. **Power** 30 amp.
Washrooms, showers, laundry,
portadump, **pumpout.**
Adjacent: Resort accommodations and
golf course. Health spa, marine chandlery,
service, repairs, snacks. Access to Blaine
by ferry through summer–week-ends.

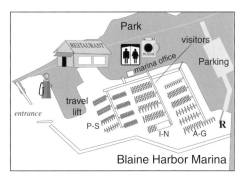

Blaine Harbor Marina

Blaine Harbor Marina

Dock Manager
235 Marine Drive,
Blaine, WA. 98231
Phone (360) 647-6176 fax (360) 332-1043
VHF 66A Chart 18421
Moorage: 700 feet guest moorage plus
slips. **Fuel:** gas, diesel, propane, at Blaine
Marina (fuel dock 332-8425).
Power 30,50,100 amp.
Washrooms, showers, portadump,
pumpout.

Customs–phone in.
Adjacent: Haulouts, repairs, supplies,
restaurants. Launch ramp. Landscaped
parkland. Short walk to uptown Blaine.
Blaine Marina (fuel dock– 332-8425)

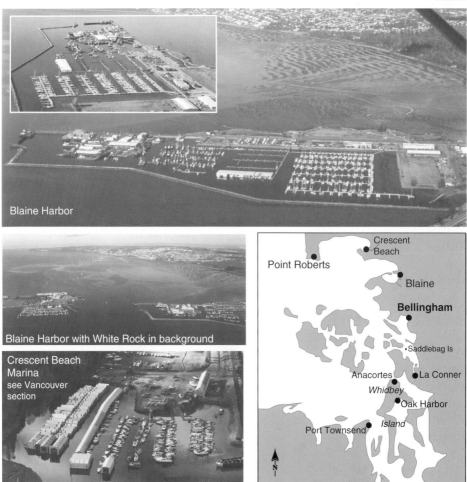

Blaine Harbor

Blaine Harbor with White Rock in background

Crescent Beach Marina
see Vancouver section

Crescent Beach

Point Roberts

Blaine

Bellingham

Saddlebag Is

Anacortes · La Conner

Whidbey

Oak Harbor

Port Townsend · Island

N

Going south from Juan de Fuca Strait or the San Juan Islands your choices are Hood Canal, Admiralty Inlet or Puget Sound. If you are in the vicinity of Crescent Beach or Point Roberts and intend to travel down Puget Sound you may find a visit to Blaine worthwhile. The town has been embellished with new paving and landscaping. The marina has many facilities and a warm welcome for visitors. The same can be said for Semiahmoo Marina on the opposite side of Drayton Harbor. This modern marina loves to have visitors. Call ahead to reserve moorage and look forward to a pleasant stay with options of golf or time in the spa. If you stay there and want to visit Blaine you can use the ferry in summer.

In the Puget Sound area most mariners are familiar with destinations such as Port Townsend known for its historic buildings and holiday atmosphere, or Anacortes for its bustling activity as a port for larger vessels, ferry traffic and business community. Check out these two places for their large, accommodating marinas. And visit other ports such as Poulsbo for its colorful Scandinavian village, Silverdale, Port Ludlow or Jarrell's Cove for remoteness from anywhere. These and other marinas and towns in the Sound and Hood Canal can provide lots of entertainment, new experiences and friendships, and a joyful boating experience. Moreover, getting to some of these places can be a lot of fun. Some state marine parks have been included in the following pages where they provide adequate or substantial visitor moorage and other facilities.

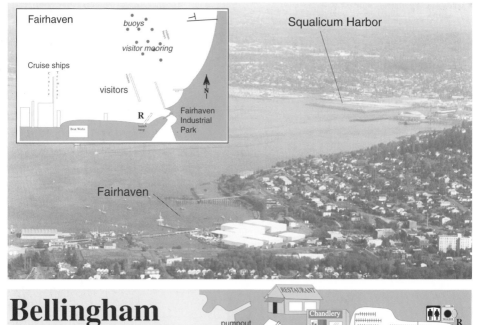

Bellingham

Squalicum Harbor/Port of Bellingham

Reed Gillig
22 Squalicum Fill WA, 98227
Phone: (360) 676-2542 fax (360) 671-6149
www.portofbellingham.com VHF ch 16.
Chart 18424
Moorage: Visitor's dock–1500 feet.
Fuel: gas, diesel, propane.
Power 20, 30, 50 amp. **Water.**
Showers, laundry, washrooms.
Portadump. **Pumpout.**
Adjacent: Marine supplies, service, haulouts. Restaurant, groceries, stores, **Launch ramp.**
Nearby Moorage:
Fairhaven. Numerous mooring buoys and a linear floating dock for visitors (by dinghy to shore) during boating season. Park, scenic and historic area adjacent. **Garbage** disposal. **Water.**
Launch ramp.

Fisherman's Cove Marina
2557 Lummi View Drive,
Bellingham, WA. 98226
Phone (360) 758-7050 fax (360) 758-2806
Chart 18421 located at Hale Passage.
Fuel dock : gas, propane.

Saddlebag Island Marine State Park.
East of Guemes Island, Padilla Bay.
Chart 18429 Mooring, camping. Watch depths all sides.

Harbor Marine Fuel
21 Squalicum Fill,
Bellingham, WA. 98225
Phone (360) 734-1710
Chart 18421
Fuel dock : ice, oil, gas, diesel, snacks.

La Conner

La Conner Marina

Russ Johnson
613 N. 2nd Street, PO Box 1120
La Conner, WA, 98257
Phone: (360) 466-3118 fax (360) 466-3119
VHF ch 68. Chart 18427
*Fuel adjacent: gas, diesel, propane.
Moorage: 2300 foot guest dock plus slips.
Power 30 amp. **Water. Showers, wash-**
rooms, laundry. Pumpout.
Swinomish Yacht Club adjacent south.
Nearby: Stores. marine supplies, service,
light boat launcher to 7500 lbs (roller
equipped trailers), 55 ton travel lift. Boat
storage. historic town of La Conner–stores,
gifts, arts and crafts, restaurants. Moorage
also available at La Conner public docks.

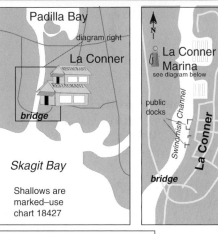

*La Conner Landing Marine Services. Fuel dock,
P.O. Box 1020. La Conner, WA., 98257. (360) 466-4478. washrooms,
pumpout. Store: groceries, beer and wine, fishing equipment, bait, ice.

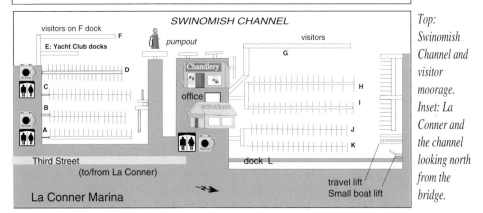

Top: Swinomish Channel and visitor moorage. Inset: La Conner and the channel looking north from the bridge.

Cap Sante Boat Haven–entrance

Anacortes

Cap Sante Boat Haven

P.O. Box 297, 1019 Q Avenue,
Anacortes, WA, 98221
Phone: (360) 293-0694 fax (360) 299-0998
VHF ch 66A.
Charts 18421, 18427
Moorage: guest dock plus slips. **Call.**
Fuel at Cap Sante Marine: gas, diesel,
propane. **Power** 20, 30, 50 amp. **Water.**
Showers, laundry, washrooms. Pumpout.
Portadump.
Nearby: Food and other stores, marine

supplies, service, historic town of
Anacortes–stores, gifts, arts and crafts,
restaurants.

Adjacent: Cap Sante Marine, fuel dock,
launching and service center located at
Cap Sante Boat Haven. **Marine Service
Center,** south of cap Sante, has free
pumpout, some moorage, 30 amp power,
showers, washrooms fuel dock with
gasoline, diesel and propane. Full haulout
facility and repair yards.

Cap Sante Boat Haven

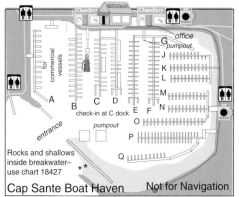
Cap Sante Boat Haven   Not for Navigation

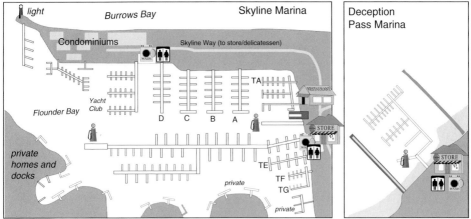

Not for Navigation

Skyline Marina

Skyline Marina (Penmar Marine)
2011 Skyline Way, (Flounder Bay),
Anacortes, WA, 98221
Phone: (360) 293-5134 (888) 973-6627
www.penmar.com **VHF ch 16, 68**
Chart 18427 See photo page 251.
Moorage: 2300 foot guest dock plus slips.
Fuel docks: gas, diesel. **Power** 20, 30
amp. **Water. Garbage disposal.**
Showers, laundry, washrooms. Pumpout.
Adjacent: Stores, marine supplies,
fishing tackle, bait, charts, books, service,
repairs. Haulouts to 50 tons. Restaurants
and groceries nearby. Four miles to town.

Deception Pass Marina
Dundee Woods
200 W. Cornet Bay Road,
Oak Harbour, WA, 98277
Phone: (360) 675-5411
www.penmar.com **VHF ch 16, 68**
Chart 18427
Moorage: guest dock plus slips.

Fuel dock: gas, diesel, kerosene, stove oil,
propane. **Power** 30 amp. **Water.**
Garbage disposal.
Laundry, washrooms. Pumpout.
Adjacent: Store, fishing tackle, bait,
charts, books, groceries, haulouts.

Nearby:
• **Deception Pass Marine State Park**
(Sharpes Cove, Bowman Bay) 128 foot
guest dock. Picnic sites, campsites,
washrooms, showers, portadump. Mooring Buoys located at Skagit Island and
Hope Island.

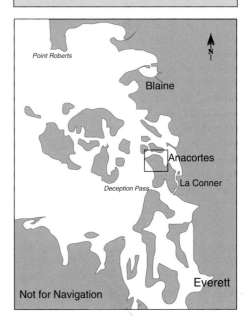
Not for Navigation

Whidbey Island area

Oak Harbor Marina

Dave Williams
**865 SE Barrington Dr., Oak Harbor,
WA, 98277   Charts 18428, 18441
Phone: (360) 679-2628 fax (360) 240-0603**
*email: ohmarina@whidbey.net
www.whidbey.net/ohmarina.* **VHF ch 16.
Visitor moorage.** Check depth at low tide.
Fuel: gas, diesel, propane. **Power** 20, 30
amp. **Water.
Showers, laundry, washrooms.** Pumpout.
Nearby: Stores, marine supplies, service,
haulouts, **launch ramp.** Access to Oak
Harbour.

Coupeville Wharf

Jack Parker–harbormaster
**Port of Coupeville, P.O. Box 577
Coupeville, WA, 98239-0577
Phone: (360) 678-5020 Fax (360) 678-8436
Chart 18441   Portadump nearby.
Moorage.** Shallow at low tide. **Fuel:** Gas,
diesel. **Water. Showers, washrooms.
Adjacent:** Store and deli, ice, charts,
books, art gallery. **Launch ramp** nearby
at Captain Coupe park.

Fort Worden Marine State Park
Port Townsend. **(360) 385-4730. Charts
18441, 18464. Dock space. Washrooms,
showers, laundry. Launch ramp.** Mooring buoys. Scuba Diving. Marine Science
Center. Campsites.

Oak Harbor

Tulalip Marina

Manager
**7411 Tulalip Drive, Marysville,
WA, 98270
Phone: (360) 651-4999
Chart 18441
Moorage. Water. Fuel: gas, diesel.
Power** 50 amps.
Washrooms. Pumpout.
Nearby: Store, cafe, high-tide launch
ramp.

Langley Marina

Manager
**P.O. Box 681, 202 Wharf St., Langley,
WA, 98260   Chart 18441
Phone: (360) 221-1771 Chart 18441
Water. Showers, washrooms.**
Portadump.
Adjacent: Store. charts, marine supplies,
service, repairs, fishing supplies.
Dive shop.

Oak Harbor

Oak Harbor Marina

to shops office

WASH

launch ramp

pumpout

A

R

visitors

B

C

D

E

pumpout

visitors

F

entrance

F dock

picnic sites along outer float

entrance

Oak Harbor Marina on Whidbey Island. Pictured lower is the main guest dock adjacent the manager's office.

Langley Boat Harbor

Box 366 Langley, WA. 98260
Phone (360) 221-4246 Chart 18441
email: langleycity@whidbey.com
Moorage, 20, 30 amp power, water,
washrooms, showers, pumpout.
Launch ramp.
Nearby: Post office, restaurant, liquor
store, groceries. Arts and Crafts, book-
store, pharmacy. Accommodations.

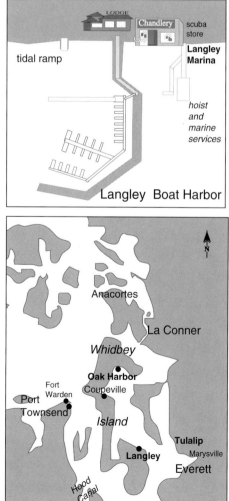

LODGE

Chandlery

scuba store

tidal ramp

Langley Marina

hoist and marine services

Langley Boat Harbor

Port of Everett Marina

P.O. Box 538 , 1720 W. Marine View
Drive, Everett, WA, 98206
Phone: (425) 259-6001 fax (425) 259-0860
www: marinaportofeverett.com
VHF ch 16, 69   Chart 18444, 18443
Moorage: 1800 foot guest dock plus slips.
Fuel docks: gas, diesel.
Power 20, 30 amp**. Water. Garbage**
disposal. Showers, laundry, washrooms.
Pumpout. Portadump.
Adjacent: Village restaurants and shops.
Marine stores, fishing tackle, bait, charts,
books. Wheelchair access docks. Haulouts,
storage, repairs, service.
Nearby: Launch ramp at nearby Everett
Marine Park. Watch depths at marina.

N

Anacortes

La Conner

Whidbey

Oak Harbor

Fort
Warden

Coupeville

Port
Townsend

Island

Tulalip

Langley

Marysville

Everett

Hood
Canal

261

Point Hudson Marina

Port Townsend

Charts 18464, 18441   VHF 09

Point Hudson
Resort & Marina

Forrest Rambo, General Manager
103 Hudson St.
Port Townsend, WA 98368
email: pthudson@olypen.com
Phone: (360) 385-2828 fax (360) 385-7331
Moorage: slips to 40' lineal slips to 65'.
Water. Power 20, 30 amps.

Fuel: 1 mile south at Fish'n' Hole Marine
(Port of Port Townsend).
Laundry, showers, washrooms. Pumpout. **Launch ramp**.
Nearby: Restaurants. Stores, groceries,
marine store, service and repairs adjacent.
Fleet Marine chandlery adjacent to
harbor–check for haul outs and service.
Check in at marina office on northeast
side of the marina. This is a quaint,
historic town with many antique stores,
arts and craft shops, classic restaurants
and specialty stores.

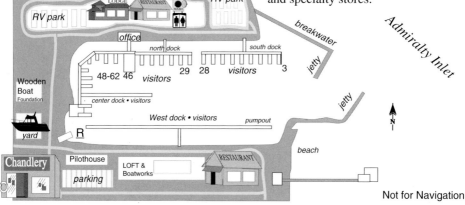

Not for Navigation

262

Port Townsend Boat Haven

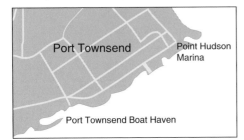

Port Townsend

Point Hudson Marina

Port Townsend Boat Haven

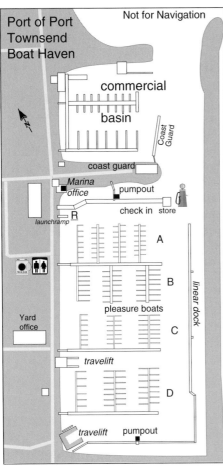

Not for Navigation

Port of Port Townsend Boat Haven

commercial basin

Coast Guard

coast guard

Marina office

pumpout

check in   store

launchramp   R

A

B

pleasure boats

linear dock

Yard office

C

travelift

D

travelift   pumpout

WASH

Port Townsend Boat Haven

Ken Radon
**P.O. Box 1180, 2601 Washington Street,
Port Townsend, WA 98368
Phone: (360) 385-2355 fax 385-3988
Charts 18464, 18441 VHF Ch 09 & 66A**
email: info@portofpt.com
www: www.portofpt.com
Moorage: transient slips and other.
Water. Power 20, 30, 50 amps.
Fuel: gas, diesel (no mooring at dock).
Laundry, showers, washrooms. Pumpout. Portadump. Customs. **Launch ramp**.
Haul outs to 300 tons.
Nearby: Restaurants. Stores, groceries, marine store, service and repairs adjacent.

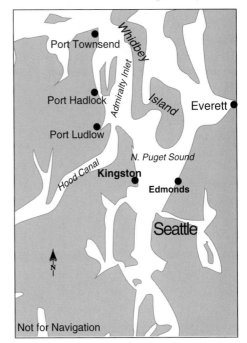

Port Townsend

Whidbey

Admiralty Inlet

Port Hadlock

Island

Everett

Port Ludlow

N. Puget Sound

Hood Canal

Kingston

Edmonds

Seattle

Not for Navigation

Port Hadlock

Port Ludlow Marina.
*Inset right: Port Hadlock Marina,
facing north.*

Fort Flagler Marine State Park
Marrowstone Island. Chart 18464.
Visitor dock. Washrooms, showers,
portadump. Launch ramp. Mooring
buoys. Scuba Diving. Mini store. Campsites. Boat rentals. Fishing supplies.

Mystery Bay Marine State Park
Kilisut Harbor, Marrowstone Island.
Chart 18464. Visitor dock. Pumpout,
portadump. **Launch ramp.**

Port Hadlock Bay Marina
Randy Pratt
P.O. Box 1369. 310 Alcohol Loop Rd.
Port Hadlock, WA 98339
Phone: (360) 385-6368 1 (800) 785-7030
Fax (360) 385-6955 Charts 18464, 18441
Moorage: some transient moorage.
Water. Power 30, 50 amps.
Fuel: gas, diesel, CNG. stove oil, propane.
showers, washrooms. Pump-out.
Nearby: Old Alcohol Plant Lodge with
restaurant and hotel facilities.

Port Ludlow Marina
Dean Kelley
1 Gull Drive, Port Ludlow,WA 98365
Phone: (360) 437-0513 1 (800) 308-7991
Charts 18477, 18473, 18441 Ch 16 to 68
Moorage: Visitor docks and other. **Water.**
Power 30, 50 amps. **Fuel:** gas, diesel,
CNG. stove oil, propane.
Laundry, showers, washrooms.
Pump-out. Portadump.
Nearby: Restaurants. Golf course shuttle.
Marina store, groceries, books, fishing
tackle, bait, ice, some marine supplies.

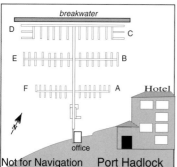

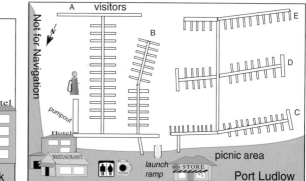

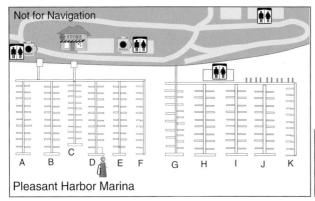

Pleasant Harbor

Quilcene Boat Haven

Hood Canal

Quilcene Boat Haven

Ken & Peggy Dressler
1731 Linger Longer Rd.
P.O. Box 98, Quilcene, WA. 98376
Phone (360) 765-3131 Fax (250) 765-3935
Guest moorage available. **Fuel:** gas, diesel.
Power 20, 30 amp. **Washrooms, showers,**
portadump, **pumpout. Launch Ramp.**
Adjacent: Ice, supplies. repairs, service.
Camping. Barbeque. Town less than 1 mile.
Shrimpoing popular in April and May.

Pleasant Harbor Marina

Chuck and Betty Finnila
308913 Highway 101, Brinnon WA 98320
Phone (360) 796-4611 Fax (360) 796-4898
VHF 9, 16. Charts 18476
Moorage: Guest moorage available.
Fuel: gas, diesel. **Power** 30, 50 amp.

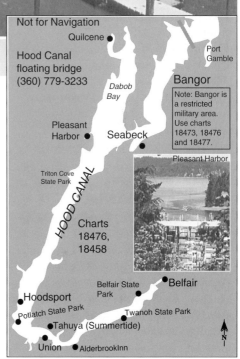

**Washrooms, showers,
laundry, portadump,
pumpout.
Adjacent:** Hot tub, Boaters
Lounge, swimming pools,
espresso bar. Ice, fishing and
marine supplies. repairs,
service. Gifts, marine store.
Beer and wine. Order-in or
take-out Pizza. Check at office.
**Nearby: Pleasant Harbor
Marine State Park.** (360)
796-4415. Guest dock 218 feet.
Portadump. Pumpout. Toilet.

Not for Navigation

Pleasant Harbor Marina

Hood Canal Marina at Union

Seabeck Marina

Mark Sjostrom
**P.O. Box 310, 15376, Seabeck Hwy NW,
Seabeck, WA. 98380
Phone (360) 830-5179 Fax (360) 830-5504
Charts 18473, 18476, 18477
Moorage:** By reservation in season.
Water. Fuel: gas, diesel. **Washrooms,**
portadump. **Adjacent:** Ice, groceries,
fishing supplies, marine hardware.
Haulouts, repairs, service. Nearby park,
camping.

Hoodsport Marina

**24080 Highway 101, Hoodsport, WA.
98548. Phone (360) 877-9657
Adjacent:** Restaurant–free use of public
dock (check its condition).**Washrooms.
Nearby:** Grocery store. Motel and Resort
(N Hwy 101 (360) 877-5301. Underwater
park, scuba diving, scuba air station.
Gasoline available nearby.

Twanoh State Marine Park
**Near Belfair (360) 275-2222
Mooring** buoys, pumpout, portadump.
192 foot dock for overnight use. Launch
ramp, playground, picnic areas, campsites, tennis courts, hiking trails.

Potlatch State Marine Park
**(360) 877-5361
Near Hoodsport Chart 18476
Washrooms, showers.
Adjacent:** Park, picnic sites, hiking trails,
scuba diving, launch ramp Mooring buoys.

Hood Canal Marina

**P.O. Box 86,
E 5010 Hwy 106,
Union, WA. 98376
Phone (360) 898-2252 Fax (360) 898-8888
Moorage:** Guest moorage–check in ahead.
Fuel: gas. **Power** 30 amp. **Washrooms,
showers.**
Nearby: Groceries, supplies. repairs,
marine service.

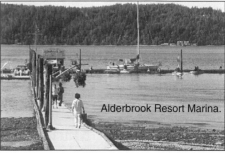
Alderbrook Resort Marina.

Alderbrook Resort, Golf Club
E 7101 Hwy 106, Union. WA 98592.
(360) 898-2200 **Fax (360) 898-4610**
www:*alderbrookinn.com*
Large boats reservations. Power, water,
pump-out, showers. Hotel rooms, cottages,
indoor pool, 18 hole golf course, restaurant, banquet facilities, watercraft rentals.

Summertide Resort & Marina
**NE 15781, Northshore Rd.,
Tuhuya WA. 98588
Phone (360) 275-9313 Fax (253) 925-9277
Moorage:** seasonal by reservation.
Boats to 22 feet. **Washrooms, showers,
laundry. Adjacent:** Launch ramp. RV
sites. Cottage rentals. Store–Ice, propane,
groceries, fishing supplies and licences.

Kingston

Central Puget Sound

Port of Kingston

Gary W. Johnston
P.O. Box 559 Kingston,
25864 Washington Blvd
Washington 98346
Phone: (360) 297-3545 fax (360) 297-2945
Charts 18446, 18473, 18441
Moorage: transient–slips for 44 guests.
Fuel: diesel, gas, propane. **Water.**
Power 30 amps.
Laundry, showers, washrooms. Pumpout. Portadump
Launching hoist. **Launch ramp.** Guest moorage located just inside breakwater.

Moor your boat at the check in slip and register if space is available.
The ferry from Edmonds lands next to the marina at Kingston. Lots of traffic converge here so be wary of your right of way. Watch also for the heavy motor traffic on shore as you wander into Kingston to visit stores and restaurants.

Port of Edmonds Marina

Dave Howard *dhoward@portofedmonds.org*
336 Admiral Way, Edmonds, WA, 98020
Phone: (425) 774-0549 fax (425) 774-7837
www.portofedmonds.org **VHF ch 16, 69**
Chart 18441, 18446, 18473
Moorage: 1000' visitor docks plus slips.
Fuel docks: gas, diesel. **Garbage disposal.** Pumpout. Portadump.
Power 20, 30 amp. **Water.**
Showers, washrooms, laundry.
Adjacent: Marine stores, fishing tackle, bait, charts, books. Some groceries. Restaurant. Fishing pier. Haulouts, boatyard, repairs, service.
Nearby: Restaurants and shops. (van service available).
Public beaches. Good scuba diving at nearby artificial reef.

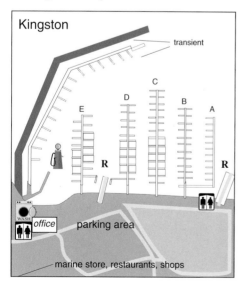

Poulsbo

Bainbridge Island vicinity

Port of Poulsbo

Barbara Waltz
P.O. Box 732, 18721 Front Street
Poulsbo. WA 98366
Phone: (360) 779-3505 Fax: 779-8090
email: port@poulsbo.net **Chart 18446**

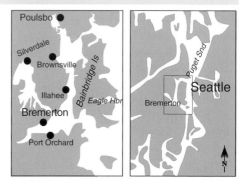

Moorage: transient slips for 130 guests.
Water. Power 20, 30 amps.
Fuel: gas, diesel. **Laundry, showers, washrooms.** Free pump-out.

Nearby: Chandlery, bistros, bakery, shops and all facilities for visitors. Poulsbo is a character town.
The town is built in traditional Viking style. It has a beautiful setting with adjacent village ethnic restaurants, bakeries, gift and book stores.

Photos top to bottom show the marina at Poulsbo, a downtown scene and the fuel dock at the marina. This Viking village has a strong appeal to tourists. Mariners will enjoy the marina and nearby facilities.

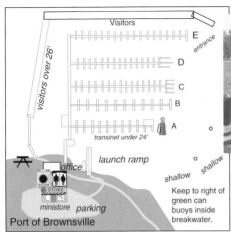

Port of Brownsville

Brownsville–visitors dock

Port of Brownsville

Ben Holland
9790 Ogle Road NE Bremerton WA
98311. Web: *www.portofbrownsville.org*
Phone: (360) 692-5498 Fax: (360) 698-8023
Charts 18446, 18449. VHF 16, 68
Moorage: 950' breakwater plus visitor
dock. **Water. Power. Fuel:** gas, diesel,
propane. **Laundry, showers, washrooms.**
Launch ramp. Free pump-out. Public
phones. **Nearby:** park, deli, store.

Illahee Chart 18449

Illahee State Park

Port Orchard Bay. **Phone:** (360) 478-6460
Visitor dock. Washrooms. Portadump.
Nearby/adjacent: Mooring buoys, picnic
tables, shelters, campsites, beach.

Eagle Harbor Waterfront Park

280 Madison Ave. N. Bainbridge
Island, WA 98110 Tammy Allen
Phone (206) 780-3733 fax (206) 780-8600
Moorage 100 ft. **Washrooms. Pumpout**.
Playground, picnic tables,
shelter.**Nearby:** Launch ramp. Linear
moorage.Downtown. Near Seattle ferry.

Winslow Wharf Marina

P.O. Box 10297 Winslow, WA 98110
Phone: (206) 842-4202 Fax 842-7785
Chart 18449 Ch 09
Some visitor slips. **Showers, laundry,
washrooms.** 20, 30 amp **power.**
Nearby: Launch ramp. pumpout,
portadump. **Chandlery adjacent.**

Harbor Marina

P.O. Box 11434, Eagle Harbor,
Bainbridge Island, WA 98110
Phone: (206) 842-6502 Fax 842-5047
Chart 18449
Some visitor moorage. **Shower,
laundry,washrooms.** 30 amp **power.**
Facilities: Pumpout. **Adjacent pub.**

Eagle Harbor Marina

5834 Ward Ave. NE., Bainbridge Island,
WA 98110 Phone: (206) 842-4003
Limited visitor moorage. **Shower,
laundry,washrooms.** 20, 30, 50 amp
power. Dive shop. Sauna, gym. Pumpout.

Port of Silverdale Marina

Silverdale, Dyes Inlet. P.O. Box 310
Silverdale, WA 98383 Phone: (360) 698-
4918 Chart 18449 Visitor moorage.
Washrooms. Nearby: Restaurants,
shopping. Adjacent: **Launchramp.**
Waterfront Park. Picnic and play areas.

Silverdale

Port Orchard

Bremerton - Port Orchard

Port Washington Marina

1805 Thompson Drive,
Bremerton. WA 98337
Phone (360) 479-3037   Chart 18449
Moorage: transient–call for slip assignment. **Water. Power** 30, 50 amps.
Pumpout. Laundry, showers, washrooms.

Photo above shows a view of the docks at Port Orchard. Right: The SS Turner Joy at Bremerton.

Port of Bremerton Marina

Port Commissioners
8850 SW State Highway 3
Port Orchard. Washington 98367
Phone: (360) 373-1035 Fax: (360) 479-2928
Charts 18448, 18449 VHF 16
Moorage: transient–call for reservations.
Water. Power 30 amps.
Fuel: at Port Orchard Marina. **Pumpout.**
Laundry, showers, washrooms.
Public phones, bus, ferry, restaurant.
Adjacent City of Bremerton. All facilities and amenities. restaurants, stores. Ferries.

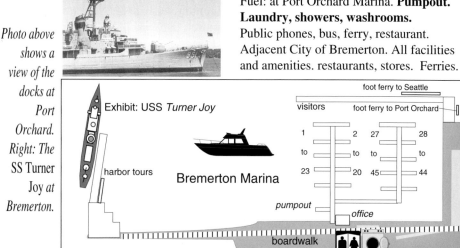

foot ferry to Seattle

Exhibit: USS *Turner Joy*

visitors   foot ferry to Port Orchard

harbor tours

Bremerton Marina

1
to
23

2   27   28
to to   to
20 45   44

pumpout

office

boardwalk

WASH

270

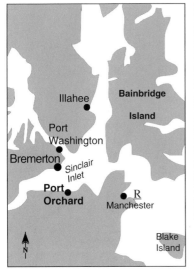

Port Orchard Marina

Steve Toms
707 Sidney Parkway
Port Orchard
Washington 98366
Phone: (360) 876-5335 Fax: (360) 895-0291
Charts 18448, 18449 VHF 16
Moorage: transient–call for reservations.
Free moorage during daytime. **Water.**
Power 30, 50 amps.
Fuel: gas, diesel. **Laundry, showers,**
washrooms. Public phones.
Nearby: Boardwalk and waterfront park.
Ferry to Bremerton, Seattle; bus, restau-
rants, shops. Marine hardware and services
off property.

Blake Island State Marine Park

Blake Island, Yukon Harbor, Puget
Sound. Phone (360) 731-8330
Charts; 18474, 18448, 18449, 18441
Moorage, water, camping, trails, scuba
diving nearby. Indian Loghouse restau-
rant. Norm Rocket, manager.

Port of Manchester

P.O. Box 304 Manchester
Washington 98353
Phone: (206) 722-3887
Chart 18448
Limited visitor moorage. washrooms.
Launch ramp.
Nearby: Restaurants, stores. Potable
water.

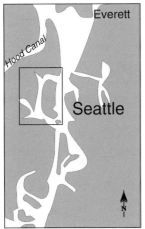

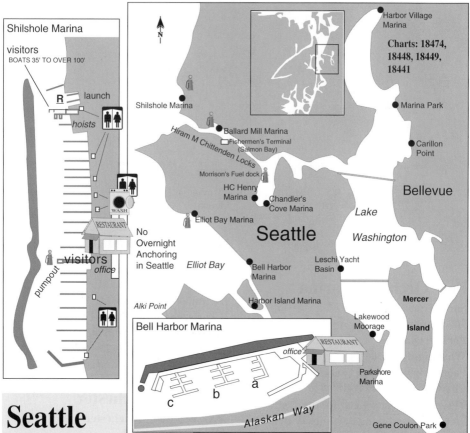

Shilshole Marina

visitors
BOATS 35' TO OVER 100'

R launch

hoists

WASH

RESTAURANT

visitors
office

pumpout

No
Overnight
Anchoring
in Seattle

Alki Point

Charts: 18474,
18448, 18449,
18441

Harbor Village
Marina

Shilshole Marina

Ballard Mill Marina

Hiram M Chittenden Locks

Fishermen's Terminal
(Salmon Bay)

Morrison's Fuel dock

HC Henry
Marina

Chandler's
Cove Marina

Elliot Bay Marina

Seattle

Elliot Bay

Bell Harbor
Marina

Harbor Island Marina

Marina Park

Carillon
Point

Bellevue

Lake

Washington

Leschi Yacht
Basin

Mercer

Lakewood
Moorage

Island

Parkshore
Marina

Gene Coulon Park

Bell Harbor Marina

office

RESTAURANT

c   b   a

Alaskan Way

Seattle

Shilshole Bay Marina

Darlene Robertson
**7001 Seaview Ave. NW,
Seattle, Washington 98117
Phone: (206) 728-3006 Fax: (206) 728-3391
Charts: 18474, 18448, 18449, 18441 VHF 16**
Email: *shilsholem@portseattle.org*
Web: *www.portseattle.org/harbor/moorage*
Moorage: transient–call for reservations.
Water. Power.
Marine supplies. **Laundry, showers,
washrooms.** Public phones. Launch ramp.
Boat yard. Haul-outs. Free pump-out.
Waste (hazardous) disposal. Security.
Nearby: Bus, restaurants, groceries,
shops. This marina offers a variety of
services to transient mariners. Its location
makes it an ideal stop for those heading
into or out of Lake Washington.

Ballard Mill Marina

Dock Manager
**4733 Shilshole Ave. NW,
Seattle, Washington 98107
Phone: (206) 789-4777
Charts; 18474, 18448, 18449, 18441**
(located in ship canal) **VHF 66A**
Moorage. Water. Power 20, 30 amp.
Washrooms. Showers. Pumpout.
Nearby: Restaurants, stores, service,
repairs, haulouts. Launch ramp.

Visitors check-in dock at Shilshole marina.

272

Bell Harbor

Elliot Bay Marina

Bell Harbor Marina

John Erik Johnson
Pier 66 2201 Alaskan Way,
Seattle Washington 98121
Phone: (206) 615-3952 Fax: (206) 615-3965
Charts; 18474, 18448, 18449, 18441
VHF 66A
Moorage, Water. Power 30, 50 amp.
Washrooms. Showers. Garbage, recycling. Pumpout.
Nearby: Pike Place Market, restaurants, stores.

Elliott Bay Marina   VHF 78A

Steve Krakenberg
2601 West Marina Place, Seattle
Washington 98199
Phone: (206) 285-4817 Fax:
(206) 282-0626
Charts; 18474, 18448, 18449.
Martin Harder - General Manager
Moorage for about 60 guests,
Water. Power 30, 50 amp.
Fuel: gas, diesel, Restaurants,
showers, laundry, washrooms, slip-side **pumpout.**

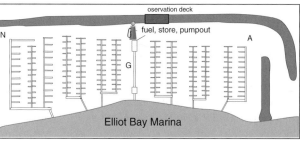

oservation deck

N

fuel, store, pumpout

A

G

Elliot Bay Marina

Fishermen's Terminal

Salmon Bay. 2100 Commodore Way
Seattle, WA 98199   (Inside ship canal)
Phone: (206) 282-5555 fax 282-8482
Moorage. **Shower, laundry, washrooms.**

Leschi Yacht Basin

120 Lakeside, Seattle, WA. 98122
Phone (206) 328-4456.

Harbor Island Marina

Dock Manager
1001, Klickitat Way #101
Seattle Washington 98134
Phone: (206) 624-5711
Charts; 18474, 18448, 18449, 18441
Moorage. Water.
Power 30, 50 amp.
Washrooms. Showers. Pumpout.

H. C. Henry Marina

Pat Craig
809 Fairview Place N.,
Seattle Washington 98109
Chart 18447
Limited guest moorage, **Water. Power**
220 only. **Pumpout.**
Nearby: Restaurants, shops, services.

Chandler's Cove

Brad Olson
901 Fairview Ave. N., # C170
Seattle Washington 98109
Phone: (425) 453-2500 Fax (425) 453-0505
Chart 18447 Limited guest moorage. Ice.
Water. Power. Washrooms. Showers.
Pumpout. **Nearby**: Restaurants. Store.

Harbor Village Marina

6155 NE 175th Street
Seattle (Kenmore).
Washington 98155
Phone: (425) 485-7557 Chart 18447
Moorage: Private. Call for reservations.
Water. Power 30, 50 amps.
Laundry, showers, washrooms. Public
phones. Pump-out station.
Nearby: Restaurant.

Marina Park

123 Fifth Ave.,
Kirkland, Washington 98032
Phone: (425) 828-1218 Fax: (425) 828-1220
Chart 18447
Visitor moorage. Washrooms.
Nearby: Launch ramp. Kirkland city
access. Ice. Liquor store, post office.

Morrison's (Fuel)

North Star Marina
2732 Westlake Ave. N.,
Seattle WA 98109 Phone: (206) 284-6600
Fuel stop. Gas, diesel and oils. Charts,
supplies, tackle. No visitors overnight.

Carillon Point Marina

Shelley Taylor
3240 Carillon Point,
Kirkland, Washington 98033
Phone: (425) 822-1700 Fax: (425) 828-3094
Chart 18447
Visitor moorage. Power 30, 50 amps.
Showers, washrooms.
Pump-out station. Portadump.
Nearby: Hotel, restaurant, shopping.

Gene Coulon Memorial Beach Park

Sylvia Allen
1201 Lake Washington Blvd.,
Renton, Washington 98055
Phone: (425) 235-2560 Fax: (425) 277-5541
Chart 18447
Visitor moorage. showers, washrooms.
Nearby: Restaurant, **Launch ramp**. Park
with facilities. Tennis, playground.
Large launching ramp.

Lakewood

Rick Camerer
4500 Lake Washington Blvd. S.,
Seattle, Washington 98118
Phone: (206) 722-3887 Fax (206) 760-5301
Limited visitor moorage. washrooms.
Laundry, gift store, marine supplies,
snacks. Picnic area. **Chart 18447.**

Parkshore Marina

Dave Jordan
9050 Seward Park Ave. S.
Seattle, WA 98118
Phone: (206) 725-3330
Visitor moorage in vacant tenant slips.
washrooms, showers, pumpout station.
Launch ramp. Use chart 18447.
Adjacent Rainier Yacht Club.

Lake Washington moorage is available on
a very limited basis. Stop at Parkshore
Marina, the Kirkland dock or possibly at Gene
Coulon Park. If you are a member of a yacht
club with reciprocal privileges you will be
able to stay on a first come basis at club
facilities on the lake.

Des Moines

City of Des Moines Marina

Joe Dusenbury
22307 Dock St.,
Des Moines, WA 98198
Phone (206) 824-5700 fax (206) 878-5940
Moorage. Large permanent marina with section for visitors.
Water. Power 20, 30 amps.
Fuel: gas, diesel, propane, stove oil, engine and outboard oils.
Pumpout. Portadump.
Washrooms. Showers. Laundry nearby.
Adjacent: Boatyard, Haul outs–30 ton travel lift, marine stores, restaurants.
Public phones. 30 ton travel lift.
Launch ramp.
Grocery store across parking lot.
chart 18474, 18448   VHF 16

Dockton Park, Vashon Island

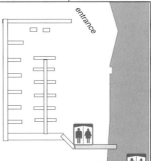

Above: The guest dock at Des Moines. Inset: Dock Carts lined up at Chinook Marina in Tacoma

Vashon Island Dockton Park

www.*metrokc.gov/parks*
P.O. Box 11 Vashon, WA 98070
Phone (206) 463-2947
Moorage. Visitor docks
Water. Pumpout Porta dump
Washrooms. Showers
Moorage adjacent to park. **Launch ramp.**

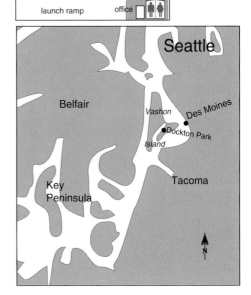

Seattle

Hood Canal

Gig Harbor □

Tacoma

Gig Harbor

Arabella's Landing

Stan and Judy Stearns
Mardella Rowland, Marina Manager
**3323 Harbor View Drive,
Gig Harbor WA 98332
Phone/fax (253) 851-1793**
www.vici.com/arabella/marina.htm
Moorage. 1500 feet visitor docks.
Water. Power 30, 50 amps. **Pumpout.**
Laundry. Washrooms. Showers.
Adjacent: Clubhouse, walkways, gardens,
wheelchair access. A quality marina with
all amenities. Stores and services nearby.
*Public dock nearby has good overnight
moorage when space is available.*

*Above: Arabella's
Landing at Gig Harbor.
Inset: Another view of
Arabella's Landing
Marina..
Below: The public dock
at Gig Harbor is close
to all facilities.
Note: Gig Harbor is a
top rated destination.*

Peninsula

N

Arabella's Landing

Gig Harbor public dock

Peninsula Yacht Basin

**8913 N Harborview Dr,
Gig Harbor WA 98335
Phone: (253) 858-2250
Moorage.** Call for slip.
Water. Power 30 amps.
Laundry. Washrooms.
No services at the marina.
Nearby restaurants, shops.

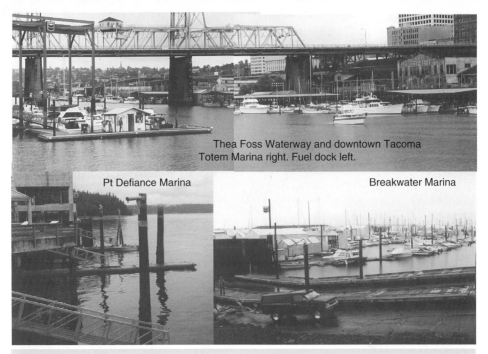

Thea Foss Waterway and downtown Tacoma
Totem Marina right. Fuel dock left.

Pt Defiance Marina

Breakwater Marina

Tacoma

Charts: 18453, 18474, 18448

Chinook Landing Marina

Dennis LaPointe
3702 Marine View Drive #100
Tacoma WA 98422
Phone: (253) 627-7676 fax (253) 779-0576
Moorage. Many slips. **VHF 79**
Pumpout
Water. Power 30, 50 amps.
Showers, Laundry Washrooms.
Marina store.

Breakwater Marina

Michael Marchetti
5603 Waterfront Drive
Tacoma WA 98407
Phone: (253) 752-6663 fax (253) 752-8291
Moorage. Many slips for visitors.
Water. Power 20 & 30 amps. **Fuel:** gas,
diesel, propane, stove oil. **Pumpout.**
Laundry. Washrooms. Showers.
Adjacent: Tidal Grid. Restaurant nearby.
Visitors: Check in at Fuel dock.

See location diagram next page

Point Defiance Boathouse Marina

Manager at restaurant.
5912 N Waterfront Drive,
Tacoma WA 98407
Phone: (253) 591-5325
Moorage. Boat rentals and visitor dock
space.
Water. Fuel: gas, premix.
Pumpout. Washrooms.
Adjacent: Public fishing pier, restaurant.
Launching ramp. gift and tackle shop.

Totem Marina

Eva Palka
Thea Foss Waterway
821 Dock St, Tacoma, WA 98402
Phone: (253) 272-4404
Moorage. Visitor docks pier 4 & 5.
Water. Power   20, 30 amps. **Fuel:** At
Totem Fuel dock opposite. **Pumpout.**
Showers, Laundry, Washrooms.
Nearby stores–groceries, restaurant,
fishing supplies, post office.
Tacoma city nearby.

Pick's Cove

Pick's Cove Marina

Dock Manager
Thea Foss Waterway
1940 East "D" Street,
Tacoma WA 98421
Phone (253) 572-3625 Fax (253) 572-0503
1 800 663-3625
web: *www.pickscove.com*
Moorage. Some transient available.
Water. Power. Fuel nearby. **Pumpout.**
Showers, washrooms.
Service, repairs, haul outs, hardware,
marine supplies, fishing equipment.

Narrows Marina

Dock Manager
9007 S. 19th St.
Tacoma WA, 98466
Phone: (253) 564-4222
Moorage. Some visitor slips.
Water. Power 20 amps.
 Fuel: gas, diesel
Washrooms. Marine
store–charts, tackle, bait,
electronics.
Adjacent: Launch ramp.

Photo above: Pick's Cove
Marina, Tacoma.
Opposite page bottom: Store at
Longbranch.

Steilacoom Marina

Shirley Wang
402 First St., Steilacoom WA 98388
Phone: (253) 582-2600
Moorage. Visitor moorage. **Portadump.**
Water. Power 20 amps.
Fuel: gas, diesel, CNG
Washrooms. Marine store
Adjacent: Park, beach.

Port of Allyn Dock

Lynch Cove. Near Belfair. (360) 275-2192.
Small dock–brief stops. **Launch Ramp.**

Lakebay Marina

Dave Roe
15 Lorenz Rd Key Peninsula,
Lakebay, WA 98349
Phone: (253) 884-3350
Moorage. Water. Power 15 amps.
Fuel: gas, propane **Washrooms.** Store–
fishing tackle etc, ice, groceries.

278

Fair Harbor

Fair Harbor   Charts: 18457, 18448.

Fair Harbor Marina
Susan and Vern Nelson
5050 Grapeview Loop Rd.,
Grapeview, WA 98546
Phone: (360) 426-4028
Moorage. Visitors docks 350 feet.
Water. Power 30 amps. **Fuel:** gas,
Laundry. Washrooms. Marine store–
groceries, hardware, fishing tackle and
bait, alcohol, kerosene, propane. Charts.
Gift shop. Some repairs and service.
Adjacent: picnic area, golf course access.
.

Port of Shelton
Shelton Yacht Club **(reciprocal only)**
West 410 Business Park Rd,
Shelton WA 98584 Phone: (360) 426-1151
Water. Power 30 amps. **Pumpout**
Laundry.   VHF 16

Longbranch

Longbranch Marina
Katie Parish
P.O. Box 111 Longbranch WA 98349
Phone: (253) 884-5137
Moorage. Visitors welcome.
Porta pottie toilets.
Water. Power 30 amps.
Laundry. Portable toilets.   VHF 16/68
Adjacent: anchorage nearby. Store across
the road–*photograph below.*

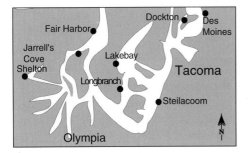

279

photo courtesy of Jarrell's Cove Marina

Jarrell Cove

Jarrell's Cove Marina

Lorna and Gary Hink
220 East Wilson Rd, Hartstene Island
Shelton WA 98584
Phone: (800) 362-8823 (360) 426-8823
Fax (360) 432-8494 Chart 18457, 18448
Moorage. 200 feet visitor docks.
Check in at fuel dock. Pumpout
Water. Power 30 amps. **Fuel:** gas, diesel,
propane. **Laundry, showers, washrooms.**
Marine store–hardware, fishing tackle,
licences, groceries, ice. books, beer.
Adjacent: 4 RV sites, game area, picnic
area, beach, public phone, point of interest
(historic log cabin).
Slip assignment at fuel dock.

This is one of the most attractive settings in the south Puget Sound area. There is lots of moorage at the marina as well as at the park on the opposite side of the cove.

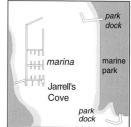

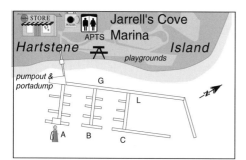

Jarrell's Cove Marine State Park,
Hartstene Island. 682 foot guest dock.
mooring buoys, washrooms, showers,
pumpout, portadump. Picnic areas.
Located opposite the marina.

Boston Harbor

Boston Harbor Marina

Don McHugh and Pam McHugh
312 73rd Avenue NE,
Olympia WA 98506   VHF 16
Phone: (360) 357-5670 Fax (360) 352-2816
Moorage. Transient. Large vessels okay.
Water. Power 20 amps.
Fuel: gas, diesel, CNG
Washrooms. Marine store–gifts, marine
supplies, fresh seafood, groceries, ice.
Adjacent: Launch ramp, picnic area,
beach, park. Kayak and boat rentals.

Boston Harbor Marina is a good place to sit and watch the sunsets
and the store has a friendly staff to welcome you to the harbor.

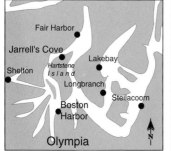

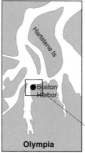

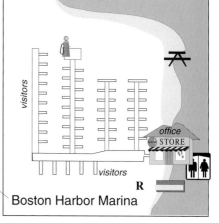

Boston Harbor Marina

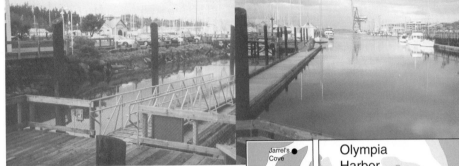

Percival Landing–Port Plaza dock on east side of marina

Olympia

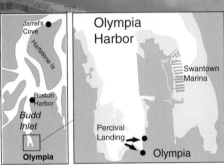

Olympia Harbor

Jarrel's Cove

Hartstene Is

Swantown Marina

Boston Harbor

Budd Inlet

Olympia

Percival Landing

Olympia

Percival Landing

Terry Meyer (360) 753-8379
217 Thurston Ave., Olympia WA 98501
Phone: (360) 753-8382
Moorage east side Port Plaza dock–public.
Water. Power 30 amp available.
Washrooms. Public phones.
Adjacent: Oyster Bar restaurant.
Nearby: Grocery store, uptown stores,
restaurants and all facilities.
This facility is adjacent to the Olympia
Yacht Club (west side). The marina
extends down the east side of the harbor
and along the south waterfront. It is
literally a downtown feature of Olympia.

Swantown Marina

Cheryl Maynard
1022 Marine Drive NE,
Olympia WA 98501
Phone: (360) 786-1400 fax (360) 753-1765
Moorage. Visitors. **Pumpout.**
Water. Power 20, 30 amps. Fuel nearby.
Also restaurants, groceries, liquor store,
post office. Chandlery, repairs, service.
Laundry. Washrooms. showers.
Launch ramp.   **VHF 65A**

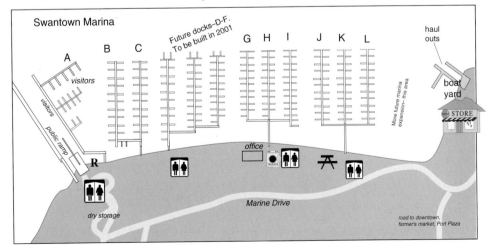

Index

284

285

Bibliography

99 Dives. San Juan Islands, Gulf Islands and Vancouver Island. Betty Pratt-Johnson. Heritage House, Surrey, BC. 1994.
101 Dives. From the mainland of Washington and British Columbia. Betty Pratt-Johnson. Heritage House, Surrey, BC. 1994.
A Guide to the Western Seashore. Rick M. Harbo. Hancock House, Surrey, BC. 1988.
BC Cruising Guide Series–Desolation Sound, Gulf Islands, Sunshine Coast. Whitecap Books, North Vancouver, BC. Bill Wolferstan.
Charlies Charts North to Alaska. Charles E. Wood. Margo Wood. Polymath Energy Consultants Ltd. Surrey B.C. 1986.
Canadian Tide and Current Tables. Pacific Coast all volumes. Ottawa-Department of Fisheries and Oceans. Annual.
Cruising Beyond Desolation Sound. John Chappel/ Naikoon Marine, Surrey, BC. 1979.
Anchorages and Marine Parks. Guide to anchorages and marine parks in British Columbia and the San Juan Islands. Peter Vassilopoulos. Seagraphic Publications. 1995.
Exploring Vancouver Island's West Coast. A Cruising Guide. Don Douglass. Fine Edge Productions. 1994.
Exploring the Inside Passage to Alaska. A Cruising Guide. Don Douglas. Fine Edge Productions. Bishop, California.1995.
Exploring the South Coast of British Columbia. A Cruising Guide. Don Douglas. Fine Edge Productions. Bishop, California. 1996.
Exploring the Gulf Islands and Desolation Sound to Port Hardy and Blunden Harbour. A Cruising Guide. Don Douglass. Fine Edge Productions. Bishop, California. 1996.
Marine Parks of British Columbia. An Explorer's Guide. Peter Chettleburgh. Special Interest Publications. Vancouver. BC. 1985.
Marine Weather Hazards Manual. A guide to local forecasts and conditions. Vancouver. Environment Canada. 1990.
North to Alaska. Hugo Anderson. Anderson Publishing Co. 1993

Northwest Boat Travel. Anderson Publishing Company. Anacortes. Annual.
Oceanography of the British Columbia Coast. Richard E. Thomson. Ottawa. Department of Fisheries and Aquatic Sciences. 1981.
Sailing Directions. British Columbia Coast (North Portion). Ottawa. Department of Fisheries and Oceans.
Sailing Directions. British Columbia Coast (South Portion). Ottawa. Department of Fisheries and Oceans.
Sea Kayaking Canada's West Coast. John Ince and Hedi Kottner. Raxas Books. Vancouver, BC. 1996.
The San Juan Islands. Afoot and Afloat. Marge and Ted Mueller. The Mountaineers. Seattle. 1988.
Waggoner. Robert Hale. Robert Hale Publishing. Seattle. Annual. *This is an excellent cruising guide with up-to-date information about marinas and other facilities. It includes planning and piloting information.* Ph (800) 733-5330.
Weatherly Waypoint Guides for GPS and Loran Navigation. Robert Hale. Robert Hale Publishing. Volumes 1–3: Puget Sound, San Juan Islands, Strait of Juan de Fuca. Gulf of Georgia, including Gulf Islands, Jervis Inlet. Desolation Sound to Port Hardy.
West Coast of Vancouver Island. Don Watmough. Whitecap Books, North Vancouver, BC.

My wife Carla and I have cruised the area this guide covers over the past twenty-five years. We have visited all areas described in the book and have stopped at and anchored in most anchorages included in the foregoing pages. Mariners who adventure beyond the known routes and popular areas will enjoy discovering for themselves others I have omitted. There are numerous books on cruising the coast and these along with your charts and reference books should enable you to extend your cruising range substantially and safely. Happy boating–Peter Vassilopoulos.

Anchorages and Marine Parks. Guide–
by Peter Vassilopoulos
$19.95

Available from Seagraphic Publications:

Anchorages and Marine Parks–*by Peter Vassilopoulos* $19.95 *(plus $2.50 S&H)*
This is a companion guide to **Docks and Destinations**. It is a *user friendly guide* to places to find sheltered anchorage overnight and to facilities and features of marine parks. The area it covers, in a south to north progression, includes the San Juan Islands and all of BC coastal waters including the west coast of Vancouver Island. The contents includes availability at marine parks by way of descriptive icons showing water, showers, toilets, picnic tables, launch ramps, camping, hiking trails and much more. It contains numerous drawings depicting anchorage layouts and their relative location on the coast and is illustrated with hundreds of aerial and other photographs. It is a best selling publication and is also available from all leading marine stores, marinas and book stores. Foreword by Sergeant Ken Burton–captain *St Roch II Voyage of Rediscovery,* photograph below.

DIVER Magazine–*Peter Vassilopoulos. Seagraphic Publication $3.50 per copy*
This Canadian magazine is published nine times a year. It contains a wealth of information about marine life, shipwrecks, underwater photography, diving medicine, personal profiles, dive travel destinations and much more. It is a national publication and covers BC extensively as well as other parts of Canada where diving is popular. It features regular dive destinations in tropical waters and provides lots of high quality colour illustrations. It is available at dive stores and selected news stands. Or by subscription or single copy from the publisher.
Subscribe at a special trial rate of $15.00 for one year–9 times a year. (includes taxes).
Order any of these books or magazines by sending payment to the publisher. Please include $2.50 for shipping and handling for books. No extra for magazine subscriptions.
Contact Seagraphic Publications
Box 1312 Delta B.C. V4M 3Y8 (604) 943-4198 *or* Box 984, Point Roberts, WA. 98281-0984

A scenic stop at the Manson's Landing docks.

Docks and Destinations

Some comments about Docks & Destinations (and Anchorages & Marine Parks)

We often refer to our copy of **Docks and Destinations** while out on the water. We ALWAYS refer to your book when we are working in our store. What a great book!
–Dan and Leah Lee, Thrifty Foods, Salt Spring Island.

Peter Vassilopoulos' nautical guidebooks are among the top ten trade bestsellers in our store this summer (1998). That's the verdict from the public!
–Merv Adey, Tanners Books, Sidney, B.C.

Our best and most informative cruising guide. Always our first recommendation to our customers looking for a cruising guide on the coast. (We use it on our own boat.)
–Brad Mah, Nikka Industries, Vancouver/Steveston.

Mariners have commented on the clarity of your book. It is well designed—succinct yet containing enough information to enable the boater to make wise cruising decisions.
–Ann Taylor, Greenway Sound.

The book has helped us find new destinations we had never heard of before. Thank you for the best boating guide on the coast.
–Jeanne and Henry Karcz, Richmond, BC.

This guide is updated when reprinted. Major updates and changes will be made periodically when new editions are published. Please write to me if you have any information or suggestions for inclusion in future editions. Your comments will be welcome.
–Peter Vassilopoulos.

The author's Monaro 27, used also for work with his Canadian national scuba diving publication, DIVER Magazine.

Canada: P.O. Box 1312 Delta, Stn A., British Columbia, Canada. V4M 3Y8
USA: P.O. Box 984, Point Roberts, WA. 98281-0984
Phone (604) 274-4333 or (604) 943-4198   Fax (604) 274-4366
email: *divermag@axionet.com* (Please contact us for updating information.)